Mike Meyers' CompTIA A+ Guide: PC Technician Lab Manual (Exams 220-602, 220-603, & 220-604)

Mike Meyers
Dennis Haley

New York Chicago San Francisco Lisbon London Madrid
Mexico City Milan New Delhi San Juan Seoul Singapore
Sydney Toronto

The McGraw·Hill Companies

Cataloging-in-Publication Data is on file with the Library of Congress

McGraw-Hill books are available at special quantity discounts to use as premiums and sales promotions, or for use in corporate training programs. For more information, please write to the Director of Special Sales, Professional Publishing, McGraw-Hill, Two Penn Plaza, New York, NY 10121-2298. Or contact your local bookstore.

**Mike Meyers' CompTIA A+ Guide: PC Technician Lab Manual
(Exams 220-602, 220-603, & 220-604)**

1 2 3 4 5 6 7 8 9 0 QPD QPD 0 1 9 8 7

ISBN-13:   978-0-07-226363-3
ISBN-10:   0-07-226363-6

Sponsoring Editor
  Tim Green

Editorial Supervisor
  Patty Mon

Project Manager
  Vasundhara Sawhney
  (International Typesetting
  and Composition)

Acquisitions Coordinator
  Jennifer Housh

Copy Editor
  Lisa McCoy

Proofreader
  Laura Bowman

Indexer
  Valerie Perry

Production Supervisor
  George Anderson

Composition
  International Typesetting
  and Composition

Illustration
  International Typesetting
  and Composition

Art Director, Cover
  Jeff Weeks

This book is dedicated to all of you who want to become great techs.

—Mike Meyers

I dedicate this book to all of my students, past, present, and future. They inspire me to do my best. I also dedicate this book to Theresa, who is always there for me when that inspiration wanes.

—Dennis Haley

About the Authors

Mike Meyers, lovingly called the "AlphaGeek" by those who know him, is the industry's leading authority on CompTIA A+ certification. He is the president and co-founder of Total Seminars, LLC, a provider of PC and network repair seminars, books, videos, and courseware for thousands of organizations throughout the world. Mike has been involved in the computer and network repair industry since 1977 as a technician, instructor, author, consultant, and speaker. Author of numerous popular PC books and videos, Mike is also the series editor for the highly successful Mike Meyers' Certification Passport series, the Mike Meyers' Computer Skills series, and the Mike Meyers' Guide to series, all published by McGraw-Hill.

Dennis Haley has worked in the Information Technology industry for over 20 years and has spent more than half of that time as a technical teacher. Dennis' responsibilities have included computer network training for the Oki Data Corporation and site director/instructor for Computer Networking Technologies. Presently he is the administrator and teacher for the E2C and Microsoft IT Academy programs at POLYTECH High School. Dennis holds a BSEET, CompTIA A+ and Network+ certifications, and Microsoft MCP, MCSA, MCSE, and MCT certifications. Dennis enjoys all aspects of technology; even his hobbies are technical, including electronic music and sound production.

Contents

Acknowledgments

Many great people worked together to make this book happen.

As our sponsoring editor at McGraw-Hill, Tim Green set the entire book in motion and stayed at the helm as the guiding hand. Thanks, Tim!

Also at Total Seminars, Dudley Lehmer was a great CEO, creating an environment for getting projects done. Scott Jernigan performed his usual magic as Editor in Chief. Michael Smyer provided excellent photographs and illustrations.

On the McGraw-Hill side, our acquisitions coordinator, Jennifer Housh, helped us keep it all on track.

To the copy editor, page proofer, and layout folks at ITC, thank you!

Finally, Tanner Allen, Tim Basher, Alex Lawson, and John Fitzgerald provided excellent sounding boards for ideas and projects that work in the real world. You're the best, guys, thanks!

Chapter 1
Essentials Review

Lab Exercises

Okay, you have completed all of the preparation and lab exercises for the CompTIA A+ certification exam 220-601 (Essentials) and have hopefully sat for and passed the exam! You now have firsthand experience with computer systems, study techniques, and actual exam question structure. There is no better way to prepare for the next exam needed to achieve the CompTIA A+ certification, the 220-602 (IT Technician), than to build and expand on the skills you have already developed.

This lab manual, the companion to *Mike Meyers' A+ Guide to Managing and Troubleshooting PCs, Vol. 2: 220-602 (IT Technician)*, covers the more advanced features of the components and techniques you'll need to explore before attempting the second exam in the series, the CompTIA A+ certification exam 220-602 (IT Technician). In this first lab, you'll start with the review of five core labs from the Essentials lab manual, building the foundation from which you can exercise the advanced skills you'll need to complete the subsequent labs.

 60 MINUTES

Lab Exercise 1.01: Study Preparation

Now that you have completed the preparation for the CompTIA A+ certification Essentials exam (220-601), you have an even better understanding of the commitment you have to make to successfully gain the skills and knowledge to be a qualified computer technician (and to pass the exam). Work through this table of skills once again to identify the areas where you should focus your study and exercises.

Learning Objectives

This lab helps you lay out a logical path for your studies. To do this, you need to deal with three issues: determining your weak points, checking your study habits, and scheduling the exam.

At the end of this lab, you'll be able to

- Identify the CompTIA A+ topics you need to learn

- Develop a good study plan

- Understand how to schedule the CompTIA A+ 220-602 (IT Technician) exam

Lab Materials and Setup

The materials you need for this lab are

- A PC with Internet access
- A telephone

Getting Down to Business

Total Seminars has been teaching CompTIA A+ certification for years, and we've developed a handy template to help you determine what you need to study and how much time you need to devote to preparing for the CompTIA A+ certification exams. This is the same table used in the CompTIA A+ certification Essentials (220-601) exam lab manual. You should find that you now have some experience performing the technical tasks, and, as such, the total amount of preparation time should be shorter.

Step 1   For each skill listed below, circle the number that corresponds to the amount of experience you have: None, Once or Twice, Every Now and Then, or Quite a Bit. You'll use that number to calculate the total number of hours you have to study for the exams.

Technical Task	None	Once or Twice	Amount of Experience Every Now and Then	Quite a Bit
Installing an adapter card	12	10	8	4
Installing hard drives	12	10	8	4
Installing modems and network interface cards (NICs)	8	6	4	2
Connecting a computer to the Internet	8	6	4	2
Installing printers and scanners	4	3	2	1
Installing random access memory (RAM)	8	6	4	2
Installing central processing units (CPUs)	8	7	5	3
Fixing printers	6	5	4	3
Fixing boot problems	8	7	7	5
Fixing portable computers	8	6	4	2
Building complete systems	12	10	8	6

Technical Task	Amount of Experience			
	None	Once or Twice	Every Now and Then	Quite a Bit
Using the command line	8	8	6	4
Installing/optimizing Windows	10	8	6	4
Using Windows 2000	6	6	4	2
Using Windows XP	6	6	4	2
Configuring NTFS permissions	6	4	3	2
Configuring a wireless network	6	5	3	2
Configuring a software firewall	6	4	2	1
Installing a sound card	2	2	1	0
Using operating system diagnostic tools	8	8	6	4
Using a Volt-Ohm Meter (VOM)	4	3	2	1

Great! You now have a good feel for the topics you need to study. Now you need to determine the total study time. First, add up the numbers you've circled. Then add the result to the number from the following table that corresponds to your experience. The grand total is the number of hours you should study to be ready for the exams.

If You Have This Much Direct, Professional Experience . . .	Add This Number of Hours to Your Study Time
0	50
Up to six months or successful completion of the Essentials (220-601) exam	30
Six to 12 months	10
More than 12 months	0

A total neophyte usually needs around 200 hours of study time. An experienced technician shouldn't need more than 40 hours.

The total number of hours for you to study is _____.

Step 2   Go to the Computing Technology Industry Association (CompTIA) Web site and download a copy of the domains (objectives) for the CompTIA A+ 220-602 (IT Technician) exam. As of this writing, you can find them at http://certification.comptia.org/resources/objectives.aspx; you'll have to fill out a short form (requiring your name, e-mail address, country of residence, and how soon you'll be testing) before you can view the objectives. Bear in mind, however, that CompTIA changes its Web site more often than TV networks invent new reality shows, so be prepared to poke around if necessary! Compare the circled areas on the table above to the CompTIA A+ objectives. Note that any single topic on the table will cover more than one objective on the CompTIA A+ exams. Circle the domains that you think parallel the weak areas you circled on the table, and don't be afraid to add or remove circles after you've seen the CompTIA A+ objectives in detail.

✔ **Hint**

If you are going to focus on one of the specialized paths for your CompTIA A+ certification—either the CompTIA A+ 220-603 exam (Help Desk Technician) or the CompTIA A+ 220-604 exam (Depot Technician)—you'll want to download the objectives for those domains.

Follow the methodology described (circle the domains that you think parallel the weak areas you circled on the form), and concentrate on those domains as laid out in the objectives for the specialized exams.

Step 3   Now that you know what topics are most important to you and how much time they'll take, you need to develop your study plan. Take the amount of time you've set aside, and determine how many days you have to prepare. Consider work, holidays, weekends, and anything else that will affect your study time. If you're in an instructor-led course, this part is easy—just use the length of the course! Then break down your textbook into manageable chunks. Again, if you're in a course, your instructor will already have done this for you. You now have your deadline—the day you'll say, "I'm ready to take the exam!"

Step 4   Following the guidance of your instructor, go online and schedule your exam with either Thomson Prometric (www.prometric.com) or Pearson/VUE (www.vue.com). You'll almost certainly need to make a phone call to do this. Make sure you have both a method of payment (credit cards or vouchers are preferred) and some form of identification when you call. In the United States, you need your Social Security number to schedule CompTIA exams. It's important that you schedule your exams *now*—setting an exam date early in the process will help motivate you to study and keep you from procrastinating!

✔ **Cross-Reference**

For details about taking the CompTIA A+ exams, go to the CompTIA Web site (www.comptia.org).

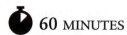 60 MINUTES

Lab Exercise 1.02: Disassembling and Reassembling the System Unit and Identifying Internal Components and Connections

You're now going to walk through the complete disassembly of the system unit. Try to do this in an orderly sequence, but, depending on the configuration of the computer you are disassembling, you may have to perform one or two of the steps out of sequence. For example, you may have to remove a CD or DVD media drive before you can gain access to remove the power supply.

When you're on the job, you'll encounter different models of personal computers manufactured by different companies. Along with learning the slightly different methods of component removal and installation, you should be able to identify the major internal parts of the PC system, regardless of the manufacturer. This lab exercise will help you practice doing that.

Ready, Set, GO!

Learning Objectives

In this lab exercise, you will locate, remove, and describe the various internal components and connectors of a standard PC system.

At the end of this lab, you'll be able to

- Remove all major components of a PC

- Recognize all major components inside a PC

- Name the function of each component

- Define the relationship of internal components to external connections

Lab Materials and Setup

The materials you need for this lab are

- A lab partner, if possible

- At least one PC that isn't vital to your (or anyone else's) home or business, not necessarily in working order but preferably less than a few years old

- An anti-static wrist strap

- An anti-static mat (optional)

- Twelve anti-static bags of various sizes

- A simple technician's toolkit

- A plastic cup or box to organize the various screws, nuts, and bolts that you'll remove

- A clean, well-lighted workspace of about 3' x 4' (a kitchen table with some newspaper spread about usually makes a fairly decent ad-hoc lab bench)

- A notepad on which to take notes and make sketches of the computer and components

- A digital camera to record the placement, configuration, connections, and connectors associated with the components you'll be removing from the system unit (optional)

Getting Down to Business

✖ Warning

Shut off the power to your system and unplug the power cord from your PC and from the wall socket before doing the following exercise.

Step 1   Disconnect all the external cables (monitor, keyboard, mouse, printer, etc.) from the PC you are going to use, and place the PC on a flat, stable surface (preferably on an anti-static mat) where you can sit or stand comfortably to inspect the insides.

Step 2   Use proper anti-static procedures while opening the case and during this entire exercise. Using whichever method applies to your case (thumbscrews, Phillips-head screws, locking tabs), remove the cover of your system unit and then lie the system down so that the open side faces the ceiling.

✔ Cross-Reference

Review Chapter 2 of *Mike Meyers' A+ Guide to Managing and Troubleshooting PCs, Vol. 1: Essentials* to confirm your understanding of proper electrostatic discharge (ESD) procedures and how to open a PC system case.

Look inside your system case. What do you see? To begin with, you'll see lots of cables and wires. Some appear to be single-colored wires, while others seem to be multiple gray-colored wires in the shape of wide ribbons. Most colored wires originate at the power supply and end at the various devices to supply the needed direct current (DC) power to run the PC. The wide *ribbon cables* attach various components and are used to transfer data. These are sometimes referred to as *logic cables* or *data cables*.

See if you can locate in your system case the major components labeled in Figure 1-1. You may have to move some of the fan shrouds, wires, and cables in order to find them—especially components on the motherboard—but remember your anti-static procedures and be gentle. Sometimes the slightest bump is enough to unseat a connection.

FIGURE 1-1 Inside a typical PC

Step 3   Now it's time to take some notes, draw some sketches, or take a few pictures. Before you start disassembling this computer, document where the components belong and what wires and cables are connected to the different components. Be prepared to take a few notes on how you actually removed the component (this will really help when you go to reinstall the components). Include as much detail as possible; it will only help in getting the system unit back together.

Step 4   To start, you'll need to clear the way—a bit like peeling an onion, layer by layer—by removing the easily accessible components and cables first.

Look inside the PC and find the expansion slots. How many total expansion cards can be plugged into your system?

Some of the expansion slots may have cards in them. These may be modem cards, sound cards, network cards, or video cards. Since expansion cards are designed to "expand" the capability of the computer system, they are designed to be installed after the system unit is assembled. For this reason, the expansion cards are a great place to begin your disassembly.

Look at the expansion cards installed in your PC, and then look at the external connectors on each. Can you match the cable to the expansion card?

Remove all installed expansion cards from your system unit. Place each card into an anti-static bag to protect it from ESD damage.

Step 5   If the computer you are disassembling is only a few years old, it will probably have multiple fan shrouds to make sure the airflow is getting to the main components to keep them cool.

Remove any fan shrouds from your system unit and place them out of the way on your workspace.

✔ **Hint**

After removing each item—especially the bulky items, such as fan shrouds, wiring, and cables—it would be good to take a few more notes or pictures. Now that you have a better view of the components underneath, you will be able to consult these notes or pictures during reassembly.

✔ **Hint**

You can complete the next three steps in the order written or out of order, whichever works best for your system unit. You'll be removing the power supply wires, the power supply, and the data cables from the components and motherboard. If one of the data cables is in the way of one of the wires, it's okay to remove the data cable first. Please remember to keep good records (notes or photos) of your configuration.

Step 6   Locate the power supply, which is a large silver box in one corner of the system unit case. Trace the colored wires leading out of it. Remember to be gentle!

Find the power plug(s) for the motherboard. If you have a newer PC, it will probably look like the one in Figure 1-2. If you have an older PC, you might see two power connectors installed side by side.

Find the power connectors for the floppy, CD-ROM (if applicable), and hard drives. Do they look like one of the connectors in Figure 1-3? They should!

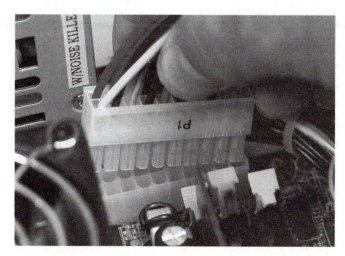

FIGURE 1-2 Power plug for the motherboard

FIGURE 1-3 Power connectors

Remove all of the power connectors from the motherboard and all data drives. Place them to the side as best as you can until you remove the power supply itself.

Step 7   If possible, remove the power supply at this point. If there are still many cables and components in the way, you can perform this step later in the lab.

Step 8   Now look at the floppy drive, which should be attached to a flat ribbon cable. (Don't worry if your system doesn't have a floppy drive—just move on and explore your other data drives.) Trace the ribbon cable to the motherboard. Do the same for all your other data drives: hard drives, CD media drives, and DVD media drives, as applicable.

These ribbon cables are about one and a half inches wide, and they are normally gray with a colored stripe on one side. The stripe—usually red—orients the cable properly to the connections on the motherboard and the floppy drive.

The cable to the floppy drive has 34 wires (conductors) and, in most cases, has a twist in the center. Its position relative to this seven-wire twist determines whether a floppy drive is the primary (or A:) drive for the system (attached to the connector at the end of the cable past the twist) or the secondary (B:) drive for the system (attached to the center connector).

✔ **Hint**

It's rare to find two floppy drives in a newer system; in fact, floppy drives are going away completely on most brand-new systems. On systems that do have floppy drives, you will not find a floppy cable at all, though you may still have a 34-pin connector on the motherboard. On systems utilizing only one floppy drive, manufacturers may use a shorter floppy cable with no twist and no second drive connector.

The type of ribbon cable that connects the hard drive(s) and CD or DVD media drive to the motherboard has 40 wires and no twist. You may even have the newest cable type, which has

80 conductors to allow for faster transmission speed of the data to and from the hard drives. Both of these cable types still have a colored edge on one side for orientation. Many current systems use much smaller, seven-wire cables for Serial ATA, or SATA, hard drives; these cables have connectors keyed like the letter L.

Step 9   After noting the current state of the ribbon cables, disconnect and reconnect each device's cable in turn. Practice this a few times. Can you plug a cable in backwards? Try it. Put the cable on the device the wrong way if you can. Older types of cables can be put on incorrectly, but newer cables and connectors have built-in keying to prevent this from happening. Make sure that the cables are properly connected when you've finished.

Now look at where the ribbon cables connect to the motherboard. Make note of the proper cable orientation. Practice disconnecting and reconnecting the cables at the motherboard. Do you have any problems if you try to plug these cables in backwards?

When you feel you have practiced enough, remove the cables and place them safely away from the computer on your work surface. Now would be a great time to make a drawing or take a photograph of the de-cluttered system unit interior.

Step 10   Most modern systems have a set of small wire and cable runs connecting front panel indicator lights—primarily the power-on and hard drive activity light emitting diodes (LEDs)—and front panel Universal Serial Bus (USB) ports to the motherboard (see Figure 1-4). Look for these individual wire connections (often collectively called *case wires*), which are usually grouped together near one corner of the motherboard. Make careful note of where each tiny connector plugs in—a photo would be incredibly helpful here—and then disconnect them all and tuck the wires out of the way.

Step 11   Now that all of the wires and cables are removed, you should have plenty of room to finish up the disassembly. You're now going to remove all the drives. Drives are usually the most cumbersome to remove due to the drive cages or frames where they're mounted (see Figure 1-5). Depending on the mounting the manufacturer has used, removing a drive may be as simple as pulling out a sliding mechanism or as complicated as opening up the other side of the system case, removing all the decorative plastic facing, and removing a handful of screws.

FIGURE 1-4 Various case wires connected to a motherboard

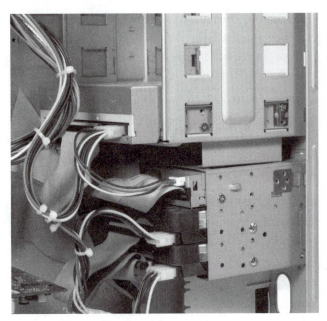

FIGURE 1-5 Typical drive configuration in a PC tower system case; note the cages or frames used for mounting the various drives

Remove the floppy drive, CD-ROM drive, DVD media drive (if present), and the hard drive(s), and set them on your work surface.

Step 12   Look in your PC and find the RAM modules. RAM comes in thin, wafer-like modules, about 3″×5″ long by one inch wide. A row of metal contacts running along one of the long edges plugs into a matching socket, which is three to five inches in length, located on the motherboard. Look for a long wafer standing on its edge; often, you'll find two or more RAM modules lined up in a row.

How many RAM modules do you have? _____

Do you have Dual Inline Memory Modules (DIMMs) or Single Inline Memory Modules (SIMMs)? _____

Making sure to follow proper anti-static procedures, remove the SIMMs or DIMMs from their slots and place them in an anti-static bag for safekeeping.

Step 13   Look in your PC and see if you can locate the CPU. Running CPUs generate a fair amount of heat, so they need their own dedicated cooling mechanisms. Because of this, when you search the motherboard, trying to find the CPU, you'll generally find it hidden under a fan/heat sink unit. Carefully remove the fan/heat sink unit from the CPU.

✖ **Warning**

Make sure that you fully understand how to remove your particular model of CPU fan before you try it!

If you were able to remove the fan, make a note of the type of CPU chip you have:

_____

If you're in a computer lab with multiple systems, examine a number of different CPU chips. Note where each CPU is located on the motherboard.

Making sure to follow proper anti-static procedures, lift the lever of the Zero Insertion Force (ZIF) socket, remove the CPU, and place it in an anti-static bag for safekeeping.

Step 14   See if you can locate any jumpers or Dual Inline Package (DIP) switches on your motherboard. Resist the temptation to play with them at this point—just make a note of what you find. In particular, look for the identifying labels on the motherboard.

Step 15   Making sure to follow proper anti-static procedures, remove the screws that secure the motherboard to the chassis or frame of the system case. Place the motherboard in a properly sized anti-static bag, and put it aside.

If you have used an area where you can leave the components, wires, cabling, and hardware for a while, you can leave the PC disassembled for later labs. If you really need to clean up the area for now, you can either follow your notes (and lab steps) in reverse order to reassemble the system or find a large box to store the disassembled computer until your next lab session.

Don't worry about the ESD-sensitive components; as long as they are in their anti-static bags, they should be fine.

Step 16   You have explored and removed nearly all the components of a typical PC system unit. To finish this lab exercise, see if you can identify all of the components in Figure 1-6.

FIGURE 1-6   Do you recognize these components inside your PC?

A _____

B _____

C _____

D _____

E _____

F _____

G _____

H _____

I _____

J _____

 **30** MINUTES

Lab Exercise 1.03: Creating and Formatting Partitions with the Windows 2000/XP Install CD

In this lab, you will use the Windows Install CD to partition and format hard drives in your system. If this were the only drive in your system, once you partitioned and formatted it with a file system, you would have a blank partition in need of an operating system to boot the computer from the hard drive. In the next lab, you will complete the process of installing the operating system.

> ✔ **Cross-Reference**
>
> For details about partitioning and formatting drives with the Windows install CD, refer to the "Partitioning and Formatting with Windows Install CD" section in Chapter 10 of *Mike Meyers' A+ Guide to Managing and Troubleshooting PCs, Vol. 1: Essentials*.

Learning Objectives

In this exercise, you'll use the Windows install CD to partition a hard drive and format the partition for use.

At the end of this lab, you'll be able to

- Set up a primary partition on a hard drive
- Format the partition with the NTFS file system

Lab Materials and Setup

The materials you need for this lab are

- A system with one hard drive that you can safely erase

- A Windows 2000 or Windows XP install CD

✖ Warning

Partitioning and formatting a hard drive destroys any data on it! Practice this lab using only drives that don't store any data that you need.

Getting Down to Business

In this exercise, you'll start the system by booting from the Windows XP install CD (you will have to configure your system CMOS to boot from the CD). You'll partition a portion of one of the hard drives and format it with the NTFS file system, as if you're preparing to install the operating system.

Step 1   Enter the CMOS setup program and configure the boot order, selecting the CD-ROM drive as the first boot device. Also, make sure that the setting called Boot Other Device (or something similar) is enabled, or your system may not recognize the CD-ROM drive as a bootable drive.

Step 2   Place the Windows XP install CD in the CD-ROM drive tray, and boot the computer. Windows Setup copies a number of files and then presents you with the screen shown in Figure 1-7. Press ENTER to set up Windows XP now.

Step 3   Press F8 to accept the license agreement and enter the main partitioning screen.

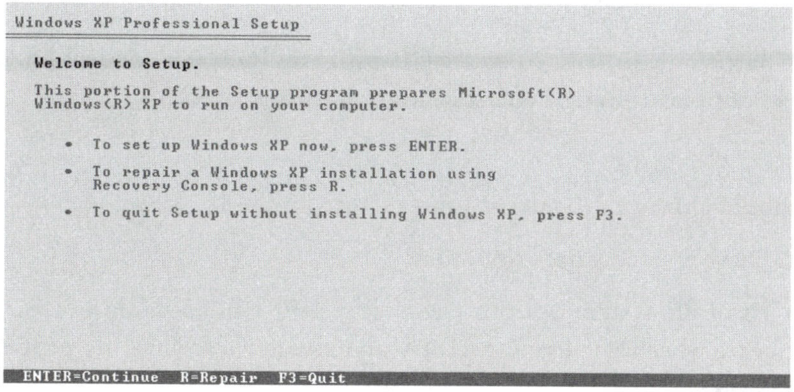

FIGURE 1-7 The first Windows Setup screen

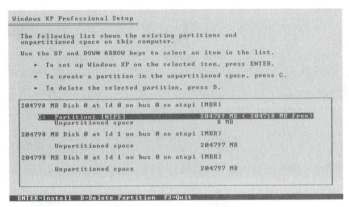

FIGURE 1-8 Partitioning screen

✔ **Hint**

If you are using a computer configured with Windows XP, Setup asks if you would like to repair this installation and advises you to press ESC if you want to install a fresh copy. Press ESC to progress to the next step—partitioning the drive.

The screen displays the installed drives and any partitions and/or file systems that have been configured on the drives prior to this session (see Figure 1-8).

Step 4   If any partitions exist on the drives you have installed to practice this lab (and if the data on these drives is expendable), delete them at this time.

To delete a partition, simply select the partition, press D to delete, and then press L to commit the delete process. The partition will be returned to unpartitioned space.

Step 5   To create a partition, follow these steps:

a)   Press C.

b)   Select the size of the partition you want to create (10 gigabytes [GB] is a good size for a system partition or a boot partition, but you should try multiple sizes).

c)   Press ENTER.

d)   The new partition should appear in the partitioning screen.

     Congratulations! You have created a partition.

Step 6   Press ENTER to see a list of file system options (see Figure 1-9). Choose a file system (NTFS is the default) and indicate whether you will perform an exhaustive formatting process or the "Quick" formatting process.

Press ENTER. Windows formats the partition and proceeds with the operating system installation. You can shut down the PC once this step is completed.

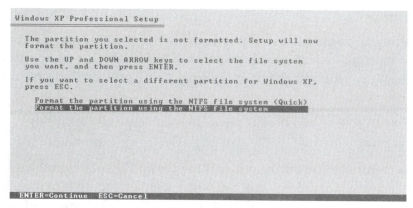

FIGURE 1-9 Format screen

Step 7   Practice deleting, creating, and formatting different combinations of partitions and file systems to become comfortable with the tools used in this exercise. Have fun!

 1 HOUR

Lab Exercise 1.04: Performing a Clean Installation of Windows XP Professional

Your boss has traditionally ordered new workstations already assembled and loaded with the desired Windows operating system. She recently decided that with her great in-house techs, she should be buying PC parts from a wholesaler instead and having you and your team build the systems. You've enjoyed choosing the various hardware components and building these custom computers, but now it's time to bring your creations to life! You need to load Windows XP Professional onto these new computers that have never seen the light of day.

Learning Objectives

You should complete at least one clean Windows installation, both for the experience and to prepare for questions asked on the CompTIA A+ exams.

At the end of this lab, you'll be able to

- Install a Windows operating system on a blank drive

Lab Materials and Setup

The materials you need for this lab are

- A working PC with a blank hard drive or with a hard drive that you can write to without negative consequences

- A Windows XP Professional CD-ROM with a valid product key

Getting Down to Business

In this exercise, you'll be putting an operating system onto a drive that doesn't currently have one. If the hard drive that you plan to use currently has data on it (even data that no one needs), then you must wipe that drive clean before you begin the exercise. Once you have a clean hard drive, you can proceed as directed.

Step 1   Insert the Windows XP CD-ROM into the CD drive, close the tray, and wait for the Welcome to Setup screen to appear.

Step 2   Follow the directions to install the operating system. Read the End User License Agreement (EULA) thoroughly. You must agree to it in order to proceed. When Setup prompts you to partition your drive, set up a single NTFS partition that uses all the available drive space. Then you'll simply need to wait and watch while Setup does its magic and reboots the computer.

Step 3   When the computer has rebooted, work through the graphical portion of the installation process by carefully reading each screen and filling in the appropriate information. Be sure to enter the product key correctly, as you won't get past that screen with an invalid key.

Step 4   When you come to the Networking Settings screen, ask your instructor (if you're in a classroom setting) whether to use Typical or Custom settings and what specific information to use.

Step 5   On the Let's Activate Windows screen, *do not* activate at this time. Instead, select No, log me off and click Next. You should see a blank Windows desktop, signifying that you've completed a successful installation of Windows XP.

 30 MINUTES

Lab Exercise 1.05: Using Windows Microsoft Management Console (MMC) Toolbox

You're about to learn how to customize your Windows toolkit! Almost every profession requires a set of tools to get the job done. Some of these tools are necessary, and some are luxuries. If you were a carpenter, you might have a toolkit where you keep your hammer, saw, screwdrivers, pliers, and so on. You could then buy new tools ("I really needed this pneumatic nail gun, and it was on sale!" is a common excuse) and add them to your toolbox—but you'd need to keep it all organized, or risk not being able to find the tool you need when you need it.

To help organize your PC technician's toolbox, Microsoft created the Microsoft Management Console, or MMC. The MMC not only organizes all of those useful tools, it also provides a consistent look and feel between different systems and even different operating systems, which makes it easier to use them.

✔ **Cross-Reference**

For details on working with the MMC, refer to the "Microsoft Management Console" section in Chapter 13 of *Mike Meyers' A+ Guide to Managing and Troubleshooting PCs, Vol. 1: Essentials.*

Learning Objectives

In this exercise, you'll learn how to create an MMC. You'll also create a desktop icon that you can use to access this customized software toolkit whenever you need it.

At the end of this lab, you'll be able to

- Create an MMC

- Add tools (snap-ins) to the MMC

Lab Materials and Setup

The materials you need for this lab are

- A PC system with Windows 2000 or XP installed

Getting Down to Business

The MMC is a shell program that holds individual utilities called snap-ins. The first time you create an MMC, you get a default blank console. A blank MMC isn't much to look at—like any new toolbox, it starts out empty.

Step 1   To create your MMC, select Start | Run, type **mmc**, and then click OK. Voilà! You've created a blank console (see Figure 1-10).

Notice that the name in the upper-left corner is Console 1.

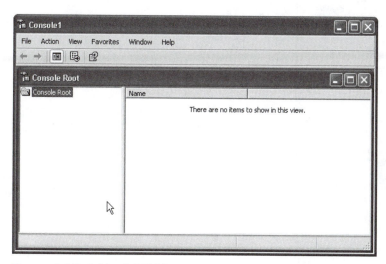

FIGURE 1-10 A blank MMC

Before you actually configure an MMC, you need to understand a few points. First, you can have more than one MMC; successive consoles will be given default names, such as Console 2, Console 3, and so on. Second, you can rename the consoles that you create and choose where to save them so that you can easily find them again. Finally, once you've created an MMC, you can modify it by adding or taking away tools—just like your toolbox at home.

Follow these steps to practice working with MMCs:

a)   Click File (Windows XP) or Console (Windows 2000) | Save As, and fill in the boxes as follows:

- **Save in** Desktop

- **File name** My First MMC

- **Save as type** Microsoft Management Console Files (*.msc)

b)   Click Save to continue. (Don't exit the MMC!)

c)   Notice in the upper-left corner of the open window that the name has changed.

d)   Find the new icon that's been created on the desktop. This icon bears the same name as your new MMC, and will enable you to access the MMC in the future just by double-clicking the mouse.

Step 2   When you add snap-ins, they'll show up in the Add/Remove Snap-in dialog box (see Figure 1-11).

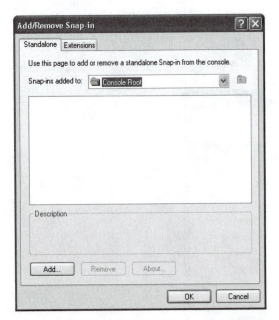

FIGURE 1-11 Adding or removing snap-ins

You'll now add some snap-ins to your MMC:

a) Click File | Add/Remove Snap-in (Windows XP) or Console | Add/Remove Snap-in (Windows 2000).

b) Click Add, and let the fun begin (see Figure 1-12). I bet you haven't had this many selections since your last visit to Sears' hardware department!

c) Add the Device Manager as your first tool. Select Device Manager from the list, and click Add.

✔ **Note**

When you add a snap-in, you have a choice of adding it for either your local computer or another computer. With the proper access permissions, in other words, you can look at the Device Manager on a networked system. More than likely, you don't have the necessary permissions to do this, so stick with the local option for now.

d) Select Local Computer and click Finish.

✘ **Warning**

I can't emphasize strongly enough that the best way to get a system administrator mad is to go snooping around on the network. As a technician, your main concern is to do no harm. If you accidentally find your way to an unauthorized area, it's your duty to report it to an administrator.

FIGURE 1-12 Adding a standalone snap-in

While you're here, you'll add one more snap-in: Event Viewer. Adding it here will provide an alternative way to access this tool:

a)   Select Event Viewer from the list.

b)   Select Local Computer and then Finish to close the wizard.

c)   Click Add to close the list window, and click OK to close the Add/Remove window.

d)   Your MMC should now show two snap-ins.

e)   Be sure to save your MMC.

You now have a toolbox with quick access to Device Manager and Event Viewer. You can use these tools in the same way as if you had navigated to them through the conventional methods.

Click Device Manager to expand the list of devices. Notice that it looks the same and works the same as it would if you opened it through Control Panel.

Step 3   If everything has worked correctly up to now, continue with this step (if you had problems creating your MMC, review the instructions or ask your instructor for assistance):

a)   Double-click the desktop icon for My First MMC.

b)   Your Device Manager and Event Log are now available directly from your desktop (see Figure 1-13).

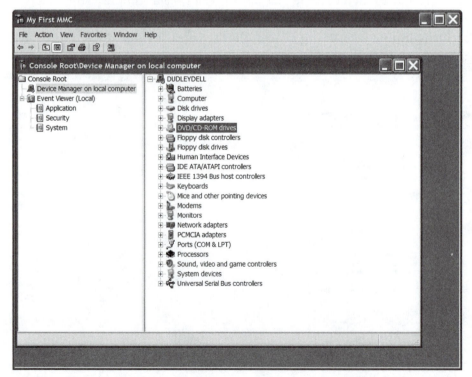

FIGURE 1-13 Accessing Device Manager from a custom MMC

✔ **Hint**

I've only scratched the surface here in showing you how to create an MMC. Your customizing options are limited only by the number of snap-ins available and your imagination. Try creating different groupings of tools to organize similar tasks, maybe all of the disk management tools together or all of the user, group, and resource tools. Be creative!

Lab Analysis Test

1.   Betsy is preparing an installation of Windows XP Professional. She has used a partitioning tool to prep the hard drive, but when she initiates the installation, she receives a blue screen with the following error message: *Windows XP requires a hard drive volume with at least 318 megabytes (333926400 bytes) of free disk space.* What's the problem?

2.   What's the purpose of the MMC?

3.   Raylene removed the case of her PC to check the type of RAM she has installed. When she put the case back on and tried to start the PC, she got a message that there's a problem with her hard drive. What is a good reason why this might have happened?

4.   Amanda argues that a hard drive must be formatted before you can set up the partitions. Samantha says the drive must be partitioned first. Who is correct and why?

5.   What happens if you don't complete the Microsoft Product Activation (MPA) for Windows XP Home Edition within 30 days of installation?

Key Terms Quiz

Use the following vocabulary terms to complete the following sentences. Not all of the terms will be used.

CD-ROM drive

electrostatic discharge (ESD)

floppy disks

GParted CD

installation

MMC

network drive

ribbon cable

snap-ins

Windows 2000 Professional

Windows XP Home Edition

Windows XP install CD

Windows XP Professional

1. If you plan to install Windows XP onto a system, it must have a _____.

2. To partition and format a hard drive when no operating system has been installed, you may use either the _____ or the _____ to boot the system and run disk setup utilities.

3. The modern hard drive may utilize technology that requires a flat, 80-wire _____.

4. The various tools in the MMC are known as _____.

5. Anti-static wrist straps and anti-static bags are used to protect devices from _____ damage.

Chapter 2

Installing and Troubleshooting CPUs

Lab Exercises

Many PC users are comfortable performing the simpler installation and upgrade tasks, such as adding random access memory (RAM) or installing a modem or sound card. When it comes to the more complicated tasks, such as installing or replacing a central processing unit (CPU), however, wise users turn to the experts—this means you!

Installing a CPU is one of the many tasks you'll find yourself performing as a PC tech. Whether you're building a new system from scratch or replacing the CPU on an existing computer, it's your job to know the important characteristics of the CPU, match the CPU to compatible motherboards, and configure the CPU on the PC.

The following lab exercises will allow you to practice removing and installing a CPU/fan assembly on a motherboard. You'll then explore the specifications of the microprocessor with a freeware program known as CPU-Z. Okay—find your anti-static wrist strap and get started with your exploration of CPUs.

 30 MINUTES

Lab Exercise 2.01: CPU Removal and Installation

You have been assisting your coworker, Joe, with the task of determining if a CPU/fan assembly that he purchased on eBay is going to work in his system. Luckily for Joe, his motherboard is compatible with his new CPU. Now he expects you to play your "Computer Expert" role and install the new CPU in his PC. As a PC tech, you must be comfortable with such basic tasks. In this exercise, you'll familiarize yourself with the procedure; using your disassembled PC, you'll practice removing and reinstalling the CPU and fan assembly.

Learning Objectives

In this lab, you'll practice removing and installing a CPU and CPU fan assembly.

At the end of this lab, you'll be able to

- Remove and install a CPU safely and correctly
- Remove and install a CPU fan assembly safely and correctly

Lab Materials and Setup

The materials you need for this lab are

- The disassembled, non-production PC you prepared in the lab exercises in Chapter 1

- Anti-static mat or other static-safe material on which to place the CPU following removal

- Anti-static wrist strap

- Thermal paste

Getting Down to Business

Time to get your hands dirty! Removing and installing CPUs is one of the most nerve-wracking tasks that new PC techs undertake, but there's no need to panic. You'll be fine as long as you take the proper precautions to prevent electrostatic discharge (ESD) damage, and handle the CPU and fan assembly with care.

✖ Warning

Be careful not to touch any of the exposed metal contacts on either the CPU or the CPU socket.

Step 1   Using the disassembled PC, determine whether the process of reinstalling and removing the CPU and fan assembly will be easier with the motherboard on an anti-static mat or installed in its case; if you prefer, reinstall the motherboard into the case before proceeding. You may find that it is easier to work with the stubborn fan assembly clamp if the motherboard is secured in the case.

Step 2   In most cases, you'll have to remove the fan assembly before you can remove the CPU. Screw-down fans are easier to remove than clip fans. Screw-down fans require only that you unscrew the securing hardware. Clip fans, found on many types of CPUs, require you to apply pressure on the clip to release it from the fan mount. Use a small screwdriver to do this, as shown in Figure 2-1. Use caution when prying the clip open, and don't forget to unplug the CPU fan!

✔ Hint

You'll discover that releasing a fan clip takes way more force than you want to apply to anything so near a delicate CPU chip. Realizing this in advance, you can be sure to brace yourself and position the screwdriver carefully to minimize the possibility of it slipping off and gouging something.

FIGURE 2-1 Using a screwdriver to remove a clip-type CPU fan from its mount

The CPU and fan assembly will have thermal paste residue on the surfaces that they were previously touching. You cannot reuse thermal paste, so you'll need to apply a fresh layer when you reinstall the CPU fan. Using a clean, lint-free cloth, carefully wipe the thermal paste residue from the CPU and fan assembly, and then place the fan assembly on an anti-static surface.

Step 3 Before proceeding, notice the orientation of the CPU's notched corner. Almost all CPUs have such a notch.

Now remove the CPU. Start by moving the end of the ZIF lever a little outward to clear the safety notch; then raise the lever to a vertical position. Next, grasp the chip carefully by its edges and lift it straight up out of the socket. Be careful not to lift the CPU at an angle, or you'll bend its tiny pins. As you lift out the CPU, make sure that the ZIF lever stays in an upright position.

The recommendation to use an older, non-production PC for the disassembly and reassembly exercises may present you with the task of working with some older technology. Pin grid array–style packages, even the early designs, are fairly similar from processor to processor. If your CPU is an Intel Pentium II or III, or an early AMD Athlon, you may have to work with a Single Edge Cartridge (SEC) package inserted in a Slot 1 or Slot A socket.

Removing an SEC CPU that uses a slot interface normally does not require removing the fan, which is usually attached to the chip cartridge itself. To remove a slot CPU, first check for and release any retaining clips that may be securing it to the slot, and then grasp the cartridge firmly on both ends and pull straight up from the motherboard.

Step 4   Now that you have the CPU chip out, examine it closely. The manufacturer usually prints the chip's brand and type directly on it, providing you with some important facts about the chip's design and performance capabilities. If your chip is an AMD Duron 1300, for example, you know that its PGA packaging fits in a Socket A (462 pins), its bus speed is 100 megahertz (MHz)—double-pumped, and it runs at 1.3 gigahertz (GHz). Make a note of the relevant specs for your chip.

What is the CPU information printed on the chip package?

✖ Warning

Always handle a CPU chip like it's a fragile old photograph: very gently, holding it only by the edges. Make sure you take *complete* ESD precautions, because even a tiny amount of static electricity can harm a CPU!

Step 5   Reinsert the CPU with the correct orientation, lock down the ZIF lever, and reattach the fan. Now remove the fan assembly and the CPU again. Practice this a few times to become comfortable with the process. When you're finished practicing, reinsert the CPU for the last time. Be sure to apply a thin film of fresh thermal paste onto the square in the center of the top of the CPU before you place the fan. Now reattach the fan assembly. Don't forget to plug the fan back in!

✔ Hint

If this was a production system, with RAM and other components installed, this would be an ideal time to turn the system back on and make sure you have the CPU seated properly. In real life, you should always test your hardware before you put the case back on!

Step 6   You may leave your CPU/fan assembly installed on the motherboard and place the motherboard on your anti-static mat. Optionally, if you reinstalled the motherboard in the case, you may leave it assembled.

 30 MINUTES

Lab Exercise 2.02: Exploring CPU Specifications with CPU-Z

Joe is impressed with your knowledge and expertise—and he's relieved that the CPU he purchased on eBay happened to work out. You explain that not only did it work out, but he has really improved the performance of his system with the upgraded CPU. In fact, to further display the characteristics of the CPU Joe has just purchased, you download a utility known as CPU-Z from www.cpuid.com.

This utility reads the specification of different PC components from information embedded in them. You launch the utility to display the parameters of the new CPU for Joe.

Learning Objectives

In this lab, you'll identify various CPU specifications.

At the end of this lab, you'll be able to

- Run the CPU-Z utility
- Recognize key characteristics of CPUs

Lab Materials and Setup

The materials you need for this lab are

- Access to a working computer with Internet access to facilitate downloading and running the CPU-Z utility
- A notepad and pencil to document the specifications
- A word-processing or spreadsheet application to facilitate the documentation (optional)

This lab is more informative if you have access to different types of systems with different classifications of CPUs.

Getting Down to Business

In the following steps, you'll download a reference utility known as CPU-Z and use it to further explore the characteristics of the CPU.

Step 1   Log on to a computer with Internet access, and point your browser to the following Web site: www.cpuid.com. Follow the directions to download the current version of CPU-Z (version 1.4 as of this writing). Unzip the file and launch CPU-Z.

Step 2   The CPU-Z utility displays a number of tabs across the top of the window (see Figure 2-2). At this time, you are only concerned with the CPU and Cache tabs.

Using the data gathered by CPU-Z, record some of the pertinent information below.

Name _____

Codename _____

Package _____

Core Speed _____

Multiplier _____

Bus Speed _____

L2 Cache _____

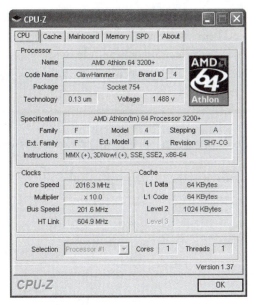

FIGURE 2-2 The CPU-Z utility

✔ **Hint**

Due to variations in CPUs, chipsets, basic input/output system (BIOS), and motherboards, CPU-Z may not be able to display all of the information about your CPU. In some cases, the information may actually be erroneous. The CPUID Web site has good documentation on some of the common incompatibilities.

Step 3   If possible, launch CPU-Z on various computers to compare the characteristics of different CPUs. Save the utility for use in future lab exercises.

Lab Analysis Test

1. Lenny informs you that he has a new processor, but the only information he can uncover on the Internet is that it is named "Conroe." What processor is Lenny using?

2. Joanna called you to say that ever since you installed her new CPU, the PC gives intermittent problems when it runs. Sometimes it just quits and freezes up. What could possibly be wrong?

3. Your cousin Trevor has been reading some CPU spec sheets online and keeps seeing the term L2 CACHE with numbers like 256K and 512K. He asks if you can explain what L2 CACHE is and what it is used for.

4. Lindsey runs CPU-Z on her system and notices that the processor's core speed is 2191.2 and the displayed multiplier is x22. What is the speed of the system clock in Lindsey's computer? How would the industry display this system clock speed?

5. Andy has upgraded the memory on his computer twice. The first time he added 256 megabytes (MB) to bring it to a total of 512 MB. He then replaced both sticks with two 512-MB sticks for a total of 1 gigabyte (GB). Now that he's a technical wiz, he's decided to upgrade his processor. What recommendations would you have for Andy?

Key Terms Quiz

Use the following vocabulary terms to complete the following sentences. Not all of the terms will be used.

alignment notch 4

Cedar Mill

clip connector

codename 2

CPU

fan assembly

land grid array (LGA)

microprocessor

Northwood

package

pin grid array (PGA)

Prescott 3

screw-down connector

thermal paste 1

Willamette

zero insertion force (ZIF) 5

1. It is important to use _____ when installing a fan assembly on the CPU.

2. Both Intel and AMD have adopted the use of a _____ to distinguish among revisions of their CPUs.

3. The codename of the final revision of the Intel Pentium 4 processor (2006) was _____.

4. When installing a PGA or LGA form-factor CPU, it is imperative that you correctly install the chip using the _____ of the socket.

5. Beginning with the Intel 486 and continuing through today's high-end processors, the _____ socket was implemented to protect the pin grid array of the processor chip.

Chapter 3
Installing and Troubleshooting RAM

Lab Exercises

One of the easiest and most cost-effective upgrades you can make to a PC is to add more memory. As such, random access memory (RAM) installation is probably the most common type of upgrade you'll perform as a PC tech.

RAM installation tasks include determining how much RAM the PC has installed, how much RAM the PC can support, what type of RAM it uses, and physically installing the RAM on the motherboard. You have already explored the various methods to determine the amount of RAM installed in the computer, the total amount that the motherboard can support, and what type of RAM is needed. The following labs are designed to give you practice working with RAM by using visual recognition of the different types and packages, and by walking you through the steps of installing RAM. You will finish up by launching the CPU-Z application and exploring the information pertaining to your system's memory.

 30 MINUTES

Lab Exercise 3.01: Removing and Installing RAM

Remember Joe, clutching a stick of RAM he got from a guy on the fourth floor? Having looked at the specs for his system, you know it takes 184-pin DDR SDRAM. Joe thinks the stick he got is the right size to fit, but you know it's 240-pin DDR2 RAM, so it won't.

Taking pity on Joe, you've found a stick of RAM for him that works with his system, and now you have to install it. Meanwhile, you can "re-inventory" that stick of DDR2 RAM into your computer!

Although RAM installation is one of the simpler PC hardware upgrades, it's still important that you follow the correct steps and take all appropriate safety precautions. You will once again practice using the disassembled, non-production system. This time, you will be removing and installing RAM sticks.

Learning Objectives

In this lab, you'll practice removing and installing RAM.

At the end of this lab, you'll be able to

- Remove RAM safely and correctly

- Install RAM safely and correctly

Lab Materials and Setup

The materials you need for this lab are

- The disassembled, non-production PC used in the lab exercises in Chapter 1

- An anti-static mat or other static-safe material on which to place the RAM

- An anti-static wrist strap

- A notepad

✔ **Hint**

If you're in a computer lab or you have access to multiple PCs, you should practice on a variety of systems.

Getting Down to Business

Removal and installation procedures vary, depending on the type of RAM your system uses. Dual inline memory modules (DIMMs) and RIMMs snap into the RAM slots vertically, while single inline memory module (SIMM) installation is a bit more involved; these modules insert at an angle and then pivot into their final locked position. The following steps describe the removal and installation procedures for DIMMs.

✖ **Warning**

Regardless of the type of RAM on your system, be certain to take measures to prevent electrostatic discharge (ESD) damage. Shut down and unplug your PC, and place it on your anti-static mat. Strap on your anti-static bracelet and ground yourself. If necessary, remove any cables or components that block access to your system's RAM before you begin.

✔ **Hint**

You should have already removed the RAM from your tear-down computer and have it safely stored in an anti-static bag. You may either install the RAM in the sockets on the motherboard, with the motherboard on the anti-static mat, or reinstall the motherboard into the case first. The following removal steps are listed for reference, especially if you have access to additional computers for exploration.

FIGURE 3-1 Removing a 184-pin DIMM (DDR SDRAM)

Follow these steps to remove DIMM or RIMM RAM from your PC:

Step 1   Locate the retention clips on either end of the RAM module.

Step 2   Press outward on the clips to disengage them from the retention slots on the sides of the RAM sticks (see Figure 3-1).

Step 3   Press down on the clips firmly and evenly. The retention clips act as levers to lift the DIMM sticks up and slightly out of the RAM slots.

Step 4   Remove the DIMM sticks and place them on your anti-static mat or in an anti-static bag.

Step 5   Make note of the following:

How many pins does your RAM have? _____

Where are the guide notches located? _____

What information is on the RAM's label?_____

Step 6   While you've got your system's RAM out, this is a good time to check the condition of the metal contacts on both the RAM sticks and the motherboard RAM sockets.

Are the contacts free of dirt and corrosion? _____

After you've examined your system's RAM and inspected the motherboard RAM sockets, reinstall the RAM as described below.

If the tear-down computer you are using is fairly old, there's a chance that it will be populated with 72-pin SIMM RAM sticks. For reference, I've included a few tips for working with this type of memory.

Follow these steps to remove SIMM RAM from your PC:

Step 1   Locate the retention clips on either end of the SIMMs. Remember that SIMMs require two RAM sticks to make a complete memory bank.

Step 2 Press outward on the clips to disengage them from the retention slots on the sides of the RAM sticks. Some motherboards don't leave you with much room to operate, so you may need a small screwdriver or needle-nose pliers to undo the retention clips. Be very careful not to touch any of the circuitry with metal tools!

Step 3 Once the SIMMs are loose, pivot their slots to a 45-degree angle, and then slide the SIMM sticks out.

To reinstall SIMM RAM, perform the following steps:

Step 1 Orient the SIMM RAM stick so that the guide notch on the end matches the guide ridge on the socket.

Step 2 Slide the RAM stick into the socket at a 45-degree angle until it seats firmly.

Step 3 Pivot the RAM upright until it snaps into place, making sure that both retention clips are secured.

To install a DIMM or RIMM RAM, follow these steps:

Step 1 Orient the DIMM or RIMM so that the guide notches on the RAM module match up to the guide ridges on the RAM socket.

Step 2 Press the RAM stick firmly and evenly straight down into the socket until the retention clips engage the retention notches on the ends of the RAM stick.

Step 3 Snap the retention clips firmly into place.

Step 4 Repeat these steps to install other RAM modules as appropriate. If you're using RIMM RAM, don't forget to install the continuity RIMM (CRIMM) sticks into any empty RAM slots.

To professionally finish a RAM installation, especially if you are on a production-level computer, follow these steps:

Step 1 Once your system RAM is in place, reattach any cables that you may have had to move, and plug the system power cable in. Do not reinstall the PC case cover until after you've confirmed that RAM installation was successful.

Step 2 Boot the system up and watch the RAM count to confirm that you correctly installed it.

✔ **Hint**

If your system has any problems when you reboot, remember that you must turn off the power and unplug the computer again before reseating the RAM.

 30 MINUTES

Lab Exercise 3.02: Exploring RAM Specifications with CPU-Z

Now that you have Joe's system up and running with double the memory it had before, you can take a moment to analyze the re-inventoried memory on your computer. You've already downloaded the CPU-Z utility from the Internet; now you'll need to launch it and examine the information on the Memory and SPD tabs.

Learning Objectives

In this lab, you'll identify various RAM specifications.

At the end of this lab, you'll be able to

- Recognize key characteristics of RAM

Lab Materials and Setup

The materials you need for this lab are

- Access to a working computer with the CPU-Z utility installed

- A notepad and pencil to document the specifications

- A word-processing or spreadsheet application to facilitate the documentation (optional)

This lab is more informative if you have access to different types of systems with different types of RAM.

Getting Down to Business

In the following steps, you'll explore the different characteristics of RAM.

Step 1 Launch the CPU-Z application.

Step 2 Navigate to the Memory tab. The CPU-Z utility displays the current statistics of the RAM installed, as shown in Figure 3-2.

Using the information gathered by CPU-Z, record the following information:

Type _____

Size _____

CAS# Latency (CL) _____

RAS# to CAS# Delay (tRCD) _____

RAS# Precharge (tRP) _____

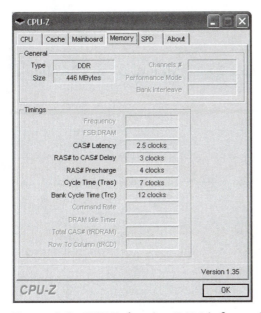

FIGURE 3-2 CPU-Z showing RAM information

Step 3   Click the SPD tab in CPU-Z.

Step 4   The SPD tab (see Figure 3-3) lists a number of technical bits of information about a particular stick of RAM. This information is contained on an additional chip on every synchronous dynamic random access memory (SDRAM) stick, called the *serial presence detect (SPD)* chip.

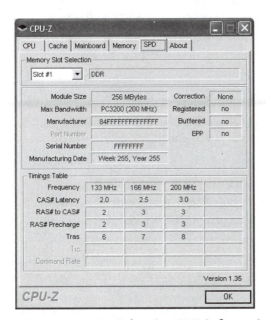

FIGURE 3-3 CPU-Z showing SPD information

Using the information gathered by CPU-Z, record the following information for each of the system's RAM modules:

	Module 1	Module 2	Module 3	Module 4
Slot #	_____	_____	_____	_____
Module size	_____	_____	_____	_____
Maximum bandwidth	_____	_____	_____	_____
Manufacturer	_____	_____	_____	_____

✔ **Cross-Reference**

To review how the SPD chip works with the system, refer to the "SPD" section in Chapter 4 of *Mike Meyers' A+ Guide to Managing and Troubleshooting PCs, Vol. 2: PC Tech.*

Step 5   If possible, launch CPU-Z on various computers to compare the characteristics of different types of RAM. Save the utility for use in future lab exercises.

→ **Try This: PC Wizard**

On a computer with Internet access, point your browser to www.cpuid.com. Follow the on-screen directions and download a copy of PC Wizard.

Extract the files into a folder and launch the PC Wizard application. Once PC Wizard is running, find and click the Mainboard icon in the Hardware area. This displays a list of components in the right pane of the application window. Click the Physical Memory item, and then browse through the information displayed in the lower portion of the window.

Using this information, can you determine the maximum size of individual RAM modules allowed on this system and the maximum amount of total memory that it supports? Does this correspond to the information you found earlier in the PC or motherboard documentation?

Note that because of variations in chipsets, basic input/output system (BIOS), and motherboards, PC Wizard may or may not provide detailed information on the RAM. In some cases, the information may actually be erroneous. The CPUID Web site has good documentation on some of the common incompatibilities.

Lab Analysis Test

1. Kevin has an old Intel 486 system that he would like to refurbish to run some of his Windows 98 games. He needs to locate some memory. What type will Kevin need for this system?

2. Theresa's Windows 2000 Professional system has 512 megabytes (MB) of RAM. She adds another stick with 512 MB of RAM, but the RAM count still only shows 512 MB. What could be causing this?

3. John's system has 512 MB of PC4200 DDR2 SDRAM. He recently installed an additional 512 MB of DDR2 SDRAM that a coworker gave him. He tells you that his system now boots up correctly and shows the correct amount of RAM, but then it freezes after several minutes. He notes that if he removes the new RAM, the system runs fine. What could be a possible reason for this?

4. Michael is using the CPU-Z utility to explore his memory specifications when he clicks the SPD tab. He turns to you and asks, "What does SPD stand for?" What is your response?

5. Dominique has just purchased a new stick of RAM, which she quickly removes from the packaging and hands to you so that you can be impressed. You carefully accept the RAM, but quickly replace it to the packaging. Why are you so concerned?

Key Terms Quiz

Use the following vocabulary terms to complete the following sentences. Not all of the terms will be used.

72-pin SIMM

168-pin DIMM

184-pin DIMM

240-pin DIMM

CRIMM

DDR RAM

DDR2 RAM

DIMM

double-data rate

dual-channel

Extended Data Out (EDO)

megabytes (MB)

RIMM

SDRAM

— SO-DIMM

SPD

synchronous

1. You will probably only see _____ RAM in older computers using Intel Pentium III processors and compatible motherboards. If you examine the RAM, you will most likely notice the inclusion of _____ modules to fill out the slots.

2. The "DDR" in DDR SDRAM stands for _____.

3. An additional chip known as a(n) _SPD_____ chip was added to all SDRAM to include additional information about the DRAM.

4. The only memory discussed in this lab to have a truly different installation method is _____.

5. The "S" in DDR2 SDRAM stands for _____.

Chapter 4
Working with BIOS and CMOS

Lab Exercises

Today's modern BIOSes are incredibly automated for most of the work we do on today's systems. The vast majority of jobs that used to require going into CMOS setup—installing hard drives, adding RAM, etc.—now work automatically. Even though many functions are now automated, the need for understanding how to configure and maintain your CMOS setup has never been more important. PCs are much more powerful, flexible, and also complicated than they were even a few years ago. Many of the most complex issues we deal with are in the proper configuration of CMOS.

As an example, let's say that your company is planning a mass upgrade from your current operating system—Windows XP Professional—to Windows Vista Ultimate. You've tested the upgrade process on a few lab computers and found that systems with an out-of-date BIOS have had problems upgrading successfully. In preparation for the Windows Vista installation, besides upgrading any older BIOS versions you find, you'll also disable any BIOS-level antivirus-checking functions. You're also aware that the prior IT manager did not use consistent CMOS passwords, so you may need to reset the passwords on a few computers.

This chapter assumes that you know the function of CMOS and can access any system's CMOS setup program. It builds from that point and takes you inside the CMOS setup program to perform basic configurations, including one of the most important: clearing CMOS passwords.

 30 MINUTES

Lab Exercise 4.01: Configuring and Clearing CMOS Setup Passwords

In many professional environments, the IT department doesn't want users to fool with any of the PC's settings, especially detailed items like the BIOS settings. The IT manager may even devise a password to prevent entry to the CMOS setup utility by unauthorized users. Unfortunately, in your organization, the IT manager has resigned and was not thorough in documenting these passwords.

When faced with a CMOS setup utility that has been password-protected and the password subsequently lost, the typical way to clear the password is to shunt a jumper on the motherboard that clears either the password or the entire contents of CMOS.

Learning Objectives

In this lab, you'll learn how to configure CMOS setup utility passwords and how to clear the contents of the password and CMOS using the onboard clear CMOS jumper.

At the end of this lab, you'll be able to

- Set a password using the CMOS setup utility

- Locate the clear CMOS jumper on the motherboard

- Clear passwords and CMOS settings using the clear CMOS jumper

Lab Materials and Setup

The materials you need for this lab are

- A working PC whose BIOS settings you can change, with access to the clear CMOS jumper on the motherboard

- An anti-static mat/wrist strap

- A notepad

Getting Down to Business

In the following steps, you'll reboot your PC and access the CMOS setup program using a key combination. You will then navigate to the password or security menu and configure a CMOS setup utility password. Then you'll verify the password by rebooting the computer and entering CMOS setup. Finally, you'll open up the case and reset the CMOS settings by physically shunting the clear CMOS jumper.

Step 1 Reboot your system and use the appropriate key or key combination to enter the CMOS setup program.

Step 2 Once you've entered the CMOS setup program, navigate to the Security or Password menu (see Figure 4-1). Select the supervisor password, and enter a four- to eight-character password. Save changes and exit CMOS setup.

Record your password here:_____

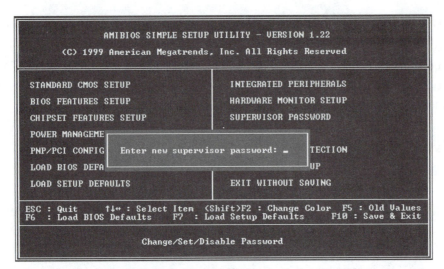

FIGURE 4-1 AMIBIOS supervisor password setup

✔ **Hint**

Typically, two types of passwords can be set in CMOS. The *supervisor* password restricts access to the CMOS setup program so that only authorized personnel can change or modify BIOS settings. Organizations, especially schools, will usually configure a supervisor password to keep curious users from causing system errors.

The *user* or *system* password restricts access to the PC itself, and is required every time the system boots (before an operating system is even loaded). This type of password is often used when an individual's PC is located in a public area.

Step 3 Reboot the PC and press the key or key combination required to enter the CMOS setup program. If you completed Step 2 correctly, you should be prompted to enter a password. Enter the password you configured in Step 2, and press ENTER. The main menu of the CMOS setup program will appear.

Discard changes and exit the CMOS setup program.

✖ **Warning**

The next step will erase all CMOS settings! While you are in the CMOS setup program, take the time to write down important settings, like the CPU soft menu settings, boot order, which integrated peripherals are enabled/disabled, and the power management setup. While the system should run fine using the default settings, taking notes now will help you get back to any custom settings that may have been configured.

FIGURE 4-2 The clear CMOS jumper on a motherboard

Step 4

> ✖ **Warning**
>
> Any time you remove the cover from your PC, remember to follow all proper safety and
> ESD precautions.

Shut down the PC, and unplug the power cord from the PC and the wall outlet. Remove the case from the PC, and, referring to the PC or motherboard documentation, locate the clear CMOS jumper. Follow the instructions included with the documentation and move the jumper to clear the CMOS (see Figure 4-2).

Step 5   Replace the PC case cover, plug the system back in, and start the system. Press the appropriate key(s) to enter the CMOS setup program.

Were you prompted for a password? _____

Do you need to configure any of the other settings? _____

 **30** MINUTES

Lab Exercise 4.02: Configuring BIOS Settings

If you find any issues when you examine the BIOS settings using the CMOS setup program, you'll need to reconfigure the settings. Remember, too, that you're preparing the PC for an upgrade to Windows Vista. BIOS-level virus checking is known to cause problems with the Windows Vista installation process, so Microsoft advises that you disable it.

Many BIOS functions are unchangeable and, therefore, are inaccessible via the CMOS setup program. These include things like keyboard and floppy disk drive recognition. Other things are under your control. These include the previously mentioned things like boot sequence order and the date/time, but also some potentially hazardous settings, such as BIOS shadowing and memory timing.

✔ **Hint**

If you're not absolutely certain what a particular setting does, the best course of action is to leave it alone! If you have any doubts, you can always exit the CMOS setup program without saving.

Learning Objectives

In this exercise, you'll access the CMOS setup utility, navigate it to find the various BIOS settings you would commonly need to modify, and practice disabling BIOS-level virus checking.

At the end of this lab, you'll be able to

- Modify the BIOS settings

Lab Materials and Setup

The materials you need for this lab are

- A working PC whose BIOS settings you can change

- If possible, a BIOS that includes virus checking

Getting Down to Business

In the following steps, you'll learn how to navigate to the CMOS setup program configuration screen that has the virus-checking option. This example uses the Award BIOS CMOS setup program. Your CMOS setup program may vary, but all BIOS makers and versions should offer the same options.

✔ **Cross-Reference**

For more details about the features of CMOS setup programs, refer to the section called "A Quick Tour Through a Typical CMOS Setup Program" in Chapter 5 of *Mike Meyers' A+ Guide to Managing and Troubleshooting PCs, Vol. 1: Essentials.*

Step 1   Enter your CMOS setup program.

Step 2   Check your notes and navigate to the configuration screen that has the BIOS-level virus-checking options. It's not always obvious where to find this option, so take your time and use the Help screens if available. As Figure 4-3 shows, virus checking can be disabled in this BIOS from the Advanced BIOS Features screen. Don't hesitate to explore, and don't be too shocked if your BIOS does not have this option—although virus checking is common, it is not universal.

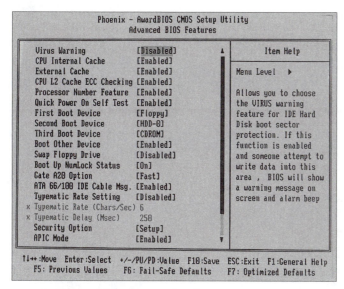

```
                Phoenix - AwardBIOS CMOS Setup Utility
                        Advanced BIOS Features

    Virus Warning            [Disabled]    ▲  │        Item Help
    CPU Internal Cache       [Enabled]        │
    External Cache           [Enabled]        │  Menu Level    ▶
    CPU L2 Cache ECC Checking [Enabled]       │
    Processor Number Feature [Enabled]        │  Allows you to choose
    Quick Power On Self Test [Enabled]        │  the VIRUS warning
    First Boot Device        [Floppy]         │  feature for IDE Hard
    Second Boot Device       [HDD-0]          │  Disk boot sector
    Third Boot Device        [CDROM]          │  protection. If this
    Boot Other Device        [Enabled]        │  function is enabled
    Swap Floppy Drive        [Disabled]       │  and someone attempt to
    Boot Up NumLock Status   [On]             │  write data into this
    Gate A20 Option          [Fast]           │  area , BIOS will show
    ATA 66/100 IDE Cable Msg. [Enabled]       │  a warning message on
    Typematic Rate Setting   [Disabled]       │  screen and alarm beep
  x Typematic Rate (Chars/Sec) 6              │
  x Typematic Delay (Msec)    250             │
    Security Option          [Setup]          │
    APIC Mode                [Enabled]     ▼  │

  ↑↓→←:Move  Enter:Select  +/-/PU/PD:Value  F10:Save  ESC:Exit  F1:General Help
       F5: Previous Values    F6: Fail-Safe Defaults   F7: Optimized Defaults
```

FIGURE 4-3 Disabling BIOS-level virus checking

Step 3 Follow the screen prompts to navigate to the correct configuration screen, and find the virus-checking setting option. Highlight the option (either using the arrow keys or mouse), and change it from Enabled to Disabled. Once again, your CMOS setup program's wording or appearance may be different, but the option to turn off BIOS-level virus checking should be common to all modern BIOSes.

Step 4 Save and exit the CMOS setup program. After you exit, the system will reboot automatically. You have just made a change to the BIOS.

The process you just followed is the same process you'll use for any changes you make to the BIOS. Be sure to save the settings before exiting the setup utility.

Lab Analysis Test

1. After running Windows XP for a few years, Chris has decided to perform a clean installation of Windows 2000. After backing up his important files, he places the Windows 2000 CD-ROM in the CD-ROM drive and reboots his computer—but it just boots into Windows XP like normal. What setting will he most likely need to configure in the BIOS to correct this situation?

   BOOT ORDER

2. Arnold has just installed a new sound card. He boots his system to install the drivers, but his system does not recognize the new card. What BIOS settings might you change using CMOS setup?

   TURN OFF on-Board AUDIO

3. Alex has just finished making changes to the BIOS-level virus checking and would now like to save these changes. Name two ways to save the BIOS settings after you've made changes in the CMOS setup program.

Key Terms Quiz

Use the following vocabulary terms to complete the following sentences. Not all of the terms will be used.

AMI

Award software

BIOS (basic input/output system)

BIOS ROM

CMOS (complementary metal-oxide semiconductor)

CMOS setup program

DELETE key

PAUSE/BREAK key

Phoenix Technologies

1. The system BIOS is stored on nonvolatile memory called _____.

2. Technicians configure the BIOS using the _____.

3. Press the _____ to suspend operation of the power-on self test (POST).

4. _____ provides the primary interface between the operating system's device drivers and most of the system's hardware.

5. A common way to enter CMOS setup is to press the _____ during startup.

Chapter 5
Installing Internal Devices

Lab Exercises

In these lab exercises, you'll learn how to install and remove expansion cards properly and configure and/or repair the device drivers for these cards. This will help you gain confidence in handling expansion card issues in the real world.

For the purposes of this chapter, suppose that you've befriended the owner of a small Internet café. Currently, the café has 12 PCs of various makes and models, all running Windows XP Professional. Paul, the owner, wanted the systems to perform well, so he ensured that each one had at least 2.8-gigahertz (GHz) processors and 512 megabytes (MB) of memory. However, in an attempt to keep the initial cost under budget, he purchased the systems without upgraded graphics or sound, so they are using the onboard graphics and sound.

Paul has noticed that many of the patrons seem to be using the systems to play games against each other in addition to the normal Internet surfing. Some of them have asked if there's any way to improve the performance of the systems so that they can play more advanced games. Paul has been thinking of branching off into hosting local area network (LAN) parties anyway, so he asks you to look into what it will take to upgrade the computers.

You would enjoy recommending that Paul buy new PCs with the latest high-performance components—what tech wouldn't want to play with the latest and greatest tech toys?—but since the computers are fairly new and well appointed, you decide to experiment with some upgrades. Because PC games are graphics- and sound-intensive, you believe that installing individual cards, such as an AGP or PCIe graphics card and a PCI sound card, will improve the overall performance. You verify that the computers have PCI and PCIe expansion slots, so you ask Paul for some cash up front and purchase a couple of video cards and sound cards. You drop them in two of the computers to test your theory.

 **30** MINUTES

Lab Exercise 5.01: Installing Expansion Cards

There are five steps to installing any expansion card device properly:

1. Arm yourself with knowledge of the device before you install it. Is the device certified to run on the Windows operating system that you're running? Is it compatible with your motherboard and other hardware? Be sure to check the Windows Marketplace, formerly known as the Hardware Compatibility List (HCL), before you do anything. The Windows Marketplace (found at http://testedproducts.windowsmarketplace.com) is the definitive authority on which devices are guaranteed to work on modern Windows operating systems.

2. Remove the cover from your PC case and install the device. As always, follow all electrostatic discharge (ESD) and safety precautions, and handle the card with care.

3. Assign system resources to the device. In approximately 99.73 percent of the cases (a rough estimate), you'll never have to do this, because plug and play (PnP) takes care of it for you, but if you're mixing old components with new, you may have to assign resources manually to accommodate the old, non-PnP device.

4. Install device drivers for the component. Windows comes with many device drivers preinstalled, so it may try to help you by installing the driver that it thinks the device needs. In most cases, you should visit the card manufacturer's Web site, download the latest drivers for the card and your operating system, and then install the updated drivers.

5. Verify that the device is functional and that it's not creating any conflicts with other devices on your system.

   The following exercise is a somewhat abridged version of this procedure, because instead of installing a new device, you'll remove and reinstall devices that are already on your system.

✔ **Cross-Reference**

To review the details of device installation, refer to the "Installing Expansion Cards" section in Chapter 5 of *Mike Meyers' A+ Guide to Managing and Troubleshooting PCs, Vol. 2: PC Tech.*

Learning Objectives

In this lab, you'll practice removing and installing internal expansion cards.

At the end of this lab, you'll be able to

- Remove and install expansion cards in a system correctly and safely

Lab Materials and Setup

The materials you need for this lab are

- At least one working computer that is running Windows and has expansion cards installed
- Screwdriver
- Anti-static mat and wrist strap
- Anti-static storage bags
- Notepad

✔ Hint

You may be asking yourself, "Hey, how come I'm not reinstalling the cards into this disassembled PC I have sitting here?" Well, that's a good question! In the next chapter, you will be practicing removing the motherboard from the case and reinstalling it. This process would be complicated by having a card or two sticking out of the motherboard.

When you install expansion cards, it's important that you secure them with screws to the system case. This not only keeps the cards from working loose, but also ensures that proper grounding is taking place. You've already installed the CPU and the RAM onto the motherboard, but as you can see, these will not hinder the installation and removal of the motherboard.

When you complete the practice on the motherboard, you will then be instructed to check back with this chapter and complete the installation of the expansion cards on the disassembled PC.

As usual, if you have access to more than one system, take advantage of it.

Getting Down to Business

In this exercise, you'll remove the expansion card devices from your PC. You'll then make note of any important information you can find on the device's label: device maker, version, and so on. You will then visit the manufacturer's Web site to check for any updated drivers for the device in your version of Windows. Lastly, you'll reassemble and restart the system, and install the updated drivers.

Shut down the system and unplug the power cable. Then place it on your anti-static mat. Remove the PC case cover, strap on your anti-static wrist strap, and you're ready to start.

Step 1 Take a few moments and draw a sketch showing which device is installed in which slot on the motherboard.

Step 2 Remove the cards one at a time from your system. For each card, follow these procedures:

a) Remove the retaining screw and store it safely.

✔ **Hint**

You'll see two main types of screws used in PCs. At first glance, they may look all the same, but while these screws are the same overall size, they have different sizes of threads. Screws with the larger threads, commonly called *coarse-threaded* screws, are generally used to secure expansion cards, power supplies, and case covers. Screws with the smaller threads, commonly called *fine-threaded* screws, are typically used to secure storage devices, such as hard drives, floppy disk drives, and CD media drives, into their respective bays.

b) Taking hold of the card by its edges, carefully and firmly pull it straight up and out of its slot.

✔ **Hint**

These cards can be difficult to remove. If a card seems stuck, try rocking it back and forth (from front to back in the direction of the slot, not side to side).

c) Holding the card only by the edges and the metal flange, place it in an anti-static bag for safekeeping.

Step 3 Examine each of the cards you removed from your system and record the pertinent information:

- Do any of the cards have writing or labels on them? If so, what information do these labels provide?

- Can you identify the manufacturers of the cards? List each card with its manufacturer.

- Are there any version numbers or codes on the cards? List this information for each card.

- If there are any jumpers or dual inline package (DIP) switches on any of the cards, how are they set? You might want to make a quick drawing of the switches and their current positions.

- Can you locate a key or legend that shows you how to set the jumpers or DIP switches? If so, make a note about where you found this information—was it in the instruction manual or printed directly on the expansion card circuit board?

Step 4 Reinstall the expansion cards in your system. For each card, follow these procedures:

a) Check your notes to confirm where to reinstall the card.

b) Align the card over its motherboard slot, making sure that the metal flange is aligned properly with the case slot. Holding the flange with one hand, place the heel of your hand on the top edge of the card and push the card firmly into the expansion slot.

c) Once the card is in the slot and the flange is flush with the case, replace the screw that holds the card in place.

✖ Warning

After all of the expansion cards have been reinstalled, take a look at the back of your system (where you can see input/output connections for the cards). Are there any holes where no cards are installed and a slot cover that has not been used? It's important to install slot covers wherever an expansion card is not installed. This ensures that air will flow properly through the computer case, keeping your critical components cool.

Step 5 Restart your PC and use Device Manager to confirm that each device is working properly. If there is a missing driver, you'll see a yellow circle with a black exclamation point next to the device listing. If there is a resource conflict, the problem device will be disabled and a red X will appear next to its listing.

Step 6 Now download and install the latest device drivers for each of your expansion cards. You can use many methods to accomplish this task, but the two that follow are the most common:

a) If your working PC is connected to the Internet, you can use the Update Driver Wizard from the device's Driver tab in Device Manager to connect to the Windows Update Web site. Open Device Manager and select *View device by type*. Locate the device that matches the expansion card you have installed, and open its Properties dialog box. Select the Driver tab (see Figure 5-1), and then click Update Driver. This displays the Hardware Update Wizard, shown in Figure 5-2; from here, you can follow the directions to download the signed driver from the Windows Update site.

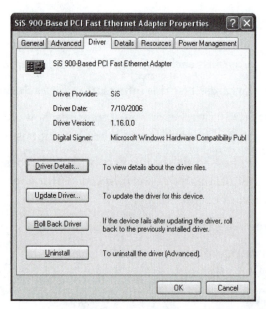

FIGURE 5-1 The Driver tab from the device's Properties dialog box in Windows

FIGURE 5-2 Accessing the Windows Update site

b)   If your working PC is not connected to the Internet, or if the device does not have a signed driver available on the Windows Update site, you will have to follow these instructions before clicking Update Driver. Using a computer with Internet access, find and connect to the manufacturer's Web site. Using the model number of the device, locate and download the correct driver for the operating system on the PC where the device is installed. Save the driver to a floppy disk or Universal Serial Bus (USB) thumb drive, remove the floppy or thumb drive from that system, and insert it into your working PC. Open Device Manager and select *View device by type*. Locate the device that matches the expansion card you have installed, and open its Properties dialog box. Select the Driver tab, and then click Update Driver. When prompted to connect to the Internet, choose *No, not this time*, and follow the directions to locate and load the new device driver (see Figure 5-3).

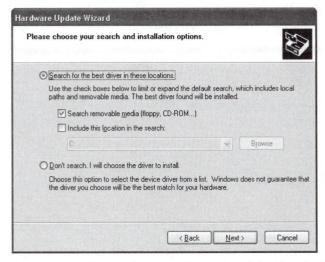

FIGURE 5-3 The Hardware Update Wizard finding device drivers on removable media

> **✔ Hint**
>
> Many manufacturers include installation wizards for their devices, so this is yet another method that may be used to update device drivers. Many times, the manufacturer will include related applications along with the drivers to enhance the performance of the device. A good example of this is an inkjet printer that includes the driver and utilities for adjusting print quality, performing printer maintenance, and so on.

 **30** MINUTES

Lab Exercise 5.02: Using Driver Rollback

Increasing the performance of your PC through the installation of expansion cards (sound cards, video cards, wireless networking, Bluetooth devices, etc.) is easier than it has ever been. Assuming, of course, that you're starting with compatible hardware, Windows XP will detect the new device and install the correct driver with little prompting. Often, Windows already has a usable driver and will install it without any action on your part. To achieve increased performance, usually it is just a matter of updating the driver via the Internet. If the driver turns out to be corrupted or not compatible with Windows XP, using driver rollback can usually get you back up and running.

A new driver may cause unexpected problems with your operating system. Because of this, Windows XP introduced a feature that enables you to roll back to the previous (working) driver if something should go wrong with a driver update. In this exercise, you'll look at the properties of a device, update the driver, and implement driver rollback.

Learning Objectives

Updating and repairing device drivers is one of the basic skills required when working with expansion cards. The following lab exercise walks you through the process.

At the end of this lab, you'll be able to

- Update a device driver in Windows XP
- Roll back to a previously working driver in Windows XP

Lab Materials and Setup

The materials you need for this lab are

- A working PC with Windows XP installed
- An Internet connection

Getting Down to Business

The following steps cover the process of updating device drivers and the steps to roll back (uninstall) device drivers that turn out to be incompatible.

Step 1 Often, when you install a new expansion card, Windows (especially Windows XP) will have a perfectly suitable driver for the device. However, if you would like to update the driver to address a problem, improve performance, or just add a new feature, this step will take you through the process of updating new drivers:

a) Begin by verifying Internet connectivity for the system you will use to update the device.

b) Go to Device Manager, and expand the appropriate device category. Locate the device you want to update (say a 56K modem).

c) Right-click the device and select Properties.

d) Click the Driver tab, and click the Update Driver button (see Figure 5-4). This launches a wizard similar to the Add New Hardware Wizard.

✔ **Hint**

In Windows XP, you can right-click the device in question in Device Manager and update the driver without accessing its properties.

When prompted with *Can Windows connect to Windows Update to search for software?* select *Yes, this time only,* and then select *Install the software automatically.* Windows will search the

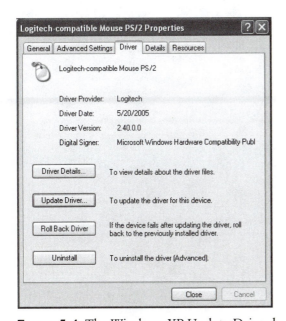

FIGURE 5-4 The Windows XP Update Driver button

Windows Update Web site and either install the driver or report that there is no newer driver for the device.

✔ **Hint**

If Update Driver does not find a newer driver than the one already installed, when you invoke rollback driver, it will inform you that there are no backup drivers available. You may want to check with the manufacturer's Web site to verify that the installed driver is the latest. The next step in the lab will be much more authentic if you are able to locate an updated driver for the device.

Step 2 If a driver is corrupt, or if the wrong driver is installed, Windows has a bad habit of stopping dead in its tracks, rendering your PC useless. Windows XP has a feature that keeps track of the drivers you install on a system and allows you to roll back to a previous one when a new one isn't working as it should:

a) Go to the Device Manager, and locate the device you want to roll back.

b) Right-click the device and select Properties.

c) Click the Driver tab. You can revert to the previous driver by clicking Roll Back Driver (see Figure 5-5).

FIGURE 5-5 Windows XP's Roll Back Driver button

Lab Analysis Test

1. When you examined the two computers from the Internet café, you were pleased to find that one of them had a PCIe × 16 expansion slot. What is the advantage of the PCIe expansion bus, and how will it contribute to providing a solution at the Internet café? *It allows better video cards to be used.*

2. Ray is using the Device Manager to search for updated drivers for his sound card. He selects all of the manual options, but is unable to find a suitable upgraded driver. What type of file is the Windows Update Driver Wizard looking for? *.inf*

3. You've installed a network interface card (NIC) and a PCI FireWire controller card on Susan's Windows XP Professional system. The system starts up fine, but when you check Device Manager, you see a yellow circle with a black exclamation mark beside the NIC icon. What is the problem? *The two devices are conflicting with each other in the drivers. Need to install Drivers*

4. Given the scenario in the previous question, what steps should you take to rectify the problem? *Need to install the Drivers for both devices*

5. Tim has installed a PCIe 10-gigabyte (GB) NIC. He boots the computer and navigates to Device Manager, only to find that there is a red X icon next to this device. What should Tim do next? *Install or update the driver. Enable the device.*

Key Terms Quiz

Use the following vocabulary terms to complete the following sentences. Not all of the terms will be used.

.inf

AGP

device drivers

DMA

expansion card

I/O address

IRQ

ISA

PCI

PCIe

rollback driver

system resources

memory address

1. When device drivers are installed, the type of file the installation wizard looks for ends with the _____*.inf*_____ extension.

2. After updating a device driver, Windows XP sometimes locks up. To correct this situation, you might implement _*roll back driver*_.

3. Often, _*device drivers*_ are updated to improve performance, add features, or improve compatibility of an expansion card.

4. Currently, high-end graphics cards are usually inserted into either a(n) _*AGP*_ or _*PCIe*_ slot.

5. The Hardware Update Wizard makes it easy to update the ~~IP Address~~ _*Device Drivers*_ for a device.

Chapter 6
Installing and Troubleshooting Motherboards

Lab Exercises

As you discovered in the labs for the CompTIA A+ certification exam, Essentials (220-601), there are basically two occasions when replacing a motherboard is required. The first, of course, is when the motherboard malfunctions or is damaged; modern motherboards aren't made to be repaired, so when they go bad, they must be replaced as a whole unit. The other is when you want to upgrade the PC to a more powerful CPU than its current motherboard supports. In either of these cases, you've got a bit of work ahead of you! Installing a motherboard requires more effort than any other type of installation: more preparation, more time performing the installation, and more clean-up afterward. Still, you shouldn't be intimidated by the prospect of replacing a motherboard—it's a common and necessary part of PC repair. In this chapter, you'll go through the process of removing and reinstalling one.

In the following exercises, you'll make preparations for the actual motherboard removal and installation, including labeling cables and connectors, and removing the motherboard from a working PC. You'll then reinstall the motherboard and launch the trusty CPU-Z utility to explore the specifications of the motherboard.

 15 MINUTES

Lab Exercise 6.01: Removing and Labeling Components and Cables

Once you've decided a system will need new a motherboard, you can't just rip the old one out. To get to the motherboard, you have to first remove the installed expansion cards and cables. Many of us have had the experience of taking something apart only to wind up with leftover parts after we put it back together. To avoid this result when you disassemble a PC, you should get into the habit of properly storing and labeling any parts that you remove from the system. This includes everything from the major components to the screws that hold them in place and the cables that connect them to the motherboard.

> **✔ Hint**
>
> If you are using the disassembled, non-production computer for this lab, you have already removed and organized the components and cables. Use this step to review the labeling and storage of components and cables in preparation for removal and installation of the motherboard. If you are using a second computer for this exercise, make use of this lab to build the "good habit" of organization. Of course, you don't need to attach a label to each individual screw, but do keep them organized in labeled containers to avoid confusion!

Learning Objectives

In this lab, you'll remove and label expansion card components, cables, and connectors in preparation for removing the motherboard.

At the end of this lab, you'll be able to

- Remove and label expansion cards
- Remove and label data cables and connectors
- Remove and label power cables

Lab Materials and Setup

The materials you need for this lab are

- A working, non-production computer
- The motherboard book or online documentation for the motherboard
- Post-it notes and a pen
- Screwdriver
- Anti-static mat
- Anti-static wrist strap
- Anti-static bags

Getting Down to Business

Starting with your system shut down (and, as always, the power cable unplugged from the wall and the case), set your system on the anti-static mat, remove the PC case cover, and strap on your anti-static wrist strap. Have your labeling materials handy, and perform the following steps.

Step 1 Following the procedure laid out in Lab Exercise 5.01 in the previous chapter, remove any expansion cards from the PC. Label each one with a Post-it note that identifies the card, and store it in an anti-static bag.

Step 2   Disconnect and label the following data cables:

- Hard drive cables

- CD- or DVD-media drive cables

- Floppy disk drive cable

- Sound cable (runs from the CD- or DVD-media drive to the sound card)

- USB front panel connector dongle (if applicable)

Step 3   Disconnect and label the following power cables:

- Hard drive cables

- CD- or DVD-media drive cables

- Floppy drive cable

- Power plugs for the CPU fan, power supply fan (if present), and case fan (if present)

- Motherboard power (P1 and/or P4 on ATX motherboards)

Step 4   Disconnect and label the front panel control wires (also called the harness wires) from the motherboard. Be certain to use the motherboard book to properly label these wires! Front panel control wires typically include the power button (on ATX motherboards), reset button, front panel LEDs—power, hard disk activity, and so on—and system speaker.

✔ Hint

> To label wires, use the small Post-its, or cut the square ones into strips. Fold the sticky part of the Post-it over the wire, and stick it to the back to make a tag you can write on.

Step 5   Depending on your system, you may have to remove other devices to ensure that you have sufficient clearance to lift the motherboard out of the PC case in the next exercise. Visually confirm that there aren't any components blocking a path for easy removal. Are any hard drives or CD- or DVD-media drives in the way? Is the power supply in the way? Remove anything that could block the motherboard's exit or bump into important attached components—namely the RAM or CPU fan—during removal.

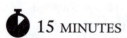 15 MINUTES

Lab Exercise 6.02: Removing a Motherboard

With all of your PC components and cables safely tucked away, the next step in your upgrade job is to remove the old motherboard so that you can replace it. Techs will tell you that motherboard removal is the exercise that separates the geek from the meek and the true PC tech from the wannabe, but don't let that intimidate you! Motherboard removal is completely straightforward and simple.

✔ **Hint**

Once again, if you're using the disassembled non-production computer, you have already removed the motherboard from the case, but you should use this exercise to review. If you're using a different computer for this exercise, follow the instructions.

Learning Objectives

In this lab, you'll remove your PC's motherboard.

At the end of this lab, you'll be able to

- Remove a motherboard safely and correctly

Lab Materials and Setup

The materials you need for this lab are

- The non-production, working computer on which you performed Lab Exercise 6.01
- Phillips-head screwdriver
- Anti-static mat and anti-static wrist strap
- Large anti-static bag

Getting Down to Business

Following the same ESD procedures listed in the previous exercises, you'll now remove the mounting screws for the motherboard and lift it out of the PC case.

Step 1 Locate and remove the screws holding the motherboard to the frame of the case. There are most likely six to nine screws, which may also have small washers. Be sure not to lose these washers, as they help prevent overtightening the screws during installation. Some systems may use small plastic or metal supports called *standoffs* between the motherboard and the frame. Remove these and store them in a labeled container.

✖ **Warning**

Remember to handle the motherboard as you would any printed circuit board: gently, by the edges, as if you were holding a delicate old photograph.

Step 2 Carefully remove the motherboard from the PC case and place it on your anti-static mat. You should place the motherboard in a large anti-static bag for the best protection.

 **30** MINUTES

Lab Exercise 6.03: Installing a Motherboard

Now that you've removed the old, inadequate motherboards from your client's systems, you get to the real test of your tech skills: installing the new motherboards and reconnecting everything so that the computers work! Once again, however, there's no need to be intimidated. Everything you need to install a motherboard (in your case, probably the motherboard you just removed in Lab Exercise 6.02) is right in front of you.

> Over the last few labs, you have concentrated on hardware removal and installation, using either the disassembled non-production system or a working non-production system—or, in some cases, both. It is easy to become casual or even careless about technique and organization, since these computers are non-critical.
>
> One of the really important concepts to remember is that all of these efforts—the studying, the labs, and the CompTIA A+ certification itself—are designed to help you become the highest-quality tech that you can be! It's important that you develop and practice patience, attention to detail, and finesse while working through the lab exercises.
>
> To this end, when you remove and replace a motherboard in a system, you interact with almost every component of the computer system. In the field, you must not only successfully disassemble/assemble the hardware, but also verify that the system powers up and operates properly afterward. Many competent techs, when installing a new motherboard, will check for proper operation along the way. Here's a good checkpoint: After you've installed the CPU and RAM, configured any jumpers or switches, and installed the motherboard in the case, insert the power connections and test the system. A POST card is a real timesaver here, but you can also connect the PC speaker, graphics card, monitor, and keyboard to verify that the system is booting properly.

Learning Objectives

In this lab, you'll install a motherboard. You can use the motherboard and system you disassembled in Lab Exercises 6.01 and 6.02.

At the end of this lab, you'll be able to

- Install a PC motherboard and connect all its associated components

Lab Materials and Setup

The materials you need for this lab are

- The disassembled, non-production PC used in the lab exercises in Chapter 2
- A working, non-production system from which the motherboard has been removed

- Components and cables previously connected to the removed motherboard

- Motherboard book or online documentation for the motherboard

- Anti-static mat

- Anti-static wrist strap

- Notepad and pen

Getting Down to Business

Physically installing the motherboard itself is mostly a matter of being careful and methodical. The more complex part of the task is reattaching all the cables and cards in their proper places.

✖ Warning

Motherboards are full of delicate electronics! Remember to follow the proper ESD and safety procedures.

✔ Hint

When installing a motherboard, it's handy to use your notepad to check off assembly steps as you go along.

Step 1   Carefully line up the motherboard inside the PC case, and secure it in place with the mounting screws. Be sure to use the washers and plastic/metal standoffs, if supplied.

Step 2   Insert the front panel control wires in their appropriate places. These should include your power button (on ATX motherboards), reset button, front panel LEDs (power, hard disk activity, etc.), system speaker, and so on. Refer to the labels and your motherboard documentation for the proper connections.

✔ Hint

At this point, if you're working on the disassembled, non-production system, skip to Step 5, install the expansion cards, and then set the system aside. You will continue to build the disassembled system in future lab exercises, where you will explore the power supply, hard drives, removable storage, and audio/video components.

Step 3   Connect all power cables to the hard drive, CD- or DVD-media drive, floppy drive, CPU fan, main motherboard, and so on.

Step 4   Connect data cables to the hard drive, CD- or DVD-media drive, and floppy drive, as well as the sound cable and USB connector dongles, if applicable.

Step 5   Following the procedure laid out in Lab Exercise 5.01 in the previous chapter, install the expansion card components.

Step 6   Now comes perhaps the most important step: double-check all of your connections and cards to make sure that they're properly seated and connected where they're supposed to be! If something is wrong, it's definitely better to discover it now than to smell smoke after you've hit the power switch.

Step 7   Finally, if you're using the working PC you previously disassembled, you can now replace the case cover on your PC and then plug the keyboard, mouse, and monitor back in. Plug the power cable back in, and turn it on. Assuming you've done everything correctly, your system will boot up normally.

 15 MINUTES

Lab Exercise 6.04: Exploring Motherboard Features with CPU-Z

Now that you've completed the analysis and upgrade of your client's systems with new motherboards and CPUs, where needed, you can verify some of the characteristics and features the motherboard manufacturer has promoted. You already downloaded the CPU-Z utility from the Internet, so you can launch that to examine the information on the Mainboard tab.

✔ **Tech Tip**

A Motherboard by Any Other Name: Over the years, motherboards have been called many names—and not just the bad names that you might use when one doesn't work properly! Early motherboards were sometimes called the *planar board*. Motherboards can be referred to as the *system board*, *mainboard*, and sometimes just *board* or *mobo*. Regardless of the name, these terms refer to the large printed circuit board (PCB) used to connect all of the components in a computer system.

Learning Objectives

In this lab, you'll identify various motherboard features.

At the end of this lab, you'll be able to

- Verify motherboard features

Lab Materials and Setup

The materials you need for this lab are

- Access to a working computer with the CPU-Z utility installed

- A notepad and pencil to document the specifications

- A word-processing or spreadsheet application to facilitate the documentation (optional)

This lab is more informative if you have access to different systems using various motherboards.

Getting Down to Business

In the following steps, you'll verify the features of your motherboard.

Step 1   Launch CPU-Z and navigate to the Mainboard tab.

Step 2   The CPU-Z utility displays some of the key features of your motherboard, as shown in Figure 6-1.

Using the information gathered by CPU-Z, record as much pertinent information below as possible:

Manufacturer _____

Model _____

Chipset _____

Southbridge _____

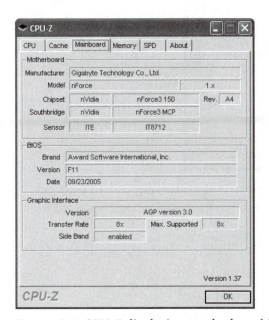

FIGURE 6-1 CPU-Z displaying motherboard information

Sensor _____

BIOS brand _____

Graphic interface version _____

Step 3   If possible, launch CPU-Z on various computers to compare the features of different motherboards.

→ **Try This: PC Wizard**

Using a system installed with PC Wizard (see Chapter 3, "Installing and Troubleshooting RAM") launch PC Wizard. Once PC Wizard is running, click the Mainboard icon. This displays a number of items (components) in the upper-right pane of the window. Click the Mainboard item to display detailed information in the lower-right pane of the window, as shown here:

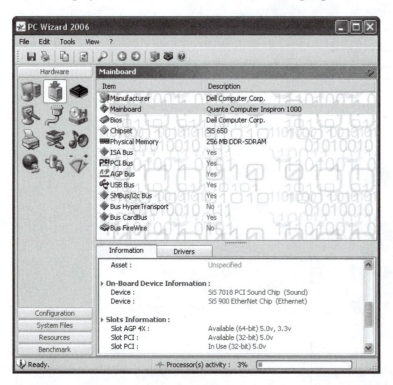

Using this information, can you determine the integrated devices supported by your motherboard? Does this correspond to the information in the PC or motherboard documentation?

Lab Analysis Test

1. When Stan reviews the Information pane of the PC Wizard utility, it indicates that there is an AC'97 Audio Controller on the motherboard. What does "onboard" represent, and what is the function of this device? Provide good detail.

2. While using CPU-Z, Melissa notices the heading "sensor." What might these sensors be used to measure on a system board?

3. Dianne is trying to install an ATX motherboard in a new, empty ATX case. She tries to set it down in the bottom of the case, but it won't fit—the ports on the side are too low to poke out the back of the case, and she can't make the screws work at all. What has she forgotten?

4. After Erik reassembled his PC and turned it on, he noticed that the green LED and the disk active LED never light up, but everything seems to work okay. What is the problem?

5. Devon has installed one or two new motherboards in the past, and has now been asked to upgrade an existing system. He tackles the project enthusiastically, disconnecting every device, power connection, and data cable. As Devon begins to install the new board, you notice the pile of cables, devices, and even the old motherboard next to the case. How should Devon change his technique? Why?

Key Terms Quiz

Use the following vocabulary terms to complete the following sentences. Not all of the terms will be used.

anti-static mat

AT

ATX

BTX

chipset

CPU-Z

FlexATX

harness wires

microATX

motherboard book

P1 power connector

P4 power connector

P8/P9 power connector

standoffs

1. The power supplies for modern ATX motherboards connect using the _____.

2. Some systems may use small plastic or metal supports called _____ between the motherboard and the frame.

3.   The set of wires that connects many of the front panel switches and indicator light-emitting diodes is known as the _____.

4.   Once the motherboard is removed from the case, it should be carefully placed on a(n) _____ to protect it from ESD damage.

5.   _____ is a handy utility that allows you to display some of the key components and specifications of the motherboard.

Chapter 7

Installing and Troubleshooting Power Supplies

Lab Exercises

Removing and installing a PC power supply is a fairly straightforward process. The various versions of the ATX power supplies are, by far, the most common power supplies you will see on desktop computer systems. These include ATX (with a 20-pin P1 power connector), ATX 12V 1.3 (which added the AUX 4-pin connector commonly referred to as P4), and ATX 12V 2.0 (which added the 24-pin P1 connector). Server motherboards often require much higher voltage, so you may start to see the Server System Infrastructure (SSI)–developed, non-ATX–standard motherboard with a power supply named EPS 12V; it uses a 24-pin P1 connector, a 4-pin P4 connector, and a unique 8-pin connector.

Suppose a client calls you, saying that her PC keeps locking up. After walking her through a few simple troubleshooting steps, you rule out a virus or a misbehaving application. This leaves hardware as the likely culprit, and in all likelihood, it's the power supply. In these lab exercises, after previously determining that the power supply is the failed device, you'll practice the procedures for replacing it.

After replacing the PC power supply, you will research some options to protect the power supply (and PC) from the damage that power spikes, surges, and drops can cause.

✔ **Hint**

> The CompTIA A+ 220-602 (IT Technician) exam will typically refer to the power supply using the abbreviation PSU (power supply unit) or the acronym FRU (field replaceable unit). FRU can describe any component that would be replaced in the field by a technician.

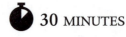 **30** MINUTES

Lab Exercise 7.01: Replacing a Power Supply

Let's assume that you've found a variance in the 12 Volt range that explains your client's system lockups. You know that power supplies aren't user-serviceable components—you don't fix them; you replace them as a unit—so it's time to replace her power supply. Next to the motherboard, the power supply is the most time-consuming component to replace, simply because of all those wires! Nonetheless, replacing it is a simple operation, as described in the following sections.

Learning Objectives

At the end of this lab, you'll be able to

- Determine the total wattage requirements of the system and select the proper power supply

- Replace a power supply

Lab Materials and Setup

The materials you need for this lab are

- A non-production PC computer system

- A working PC with an ATX power supply (optional)

- A Phillips-head screwdriver

- A labeled container for holding screws

Getting Down to Business

One of the areas where PC manufacturers cut corners on lower-end systems is power supplies. High-end systems typically come with higher-wattage power supplies, whereas entry-level PCs typically have lower-wattage power supplies. This might not be evident until you add power-hungry components to the system, placing a heavier load on the power supply and causing an early failure.

In the following steps, you'll determine the wattage of the power supply on your system, calculate the power usage of your PC, and then remove and reinstall the power supply.

Step 1   To find out what the wattage rating of your power supply is, look at the label on the power supply (see Figure 7-1).

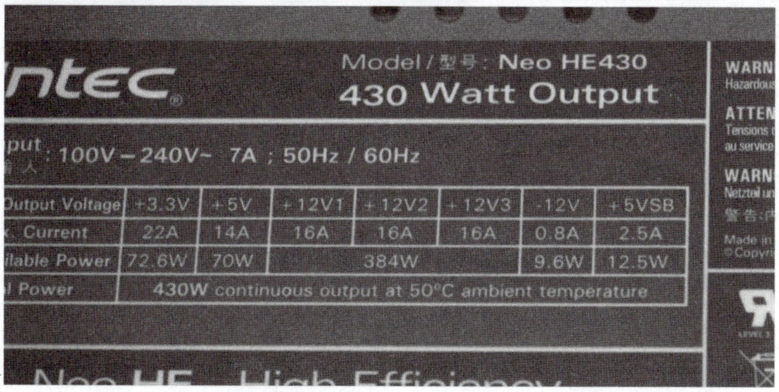

FIGURE 7-1 Typical ATX power-supply ratings label

Find the similar label on your power supply, and locate the watts rating. If you don't see a clear wattage rating, as shown in Figure 7-1, or something less evident, like the smaller "430 W" marking on the label, the power supply rating may be hidden in the model number, which, in this example, is "Neo HE430."

✔ **Hint**

All power supplies have a wattage rating. If it is not apparent on the power supply itself, search the Internet, using the model number for reference.

What is the wattage of your power supply? _____

Step 2   When it comes time to replace a power supply, don't skimp on the wattage! Modern power supplies typically range from 300 watts to 1000 watts or more. Three hundred-watt power supplies are the bare minimum you would use on a system that has only a few installed components (such as a single hard drive and CD- or DVD-media drive), while the 1000-watt models are usually found on server systems that have multiple hard drives (such as a Redundant Array of Inexpensive Disks [RAID] array), multiple processors, or other power-hungry components. Many gaming systems with high-performance graphics, dual-core processors, and Serial Advanced Technology Attachment (SATA) RAID configurations will use PSUs that provide 550 to 650 watts to meet these systems' power requirements. As a general rule, get the highest-wattage replacement you can afford while maintaining compatibility with your system. Remember, the system will only draw the current it requires, so you will never damage a system by installing a higher-wattage power supply.

✖ **Warning**

Never replace a PC's power supply with one of lower wattage!

Use Table 7-1 to calculate the overall wattage needed for your system. Add the numbers for each component, and determine the lowest and highest wattage requirements.

If the highest total exceeds the power-supply wattage rating, you may run into problems. When selecting a new power supply, you should multiply the load by a factor of 1.5. The multiplier provides a safety factor and allows the power supply to run more efficiently. A power supply is more efficient at 30 to 70 percent of its full capacity rating. Thus, a 450-watt PSU works best when only 135 to 315 watts are being used.

What wattage is appropriate for your system? _____

Component	Requirement	Voltage(s) Used
PCIe video card	45 to 75 W	3.3 V
AGP video card	30 to 50 W	3.3 V
PCI card	5 to 10 W	5 V
10/100 NIC	4 W	3.3 V
SCSI controller PCI	20 W	3.3 V and 5 V
Floppy disk drive	5 W	5 V
7200 rpm IDE hard drive	5 to 20 W	5 V and 12 V
7200 rpm SATA hard drive	5 to 20 W	5 V and 12 V
10,000 rpm SCSI drive	10 to 40 W	5 V and 12 V
CD/DVD media drive	10 to 25 W	5 V and 12 V
Case/CPU fans	3 W (each)	12 V
Motherboard (without CPU or RAM)	25 to 40 W	3.3 V and 5 V
RAM	10 W per 128 MB	3.3 V
Pentium 4 processor	70 W	12 V
Pentium D processor	65 to 104 W	12 V
AMD Athlon 64 X2 processor	92 W	12 V

TABLE 7-1   Wattage and Voltage Needs for Common PC Components

✔ **Hint**

Depending on the design of your PC case, you may have to remove data cables or components before you can get to the power supply. Make certain that you have plenty of room to work inside the case!

Step 3   Shut down the system and remove the IEC-320 power cable from the back of the power supply. Then remove the power supply:

a)   Disconnect the Molex, SATA, and mini-connectors from your drive devices. Then unplug the main power connector from the motherboard.

b)   If your power supply uses a P4 connector, disconnect it from the motherboard.

c) Unscrew the four screws holding the power supply to the PC case (remembering to support it while you remove the last one!), and remove the power supply from the case. Store the screws in the labeled container.

Step 4 Take this opportunity to inspect and clean the power supply. Check for any rust or corrosion on the power supply casing or on any of the contacts. Inspect the wires for damage or frayed insulation. Use canned air to blow dust and dirt out of the intake and exhaust vents.

Step 5 Reinstall the power supply by performing the preceding steps in reverse order. If you had to remove data cables or other components to get at the power supply, be sure to reattach them.

 **30** MINUTES

Lab Exercise 7.02: Implementing Power Protection

You've successfully fixed your client's power-problem–plagued PC (say that five times fast!), but now you've noted that she has nothing in the way of power protection for her system, nor do any of her coworkers. None!

When you mention this to her, she tells you that her boss never really saw the point of spending money on surge protectors, uninterruptible power supplies, or any of "that stuff." With a straight face, she asks, "Do those things really do any good?"

Now it's your task to sell the boss on the idea of power protection. To do this, you must explain the types of power problems that lurk in the bushes, just waiting to pounce on unwary users without power protection, and suggest precautions that they can take to prevent power-related damage.

Learning Objectives

At the end of this lab, you'll be able to

- Explain the need for power protection

- Explain the types of power protection available for a PC

✔ **Cross-Reference**

For details on power protection, refer to the "Surge Suppressors" and "UPS" sections in Chapter 7 of *Mike Meyers' A+ Guide to Managing and Troubleshooting PCs, Vol. 2: PC Tech*.

Lab Materials and Setup

The materials you need for this lab are

- A working PC

Getting Down to Business

Too often, PC users take the electricity that powers their system for granted. After all, there's not much you can do about the electricity, is there? Not so! Armed with the knowledge of the types of power conditions that can affect your PC, you can best determine what precautions to take.

Step 1   Describe the following types of power conditions and the type of damage they can cause:

Power spike

_____

Brownout

_____

Blackout

_____

Step 2   Describe the following types of power-protection equipment:

Surge suppressor

_____

Online uninterruptible power supply (UPS)

_____

Standby UPS

_____

Lab Analysis Test

1. George has purchased a number of CD-RW drives for his computer system to facilitate duplication of his own music recording. He now finds that the computer is more prone to lock-up, especially when he is burning multiple CD-Rs at a time. What might you suggest to George for his next upgrade? Why?

2. Athena lives in an area where the power is often interrupted. She bought a good surge protector strip, but that does not seem to help. What does she need to prevent her system from shutting down unexpectedly?

3. Andy has learned the power equation $P = I \times E$, and he would like to use it to determine how many computers he can plug in to a 15A power strip. You explain that the computers he uses in the computer lab have 430-W power supplies. How many can he power through one 15A power strip?

4. One of your clients has an older Pentium 4 system with a single Integrated Drive Electronics (IDE) hard drive and 512 megabytes (MB) of random access memory (RAM). He has been using this PC as his main workstation, but has purchased a newer system, and now wants to redeploy the older system as a file server on his network. He has ordered a PCI SCSI controller board and three SCSI hard drives so that he can configure a RAID array, as well as an additional 2 gigabytes (GB) of RAM. He also ordered two Y adapters for the power supply connectors. He asks for your advice about any additional hardware he should order. What do you tell him?

5. What are the power requirements of the following system?

   - AMD Athlon 64 X2 CPU and 512 MB RAM

   - Two SATA hard drives and one floppy disk drive

   - One CD-RW drive and one DVD-ROM drive

   - PCIe video

   - PCI sound card

   - Network interface card (NIC)

Key Terms Quiz

Use the following vocabulary terms to complete the following sentences. Not all of the terms will be used.

   3.3 V

   5 V

   12 V

20-pin P1

24-pin P1

IEC-320

Molex connector

P4

P8/P9

power sags

power spikes

power strip

power supply

UPS

1. The common three-prong connector on the back of a computer where the power cord plugs in to is defined in the _____ specifications.

2. PC devices with motors, such as hard drives and CD-ROM drives, usually require _____ of direct current (DC) electricity from the power supply.

3. Two popular companies, APC and Tripp Lite, provide many models of a device known as a(n) _____ to protect computer systems from brownouts and blackouts.

4. A surge protector prevents damage from _____ in the voltage.

5. The most common power protection device used for personal computers is a surge suppressor. Surge suppressors are usually incorporated into the _____ itself.

Chapter 8
Hard Drive Technologies

Lab Exercises

Every tech must know how to connect, configure, maintain, and troubleshoot hard drives of all types. A fully operational drive requires proper hardware setup and installation, CMOS configuration, and software setup, usually performed by tools that come with the operating system. The first few labs in this chapter cover physical installation and CMOS configuration of the mainstream hard drive technology, namely Advanced Technology Attachment (ATA), in both parallel and serial flavors. You will then conduct research on the developments of the rapidly changing Small Computer Systems Interface (SCSI), primarily used for large, fault-tolerant data storage. The next exercise will have you troubleshoot installations, and finally, you'll finish with a set of labs that have you install additional hard drives, configure them as dynamic disks, and implement a Redundant Array of Inexpensive Disks (RAID) 0 stripe set.

 1 HOUR

Lab Exercise 8.01: Installing Parallel ATA Hard Drives

The local nonprofit organization where you volunteer has received a donation of 10 used PCs. Most of them have tiny hard drives, so they need an upgrade before you can distribute them to the various workers at the agency. All of the motherboards have built-in parallel advanced technology attachment (PATA) controllers; some even have the better ATA/100 controllers. Your boss breaks out a stack of donated hard drives and tells you to get to work!

Installing a PATA hard drive successfully requires little more than connecting data and power cables to the drive and plugging the other end of the data cable into the motherboard. Sounds simple enough on the surface, but because all PATA drives give you options to install two on each motherboard controller, unwary techs get tripped up here. This lab walks you through the first major step in drive installation: the physical part.

✔ **Hint**

IDE drives have several names that techs use pretty much interchangeably: IDE, EIDE, and ATA. You'll see all three terms in this lab manual and on the CompTIA A+ certification exams. Except for discussions of very old technology, the terms describe the same type of hard disk drive in use today.

Learning Objectives

In this lab exercise, you'll identify the different components of PATA hard drives and cables, and learn installation procedures.

At the end of this lab, you'll be able to

- Remove a hard drive safely and correctly
- Describe PATA cables and connectors
- Describe the geometry of a hard drive
- Calculate the capacity of a hard drive
- Describe jumper settings
- Identify the major parts of a hard drive
- Install a hard drive safely and correctly

Lab Materials and Setup

The materials you need for this lab are

- The disassembled, non-production computer system from the lab exercises in Chapter 1, with at least one PATA hard drive
- A working PC with a PATA hard drive installed
- The Windows operating system installed on the PC
- Access to one or more broken hard drives that have the covers removed for observation of the internal parts (optional)

Getting Down to Business

Grab your handy screwdriver and anti-static wrist strap—it's time to remove a hard drive! As in previous labs, if you are using the disassembled, non-production PC for this lab, you have already removed all of the hard drives, CD-media drive, and floppy disk drive (if present). You should gather together the drives you removed from the system, along with all associated cables and mounting hardware, to facilitate their reinstallation at the end of this exercise. The following removal instructions are included for clarification; however, you will use the drives and cables to work through the identification steps that follow.

Step 1   Shut down your system and remove the system cover, following proper electrostatic discharge (ESD) procedures.

Step 2   Disconnect all the ribbon cables from the hard drives and CD-ROM drives, but first note which device is connected to which cable and where the orientation stripe is located on each device. Be careful but firm. Grasp the cable as closely as possible to the connector on the drive, and pull, rocking the connector gently from side to side.

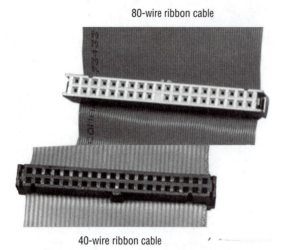

80-wire ribbon cable

40-wire ribbon cable

FIGURE 8-1 ATA cables: Comparing 80-wire and 40-wire ribbon cable connectors

Examine the connector on the end of the ribbon cable. Use Figure 8-1 to help you.

How many holes does it have for pins? _____

Are any of the holes in the connector filled in? Does the connector have a raised portion on one side so that it only fits one way? In other words, is it keyed? _____

Take a close look at the top connector in Figure 8-1.

How many connectors are on your ribbon cable?_____

Do you have a 40-wire or 80-wire ribbon cable? _____

Disconnect the power supply from all of the PATA devices by unplugging the Molex connector from each one.

✖ Warning

Molex plugs can be difficult to remove and brutal on the fingers. Little "bumps" on each side of the plug enable you to rock the plug back and forth to remove it.

Step 3   Now look at the motherboard connections, and note the orientation of the cable connectors. Disconnect the ribbon cables from the motherboard. Be careful but firm. Grasp the cable as closely as possible to the connector on the motherboard, and pull, rocking the connector gently from side to side.

Lay the cables aside for later reinstallation.

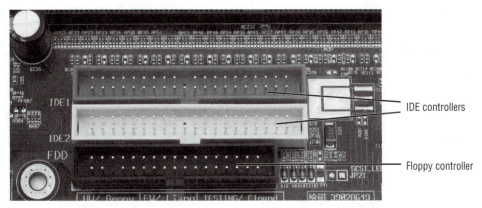

FIGURE 8-2 Viewing the PATA connectors on a motherboard

Step 4   Look at the PATA connections on your motherboard (see Figure 8-2).

How many PATA controllers do you see on your motherboard?

_____

Look closely at your motherboard, and see if you can find writing on the board next to the IDE connections. Are the interfaces grouped into pairs? Are any of them dedicated to special configurations such as RAID? _____

What color are the IDE connections on the motherboard? _____

Step 5   Remove a hard drive from the system. Be careful to note the type of screws you removed, and store them for safekeeping. Also be sure to use proper ESD procedures when removing the drive from your system.

Because of the variety of cases, caddies, bays, slots, and so on, it's not possible to give detailed instructions on how to remove the drive from your particular system. Look closely for caddy releases or retaining screws. Close inspection and a little logic will usually make it clear how to remove the drive. Make notes of how the drive comes out, as you'll have to reinstall it later.

Step 6   With the hard drive out of the system and on a static-free surface, ground yourself, pick up the drive, and examine it carefully.

Note its dimensions. It should measure about 6″ × 3.5″ × 1″. Some drives may be larger than this, measuring 6″ × 5.25″ × 1″—these are known as *bigfoot drives*. Some drives are smaller, but those are used mostly in laptops.

Look at the largest surfaces of the drive (the top and bottom). The bottom is where the printed circuit board with a read-only memory (ROM) chip is located. This circuitry is the hard drive controller. The top side of the drive normally has a label or other means of listing the specifications for the drive, but this is not always the case.

Write down all the information on the label. Be sure to include the manufacturer and the model number for future reference. Usually, the label lists the total capacity of the hard drive and the power requirements (voltage and current). On older drives, the label lists the three main measurements of hard drive geometry: the number of *cylinders*, the number of *heads*, and the number of *sectors per track*. Together, these measurements may be listed simply as CHS.

✔ **Cross-Reference**

For more information about CHS, refer to the "Geometry" section in Chapter 9 of *Mike Meyers' A+ Guide to Managing and Troubleshooting PCs, Vol. 2: PC Tech*.

Using these three measurements, you can calculate the capacity of the hard drive. The formula is cylinders × heads × sectors per track × 512 = bytes of data. (The number of bytes in one sector is 512.)

For example, an older drive has the following information on the label. What is the total capacity of this drive?

- C = 859

- H = 16

- S = 63

859 × 16 × 63 × 512 = 443,326,464 bytes

To convert this to megabytes, divide the answer by 1,048,576, as shown here:

443,326,464 / 1,048,576 = 422.8 MB

A Seagate ST310211A PATA hard drive has CHS values of 16383, 16, and 63. What is its total capacity in bytes? In megabytes? In gigabytes? (To convert from megabytes to gigabytes, divide the number of megabytes by 1024.) _____

Step 7 Look at the end of the drive where the ribbon cable connects. Find the markings for where pin 1 of the ribbon cable should go.

Is it closer to the center of the drive (near the power connector) or to the side of the drive?

_____

Does your hard drive have jumpers like the ones in Figure 8-3? _____

Notice that the drive in Figure 8-3 has the jumper set to CS (which stands for *cable select*).

Each PC system that boots from a PATA hard drive should have the hard drive located on the first PATA interface (IDE1). Normally, the jumper must be set to Master so that the system can

Figure 8-3 Locating the PATA hard drive jumper setting

recognize it as the boot drive. A second drive (hard drive or CD-/DVD-media drive) can be on the same cable, but must be set to Slave.

How are the jumpers set on your hard drive? _____

How are the jumpers set on your CD or DVD drive? _____

Can you have two master drives in the system? _____

For the purposes of this exercise, make sure you leave your hard drive jumpered as it was when you removed it.

Step 8 Locate a broken hard drive (if you're in a class, ask your instructor for one) and remove its cover.

✖ **Warning**

Never remove the cover from a functioning hard drive! Hard drives are extremely sensitive, so merely exposing the inside to the air will cause *irreparable* damage.

Notice the round polished platters that spin in the middle of the drive. This is where the data is stored magnetically.

The actuator arms that move across the platters have tiny coils of wire attached to their ends. These coils hold the read/write heads.

How many surfaces does your sample drive have (one platter = two surfaces)? _____

How many physical heads does your sample drive have? _____

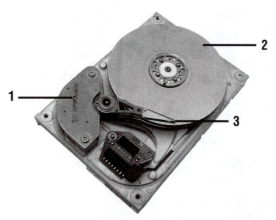

FIGURE 8-4 The internal parts of a hard drive

Both answers are most likely the same, because usually there is a read/write head for each surface.

Look at Figure 8-4 and identify the following parts by number.

Read/write heads _____

Platters _____

Voice coil motor _____

Now look at Figure 8-5 and match the numbered components.

Enhanced Integrated Drive Electronics (EIDE) controller _____

Molex connector _____

PATA connector _____

Master/slave jumper _____

FIGURE 8-5 The external parts of a hard drive

Step 9   Insert the drive back into your system, and secure it with the proper screws. Connect all the ribbon cables to all the drives, and pay attention to the proper alignment of the connectors. Connect the Molex power connectors. Leave the system case off until you verify that everything works properly.

If you used a working computer for the prior steps, you can verify that you've reinstalled the drives correctly by going to the next major step in the process of hard drive installation: CMOS configuration. Lab Exercise 8.03 in this chapter covers the CMOS details, but if you just can't wait, try Step 10. This bonus step should work on newer motherboard models.

Step 10   Turn on the system and wait for it to boot to the desktop. Double-click the My Computer icon, and confirm that the icons for the reinstalled drives are displayed. The fact that you were able to get to the desktop confirms that you've reinstalled the boot drive correctly, but do the other drives (if you have them) and your CD-ROM drive work?

✔ Hint

If you cannot boot the system, or if the CD-ROM drive does not work, the first and obvious place to start is to verify all the cable connections. Any kind of disk errors at this time were most likely caused by the technician; after all, it worked before you touched it!

 45 MINUTES

Lab Exercise 8.02: Installing Serial ATA Hard Drives

A wealthy donor has just given your nonprofit organization a dozen brand-new desktop computers. Since these are new computers, their motherboards have built-in serial ATA (SATA) controllers, but the SATA hard drives have yet to be installed or configured. You're tasked to do the job!

Installing SATA hard drives is a simple matter of plugging in the data and power cables to the drive and attaching the other end of the data cable to the SATA controller card or motherboard connection. You don't have to pull the power from the PC. You don't even have to shut down Windows. No, really—it's that simple! Let's go through the steps.

Learning Objectives

This lab is designed to introduce you to the two current flavors of SATA and walk you through the straightforward installation. At the end of this lab, you'll be able to

- Explain key features of SATA I and SATA II
- Install a SATA hard drive

Lab Materials and Setup

The materials you need for this lab are

- A newer PC system with an onboard SATA I or SATA II controller and either Windows 2000 Professional or Windows XP Professional installed

- At least one additional SATA hard drive

- A Peripheral Component Interconnect (PCI) SATA controller installed into an older PC system (optional)

Getting Down to Business

To start, you'll review the features and specifications of SATA, and then you'll compare and contrast the technology with PATA. Keep that screwdriver handy, because you'll finish with the installation and hot-swap of a SATA drive.

✔ **Cross-Reference**

For help in answering the following questions, refer to the "ATA-7" section in Chapter 8 of *Mike Meyers' A+ Guide to Managing and Troubleshooting PCs, Vol. 2: PC Tech.*

Step 1 Using your reference materials, review the features and specifications of SATA hard drive technology. Then answer these questions:

What is the speed of data transfer with ATA/133 drives? _____

What is the speed of data transfer with SATA I (SATA 1.5Gb) drives? _150 MB_____

What is the speed of data transfer with SATA II (SATA 3Gb) drives? _300 MB_____

What is the maximum length of a SATA cable? ____1M_____

How many wires are in a SATA cable? _____7_____

What is the maximum length of an 80-wire PATA cable? _____18"_____

How many drives can a single SATA cable support? _____1_____

SATA RAID has waltzed into the mainstream today. Motherboards are now being sold with a SATA RAID controller from Promise or another company built in, or you can readily buy a PCI SATA RAID controller at your local computer parts store. You'll install additional hard drives in Lab Exercise 8.06, and you'll explore the implementation of a software RAID solution in Lab Exercise 8.07.

Step 2 It's time to get working with some SATA drives. Shut down your system and remove the system cover, following proper ESD procedures.

FIGURE 8-6 Removing the SATA data cable

Step 3 Disconnect the data cable(s) from the SATA hard drive(s), as shown in Figure 8-6. Grasp the cable as closely as possible to the connector on the drive, and pull, rocking the connector gently from side to side.

Disconnect the power supply from the SATA drive(s) by unplugging the SATA connector from each one. Is the power supply a newer model with SATA connectors directly attached, or is there a Molex-to-SATA power adapter, like the one shown in Figure 8-7?

FIGURE 8-7 Molex-to-SATA power adapter

Step 4   Now look at the motherboard connections, and note the orientation of the connectors. Disconnect the data cables from the motherboard, being careful but firm. Grasp the cable as closely as possible to the connector on the motherboard, and pull, rocking the connector gently from side to side.

Lay the cables aside for later reinstallation.

Step 5   Look at the SATA connections on your motherboard (see Figure 8-8).

How many SATA connectors do you see on your motherboard?

9
_____

Look closely at your motherboard, and see if you can find writing on the board next to the SATA connectors. Are the interfaces grouped into pairs? Are any of them dedicated to special configurations, such as RAID? _____

Step 6   As in the previous exercise, remove the hard drive from the system, note the type of screws you removed, and store the screws for safekeeping. Be sure to use proper ESD procedures when removing the drive from your system.

Because of the variety of cases, caddies, bays, slots, and so on, it's not possible to give detailed instructions on how to remove the drive from your particular system. Look closely for caddy releases or retaining screws. Close inspection and a little logic will usually make it clear how to remove the drive. Make notes of how the drive comes out; you'll have to reinstall it later.

Step 7   With the hard drive out of the system and on a static-free surface, ground yourself, pick up the drive, and examine it carefully.

Note its dimensions; it should measure about $6'' \times 3.5'' \times 1''$, the same as a PATA drive. Here, too, the bottom of the drive boasts the hard drive controller, and the top of the drive is normally labeled with the drive's specifications.

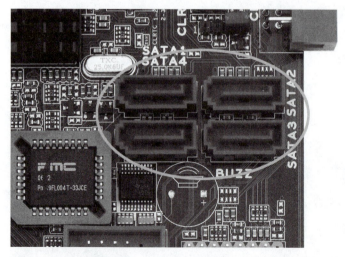

FIGURE 8-8 The SATA connectors on a motherboard

Write down all the information on the label. Be sure to include the manufacturer and the model number for future reference.

Step 8 To demonstrate one of the benefits of SATA—hot-swapping—you will now reinstall all the drives you removed and, if necessary, install an additional SATA drive to be hot-swapped. With the PC still powered down, insert all of the original drives and at least one additional SATA drive with no critical data into your system. Secure the drives with the proper screws, connect all the data cables, and connect the SATA power connectors using Molex-to-SATA adapters if required.

Leave the system case off to verify that everything is working properly and to facilitate the last steps.

✔ **Hint**

If you are performing this lab using a PCI SATA controller card, you'll have to install the expansion card and load the drivers for it. If you haven't loaded drivers for the SATA controller, you should do so now. Otherwise, this is going to be a very frustrating lab for you!

Power up the PC and boot into Windows. Windows should pick up the drive(s) with no problems at all. Check My Computer to verify that the drive is installed and functional. If the drive has no partition, then, of course, it won't show up in My Computer; if this is the case, you can use the Computer Management console to verify that the drive works.

Step 9 With Windows still running, disconnect the SATA data cable from the additional drive. What happened? _____

Step 10 Plug the data cable back in. Does Windows see the drive? _____

Step 11 Try the same hot-swap test with the SATA power cable—unplug it and then plug it back in. Does this produce the same effect as the hot-swap with the data cable?

 30 MINUTES

Lab Exercise 8.03: Configuring CMOS Settings

After installing either PATA or SATA devices, the second step you'll want to perform is the configuration of the BIOS to support these devices. On most motherboards, the BIOS automatically detects devices, so you will primarily be confirming the detection of all of the devices and configuring advanced features such as RAID, Self-Monitoring, Analysis, and Reporting Technology (S.M.A.R.T.), and boot options. Autodetection does not render CMOS irrelevant, though; you can do or undo all kinds of problems relating to hard drives using CMOS setup. This lab walks you through the important configuration options.

Learning Objectives

At the end of this lab, you'll be able to

- Configure the CMOS settings for the hard drive
- Confirm that the hard drive is installed properly

Lab Materials and Setup

The materials you need for this lab are

- A fully functioning PC with PATA and/or SATA devices installed
- A second drive with no important data on it (optional)

Getting Down to Business

There are many possible CMOS settings for the hard drive, depending on the BIOS installed on the motherboard. For example, every motherboard gives you the option to disable the built-in hard drive controllers. Why is this relevant? You can install a drive into a perfectly good system, but it won't work if the controllers are disabled!

Step 1　Turn on your system, and enter the CMOS setup utility by pressing the appropriate key(s) while your system is booting.

Select the Integrated Peripherals option from the main menu or the Drive Configuration option from the Advanced menu (you may have to hunt around for where you enable the PATA/SATA devices in your CMOS setup program), and look for the various controllers. You can enable or disable the controllers here.

✔ **Hint**

This option may look somewhat different, depending on the version of CMOS you are using. Look for a menu option such as one of these:

- Onboard Primary PCI IDE
- Onboard Secondary PCI IDE
- PCI Primary and Secondary IDE
- Onboard IDE
- Use Automatic Mode
- SATA Port 0

When the controllers are disabled in CMOS, no device attached to them can be used—not even the CD-ROM or Zip drives. This is why some systems will not let you disable the controllers at all.

If you are performing the labs in sequence and have arrived at this lab directly from Lab Exercise 8.01 or Lab Exercise 8.02, here's where you find out whether you installed and jumpered the drive correctly.

Make sure all controllers are enabled, and then look for the Autodetection option in the CMOS settings. Older systems have a separate category in CMOS, appropriately named Autodetect or something similar; newer systems have it integrated into the main settings screen. Run this utility now. If your hard drive shows up in Autodetect as the drive you thought it would be—primary master, secondary master, SATA Port 0, or what have you—then you installed and (if necessary) jumpered it properly (see Figure 8-9).

Step 2   Save your settings, exit CMOS, and reboot your PC. You should boot into Windows normally. Check My Computer to verify that you can see and access all drives.

Step 3   Reboot your PC and go into CMOS. Access the settings to enable or disable the various controllers, and disable them all. (This won't affect your data; it will just prevent drive access for the next couple of steps in this lab.)

Step 4   Save your settings, and then exit CMOS to reboot the system. Making sure there is no floppy disk in the floppy disk drive, reboot normally and watch the monitor display for messages.

What message is displayed last? _____

With most systems, the PC searches its various storage devices for a way to boot. It looks for a bootable drive (connected to an EIDE, SATA, or SCSI controller), a bootable CD or floppy disk, or a network connection—not necessarily in that order—and then stops if it cannot find the operating system. It then displays a message indicating "no bootable device" and waits for your instructions to continue.

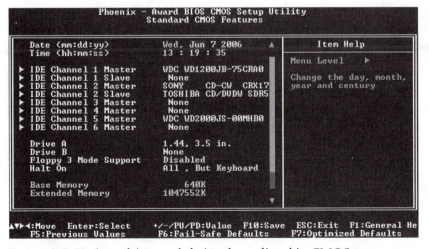

FIGURE 8-9 Various drives and their roles as listed in CMOS setup

> ✖ **Warning**
>
> If your system is connected to a network and uses the network boot option, disconnect the network cable for this exercise to get the desired results. Be sure to plug the network cable back in when finished.

If the system is not able to find a disk (because you disabled the controller), it will probably hang for a long period of time and then return a Primary Hard Drive Failure code or error message. Some systems try to recognize that you have a hard drive, regardless of the disabling of features, but this is rare.

Okay, so the system can't find your hard drive. You obviously know why—you turned off the controller!

Step 5   Reboot your system, entering the CMOS setup utility by pressing the appropriate keystroke combination while your system is booting. Navigate to the menu where you disabled all of the controllers, and re-enable them.

Step 6   Now that the controllers are enabled, go back to the Autodetection utility and look for any drives that are connected.

If Autodetection still does not see a hard drive, save your settings, reboot your system, and reenter the CMOS setup utility. Then try it again.

Do you now see all of the storage devices that are installed in the system?

Step 7   While you're still in CMOS, navigate to the menu where all of the storage devices can be configured. Use this screen (sometimes there are multiple screens) to examine the device settings and answer the following questions:

Are there any devices listed as ATA/IDE devices (Primary Master, Primary Slave, Secondary Master, or Secondary Slave)? _____

Are there any SATA controllers present? If yes, are there any SATA devices installed on the system (SATA Port 0, SATA Port 1, and so on)? _____

Is the motherboard capable of implementing RAID? If yes, how is it currently configured? _____

Exit CMOS without saving changes, and let the PC reboot.

Step 8   At this point, if you did everything as described and if you started with a known good hard drive containing a working operating system, the system will boot back into the operating system. Otherwise, you'll have to wait until you partition and format the drive to see if everything's working as it should (for example, if your instructor gave you a demo hard drive to use with nothing on it).

1 HOUR

Lab Exercise 8.04: Exploring SCSI, SAS, and SATA

As you inventory the computers that were just donated to your nonprofit organization, you discover two additional computers, both dual-CPU, Serial-Attached Small Computer System Interface (SAS/SCSI) file servers. Yippee! Your company can really put these to use. You've been hearing about the new SAS/SCSI technology, but haven't yet had the opportunity to work with it.

With the rapid changes taking place in the world of SCSI (not the least of which is SAS), you should take the time to research this technology and the best way to incorporate it into your organization.

Learning Objectives

This lab touches on important tech skills, teaching you how to research hardware so that you can provide good information to clients. With the introduction of the SATA interface, the need for SCSI implementation on desktop computers is quickly fading. However, SCSI—which is 20 years old as of this writing—still rules the hot-swappable, large-capacity, data server environment. With the introduction of SAS, which enables you to use both SAS and SATA drives simultaneously on a serial SCSI controller, it looks like SCSI could be around for another 20 years.

At the end of this lab, you'll be able to

- Explain key features of SCSI

- Explain key features of SAS

- Discuss the uses of SAS/SATA technology

- Define the levels of RAID

Lab Materials and Setup

The materials you need for this lab are

- Access to a PC system and the Internet

- A trip to the local computer store for research

Getting Down to Business

Limber up your surfing fingers, as you'll start your search on the Internet. Then you might want to make a visit to the local computer store to explore further how the technologies of SCSI and SAS are being used in today's computing environments.

Step 1   Access the Internet and search for information on parallel SCSI devices, primarily hard drives. Use keywords such as *Ultra320, white paper, controllers,* and *storage solutions.* Then answer the following questions:

What speed of data transfer can be achieved with parallel SCSI? _____

How many drives can be attached to a single controller?_____

What is the price range of parallel SCSI drives? _____

What is a SCSI chain? _____

✔ **Cross-Reference**

For more information on SCSI, refer to the "SCSI – Still Around" section in Chapter 8 of *Mike Meyers' A+ Guide to Managing and Troubleshooting PCs, Vol. 2: PC Tech.*

Step 2   Access the Internet and search for information on SAS devices, primarily hard drives. Use keywords such as *SAS hard drives, white paper, controllers,* and *storage solutions.* Then answer the following questions:

What speed of data transfer can be achieved with SAS-specific hard drives? _____

How many drives can be attached to a single controller? How many total drives can one system support? _____

What is the price range of SAS-specific hard drives? _____

What are typical revolutions-per-minute (RPM) speeds of SAS-specific hard drives?
_____

What are some of the reported mean-time-between-failure (MTBF) figures for SAS-specific drives? _____

✖ **Warning**

The system you're using should have Adobe Reader installed to view many of the data sheets on the different technologies. If it's not already installed and you're in a classroom setting, ask for permission from your instructor before downloading this or any other program, just to be sure that you're complying with school policy. You may download the current Adobe Reader from the Adobe Web site (www.adobe.com).

Step 3   One of the benefits of SAS is the ability to use SAS-specific hard drives, SATA hard drives, or both. Access the Internet and search for information on SAS implementing SATA hard drives.

Use keywords such as *SAS/SATA hard drives*, *white paper*, *controllers*, and *storage solutions*. Then answer the following questions:

What speed of data transfer can be achieved with SAS/SATA? _____

How many drives can be attached to a single controller? How many total drives can one system support? _____

What is the price range of SATA hard drives? _____

What are typical RPM speeds of SATA hard drives?

_____

What are some of the reported MTBF figures for SATA hard drives?

_____

Step 4   As you surfed around to the different sites on SCSI, SAS, and SATA hard drives, you probably noticed that many of these drives are implemented in different RAID configurations. With the overall cost of hard drives dropping, many desktop motherboard manufacturers (ASUS, Gigabyte, Intel, and so on) are incorporating RAID controllers into their motherboards. Visit a few of the motherboard manufacturers' Web sites and research their implementation of RAID. Use the following questions to refine your focus:

What are the most popular implementations of RAID used on desktop computers?

_____

How many drives are required to support the various RAID levels?

_____

Can you configure desktop RAID using both PATA and SATA drives?

_____

What are the two goals when implementing a RAID solution?

_____

✔ **Cross-Reference**

For more information on RAID, refer to the "Protecting Data with RAID," "RAID," and "Implementing RAID" sections in Chapter 8 of *Mike Meyers' A+ Guide to Managing and Troubleshooting PCs, Vol. 2: PC Tech*.

Step 5   Gather the information you've found in your Internet research and head to your local computer store. Explore the current trends, based on the systems and components your local supplier is promoting. Write a brief summary of your findings and share it with your instructor and classmates.

 45 MINUTES

Lab Exercise 8.05: Troubleshooting Hard Drive Installations

The newest tech in your office has had trouble installing hard drives properly. In fact, he's tried it on four different computers with eight different drives and succeeded only once! You've been tasked to troubleshoot his failed installations and patiently explain the proper installation process to him. What fun!

Learning Objectives

This lab walks you through the errors new techs typically make on hard drive installation, particularly with PATA drives. The lab also addresses the main problems with SATA drives—usually faulty hardware—and how to address this in the field.

At the end of this lab, you'll be able to

- Troubleshoot hard drive installation problems effectively

- Explain the proper installation techniques for PATA and SATA drives

Lab Materials and Setup

The materials you need for this lab are

- Access to a PC system with PATA and SATA interfaces

- At least one PATA or SATA hard drive (preferably two or more)

Getting Down to Business

It might seem odd to mess up a hard drive installation deliberately, but you can't hurt anything, so give it a whirl. Seeing how the PC responds to mistakes when you know specifically what's wrong can help you when you run into similar situations later in the field.

Step 1   You need a properly functioning PC for this lab to be effective, so verify first that you have a system up and running with one or more hard drives installed.

Step 2   Power down the system. Disconnect the data cable for the hard drive used to boot the system, and then power up the system. What happens? Will the PC autodetect the drive?

It is difficult to imagine not connecting the data cables to hard drives, but many times to add RAM or new devices, we have to disconnect the cables to gain access to the component. It is easy to miss reconnecting one of the cables after installing the new device.

Disconnecting the cable also simulates a broken IDE or SATA cable. These cables are somewhat delicate and can fail after a sharp crease or a crimp from the system case. If you're having unexplained problems with your drive, check the cables prior to replacing the drive.

Step 3 Power down the PC and put the cable back on properly.

Step 4 On a PATA drive, change the jumper for the primary master hard drive to the slave hard drive, and then power on the PC. What happens? Will the PC autodetect the drive? How should the jumper be installed?

Step 5 Power down the PC and put the jumper back on properly.

Step 6 Install a second PATA drive onto the primary controller, and set the jumpers on both drives incorrectly. Try variations: both as master; both as standalone; both as slave; both as cable select. Power on the PC and test each variation. What happens? Will the PC autodetect the drive? How should the jumpers be set for two PATA drives to work properly on the same controller?

 **30** MINUTES

Lab Exercise 8.06: Installing Multiple Hard Drives in Preparation for RAID

Remember those two server computers you discovered—the ones with the dual CPUs and the SAS/SCSI controllers? Well, each of them has eight 150-gigabyte (GB) SATA hard drives ready to be installed. You haven't had the opportunity to configure a RAID system before, so you ask a colleague for advice. She recommends that you install some additional drives in one of the workstations and then practice configuring RAID 0 using the software solution that comes with Microsoft Windows XP. This should help build your confidence before tackling the hardware RAID controllers on the servers.

Learning Objectives

In this lab, you will install additional hard drives—PATA, SATA, or both—in an existing system. You will access CMOS to verify that all of the drives have been recognized by the system. You will then set the system aside to be used in Lab Exercise 8.07, "Implementing Software RAID 0 with Disk Management."

At the end of this lab, you'll be able to

- Install multiple hard drives in computer systems
- Verify multiple drives in CMOS

Lab Materials and Setup

The materials you need for this lab are

- A working PC with PATA or SATA interfaces and Microsoft Windows 2000 or Windows XP installed

- At least two additional, system-compatible hard drives—PATA or SATA, as appropriate

Getting Down to Business

Even though you haven't been reminded during the last few exercises, you know that you should always take the proper anti-static precautions when opening the system case and working with the delicate components inside. Take those precautions now, and get ready to install a few extra hard drives into your system. In this exercise, you'll make sure these drives are recognized by the system; in the next lab, you'll configure them.

✔ Hint

For many of the exercises, it is important that you have a working system with either Windows 2000 Professional or Windows XP Professional installed. Obviously, you will need to keep the system partition and boot partition intact (usually, these are the same partition and are the first partition on the first hard drive of the system), with the operating system running.

Even if you have available space on the first hard drive, it is much cleaner if you can install at least two additional hard drives. That way, you can partition, format, and convert to dynamic disks to your heart's content without worrying about losing data (or the operating system).

Follow these steps to install an additional PATA drive:

Step 1 Determine on which controller, and in which order, you will be installing the drives.

Step 2 Set the jumpers properly for both the master and slave drives. (Usually, the boot device is the master drive on the primary controller, whereas the optical media drive is the master drive on the secondary controller, so the new drive is likely to be a slave to one of those drives.)

Step 3 Physically install the second drive, connecting the power and data cables properly.

Follow these steps to install additional SATA drives:

Step 1 Determine which controller you will use for the first additional drive, and connect the SATA data cable to the controller on the motherboard.

Step 2   Physically install the first additional drive, and connect the SATA power and data cables to the new drive.

Step 3   Determine which controller you will use for the second additional drive, and connect the SATA data cable to the controller on the motherboard.

Step 4   Physically install the second additional drive, and connect the SATA power and data cables to the new drive.

Follow these steps to verify the drives in CMOS:

Step 1   After installing all of the hard drives, plug the power back in and boot the computer.

Step 2   Press the appropriate key(s) to enter CMOS setup, and navigate to the configuration screen for installed devices.

Step 3   Perform autodetection, if required, and confirm that all of the installed devices are present. If any of the devices are missing (and you remembered to reboot the computer if your system requires it), power the computer down, disconnect the power, and double-check all of the cables and drive settings.

 **30** MINUTES

Lab Exercise 8.07: Implementing Software RAID 0 with Disk Management

It's finally time to flex your RAID muscles in preparation to deploy the two server computers—remember, these are the systems with dual CPUs and SAS/SCSI controllers. Windows 2000, XP Professional, and Server 2003 allow you to configure software RAID implementations using Disk Management and multiple hard drives. Windows XP Professional offers only RAID 0, a stripe set, which offers improved disk access time but no fault tolerance. At the end of this lab, you will have configured a stripe set using two disks.

✔ **Cross-Reference**

Additional information on RAID 0, 1, and 5 may be found in the "Protecting Data with RAID" section in Chapter 8 of *Mike Meyers' A+ Guide to Managing and Troubleshooting PCs, Vol. 2: PC Tech.*

This lab exercise guides you through the creation of a RAID 0 stripe set using free, unpartitioned space on the second and third hard drives installed on the Windows XP lab system. These disks will need to be converted from basic disks to dynamic disks in order to complete the implementation of RAID 0. Disk Management allows you to configure simple volumes, spanned volumes, and striped volumes on dynamic disks.

✔ Hint

Microsoft's dynamic storage provides five types of volumes: simple volumes, spanned volumes, striped volumes, mirrored volumes, and RAID 5 volumes. The first three—simple, spanned, and striped—are the only volumes currently available on Windows 2000 Professional or Windows XP Professional.

Here are the different types of volumes and their features:

- Simple volumes on dynamic disks are equivalent to primary partitions on basic disks. Simple volumes use a contiguous area of a single drive, and are represented by one drive letter or mount point.

- Spanned volumes enable you to extend the size of a simple volume to include any unallocated space (contiguous or noncontiguous) on one or more dynamic disks. Spanned volumes are represented by one drive letter or mount point, and fill the volume sequentially.

- Striped volumes use two or more dynamic disks, and spread data across all of them. Striped volumes are represented by one drive letter or mount point, and will speed up disk access times due to concurrent disk write and read operations. The more disks in the stripe set, the faster the throughput.

Learning Objectives

In this exercise, you'll use the Disk Management program to configure a RAID 0 striped volume.

At the end of this lab, you'll be able to

- Create and configure a RAID 0 striped volume

Lab Materials and Setup

The materials you need for this lab are

- A PC on which Windows XP Professional is installed on the primary hard drive and two blank hard drives that have been converted to dynamic disks

Getting Down to Business

You're in the home stretch now! Once you've worked with the Disk Management tool and converted basic disks to dynamic disks, it's just a matter of using the Disk Management New Volume Wizard, choosing the size allocated to the striped volume, and formatting the striped volume.

Step 1   Launch the Disk Management utility, and right-click the unallocated space on the first disk of the planned striped volume. Select New Volume and then select Striped (see Figure 8-10).

Step 2   The wizard asks you to select at least one additional dynamic disk for the striped volume. You will then select the size of the volume you want to create and decide what file system to use to format the striped volume.

Are there any restrictions on the size of the volume? _____

Step 3   Disk Management now allocates the space on the drives and formats them with the file system you've selected. You should now have a healthy, formatted, striped volume.

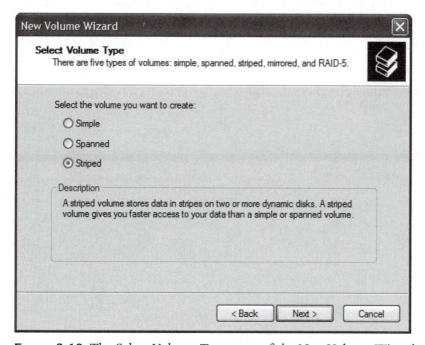

FIGURE 8-10 The Select Volume Type page of the New Volume Wizard

Step 4   Practice deleting and creating various sizes of striped volumes using various file systems. Can you format a striped volume with file allocation table (FAT)? Why or why not?

_____

_____

Lab Analysis Test

1.   Matthew has decided to use the RAID integrated into the SATA controller on his new system. He uses the system for high-end video editing, and would like to improve the performance of the system for this task. What implementation of RAID would you recommend to improve performance?

2.   In what situation(s) might it be appropriate to disable the motherboard's hard drive controllers?

3.   Brock, a new tech in your firm, informs you that the PC he's working on can't autodetect a hard drive he installed. He thinks the motherboard is broken. What's the more likely problem here?

4.   The second SATA hard drive on your company's server has just died. You have a replacement drive, but it's critical that the server remain up and functioning. What, if anything, can you do to resolve this problem and get the second drive replaced?

5.   Sean would like to install four additional hard drives in his system. His motherboard has two IDE controllers and two SATA controllers. There is one SATA drive installed, and the CD-RW drive is an IDE device. How would you configure Sean's system?

Key Terms Quiz

Use the following vocabulary terms to complete the following sentences. Not all terms will be used.

autodetect

cable select

CHS

master

PATA

platters

RAID

SAS

SATA

slave

1. A new implementation of SCSI, typically used in servers, can use SCSI devices, SATA devices, or both. This new implementation is termed _____.

2. The data in a hard drive is actually stored magnetically on disks called _____.

3. One type of IDE drive transfers data in a parallel fashion. The other type of IDE drive transfers data in a serial fashion. These two types are known as ___*PATA*___ and ___*SATA*___, respectively.

4. To secure data in servers and high-end PCs, use a(n) _____ controller.

5. A great way to determine whether a new drive is installed and configured correctly is to run _____.

Chapter 9
Installing and Troubleshooting Removable Media

Lab Exercises

Removable media storage is one of the fastest-changing components of the PC, and these days it's also very much in the public eye. With the advent of Universal Serial Bus (USB) thumb drives, MP3 players with large-capacity hard drives, and digital cameras using CompactFlash and Secure Digital memory cards, all kinds of people—from children to great-grandmothers, from artists to zookeepers—are using removable storage. With the high resolution of today's audio and video files, photographs, and games, the need for portable large-capacity storage is greater than ever.

The labs in this chapter will explore the configuration and use of optical (that is, CD- and DVD-based) drives, burners, and media. You'll also work with the fastest growing area of removable storage, the thumb drive. As of this writing, 4-gigabyte (GB) flash sticks are becoming even more affordable. The final lab in the chapter looks at some of the tech tools for troubleshooting computers that will not boot. These tools are becoming more available in the form of bootable CDs, DVDs, and even U3 bootable USB thumb drives, and you will learn how to create your own bootable devices.

 **30** MINUTES

Lab Exercise 9.01: Working with USB Thumb Drives

Your company is finally being forced to provide larger-capacity removable storage for all of the sales organization staff. In the not-so-distant past, PowerPoint presentations were moved from computer to computer via floppy disks and then CD-Rs. With the ease of use and convenient size of USB thumb drives, all sales personnel will now be issued 2-GB thumb drives. Your mission (should you choose to accept it) is to walk all of the field sales personnel through the procedures to use their new thumb drives.

✔ **Cross-Reference**

For a primer on USB flash memory drives (often called thumb drives), see the "USB Thumb Drives" section in Chapter 9 of *Mike Meyers' A+ Guide to Managing and Troubleshooting PCs, Vol. 2: PC Tech*.

Learning Objectives

In this lab, you'll learn to insert, use, and safely remove USB thumb drives.

At the end of this lab, you'll be able to

- Insert and remove USB thumb drives

- Save and transfer data using USB thumb drives

Lab Materials and Setup

The materials you need for this lab are

- A Windows XP system with USB 1.0 or 2.0 support

- A USB thumb drive

Getting Down to Business

In Lab Manual Vol. 1: Essentials, Lab Exercise 10.01, you physically removed and reinstalled a floppy drive, but as you are aware, this technology is slowly being retired. This lab exercise uses the newest technology to replace the function and ease of the floppy disk, the USB flash drive (thumb drive). You will simulate using a USB thumb drive to transfer a large file by inserting the drive into a Windows XP system, copying some data onto it, removing it, and reinserting it into a new system (or the same lab computer) and transferring the data to the new computer.

Step 1 USB thumb drives come in many shapes and colors, as well as many data capacities: 256 megabytes (MB), 512 MB, 1 GB, 2 GB, and so on. They are typically a few inches long, and most provide protection for the USB connector, either a cover of some type or a retractable mechanism as shown in Figure 9-1.

FIGURE 9-1 A USB thumb drive with a retractable connector

Boot your lab system and allow it to finish displaying the Windows desktop. Insert the USB drive and note any activity on the screen.

Did a window appear asking what you want Windows to do? _____

If yes, what were some of the options you could choose?

_____

Close the options window.

✔ Hint

Current USB thumb drives support the USB 2.0 specification, allowing a faster transfer of data (480 Mbps). Some systems (motherboards) offer both USB 1.0 and USB 2.0 ports, so when you insert the USB thumb drive into a USB 1.0 port, you may see a pop-up message in the system tray (notification area) pointing out that this device can perform faster if inserted into a USB 2.0 port.

Step 2   Open an application on your PC, such as Word or PowerPoint, and select and open a file. If you can find a file larger than 1.44 MB, you can experience firsthand the benefit of USB thumb drives over floppies.

Step 3   In the application window, select File | Save As. In the Save As dialog box, click the drop-down arrow for the Save in field. You will see a number of folders and drives where you could choose to save the file. One of these should be the thumb drive, as shown in Figure 9-2. Select the thumb drive and save the file. Close all open windows.

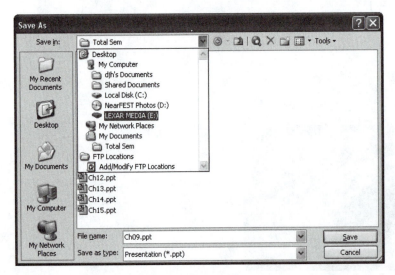

FIGURE 9-2 The Save As dialog box showing a Lexar Media thumb drive

Step 4   In the system tray, find and click the Safely Remove Hardware icon, which shows a green arrow and a gray rectangle. A tiny pop-up message appears adjacent to the icon, listing all removable devices; click the name of the thumb drive. An information balloon with a *Safe to Remove Hardware* message should notify you that you can now remove the USB mass storage device.

Remove the thumb drive from the USB port.

✔ **Hint**

If you forget to close one or more windows with a focus on the thumb drive, you will receive an error message: *The device 'Generic Volume' cannot be stopped right now. Try stopping it later.* If you receive this message, just click OK, close all open files and folders on the thumb drive, and try again.

If you have some open files or folders on the thumb drive and you just pull it out of the computer, you may receive an error message such as *Fail Write Delay.* Most of the time the files and folders will remain intact, but this is not the recommended removal method.

Step 5   At this point, if you have a second computer where you can plug in the thumb drive, it will make the lab exercise more realistic. If you don't, you can just use the same system again for this step. Insert the thumb drive into a USB port and again note any activity on the screen. This time, double-click *Open folder to view files using Windows Explorer.*

Step 6   Double-click the file you saved previously; if the file has an associated application, this should launch that application and open the file.

You have now successfully used a USB thumb drive—also referred to as a *jump drive*—to "jump" files from one computer to another.

 **30** MINUTES

Lab Exercise 9.02: Configuring Removable Media Drives

A new client has specific needs for the boot order and access to removable media in his computer center's seven computers. For the two servers, the floppy drive and USB ports will be installed, but disabled in CMOS. Three of the five workstations need the CD-ROM drive set as the first drive in the boot sequence, but the other two need the USB drive to be first in the boot sequence, with the CD-ROM drive second. It's your job to set up these PCs properly, so get to work!

Learning Objectives

In this lab, you'll use the complementary metal-oxide semiconductor (CMOS) setup program to configure the settings for the floppy drive, USB devices, and boot order.

At the end of this lab, you'll be able to

- Locate the CMOS setup screens for configuring the floppy drives, USB devices, and boot order
- Configure various scenarios for the floppy drive, USB devices, and boot order

Lab Materials and Setup

The materials you need for this lab are

- A working computer system with a floppy drive, a CD-ROM drive, and USB device support

Getting Down to Business

This lab exercise involves the floppy drive controller, CD-ROM drive, and USB controller, and shows you how to configure these devices and the boot order of these devices in CMOS.

Depending on your basic input/output system (BIOS) manufacturer and version, you may or may not be able to perform all of the following steps. Explore the different screens to discover whether you can enable/disable the floppy drive controller (FDC) and the USB controller, and which devices you can put in the boot order (floppy drive, CD-ROM, hard drive, and possibly USB devices).

Step 1   You will start by disabling the floppy drive and USB ports on the two servers. Enter the CMOS setup program by pressing the appropriate key or key combination (which you should remember from Lab Exercise 4.01/4.02) while your system is booting.

✖ Warning

> If you were to disable the USB controller on a production computer, you would disable not only USB thumb drives, but also USB keyboards and mice, as well as any cameras, external hard drives, or other USB devices in use. The disabling of the controller is overkill for keeping users from removing important information through the use of USB thumb drives. This security would most likely be configured in the security of the local computer's operating system or the network security policy. The USB controller is disabled in this lab exercise for demonstration purposes only.

Having previously browsed through your version of CMOS, you should be able to locate the screen that contains settings for the FDC and the USB controller (often called Integrated

Peripherals or I/O Device Configuration). If you can't remember which screen deals with the FDC and USB controller, browse through the CMOS screens until you find it.

Do you have an option in CMOS to disable the FDC and/or USB controller?

_____

Under what title heading did you find these options?

_____

How do you disable these settings?

_____

Do it! Disable them!

✔ **Hint**

Disabling the FDC is a good way for a network administrator to prevent users from either taking information off the network or introducing viruses into the network using floppy disks. Restricting the use of USB ports, on the other hand, can be handled more effectively in the security settings of the operating system.

Step 2   Restart your system and see if you can access the floppy drive. Did the light-emitting diode (LED) on the front of the floppy drive turn on as the system booted up?

Launch Device Manager—my favorite way is to right-click My Computer and select Manage, and then select Device Manager from the Computer Management MMC—and find the listing for Universal Serial Bus Controllers. Are they even listed as being disabled?

Step 3   Re-enter the CMOS setup utility, and turn both controllers back on. Reboot the system, and test the floppy drive and USB ports. Do they function properly?

Step 4   One of the most important aspects of removable media is that you can boot a non-functioning system from a device other than the hard drive with diagnostic and troubleshooting tools included. The next CMOS setting to play with is the boot sequence.

When you boot up a PC, the system needs to know where to get the operating system software to load into memory. The three standard places to store this software are the floppy drive, the hard drive, and the CD-ROM drive. USB thumb drives are emerging as the next big bootable media. In some cases the needed software is stored in another location, such as a network server.

Using the CMOS setup utility, you can designate the order in which your system will check the devices for the operating system software. Specifying the proper boot sequence—that is, the search order—saves time by telling the system where to look first. After all, why should your system waste time looking on the CD-ROM or USB thumb drive every time you boot, if your operating system is on the hard drive?

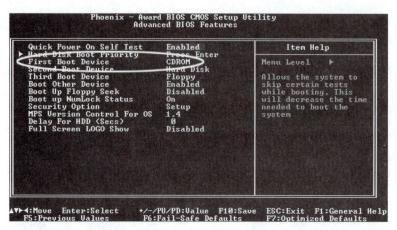

FIGURE 9-3 Boot Sequence screen from CMOS with CD-ROM as first boot device

Enter the CMOS setup utility, and look for a screen that includes a boot sequence setting.

How many different boot sequences can you configure in CMOS? _____

How many different devices can be in the search sequence? _____

Set your system to boot from the CD-ROM drive first (Figure 9-3).

Step 5   Restart your system. Typically, the boot screen will prompt you with the message *Press any key to boot from the CD*. If there is a bootable CD in the drive, the system will boot from that disc. Leave this boot order in place for the next lab exercise, in which you'll learn to create bootable CDs.

Step 6   Re-enter the CMOS setup utility, and note whether your system will allow you to boot from a USB device, such as a USB thumb drive.

If your computer is capable, you can substitute a USB thumb drive for the CD-ROM drive in the next lab exercise and create a LiveUSB of the GParted partition editor. For now, leave the CD-ROM as the first device in the boot order and shut down the computer.

 1 HOUR

Lab Exercise 9.03: Burning CDs

PCs today are used more than ever for storage of digital photographs, music, and video, in addition to more traditional types of data. Even a modest collection of MP3 files, family photos, and home video clips requires many gigabytes of space! Hard drives do have space limits, and at some point they tend to fail, so wise PC users turn to recordable CDs and DVDs. These discs provide an affordable large-capacity portable storage option; you can put your important data onto a disc, or make multiple copies of that disc to store in two or more secure locations.

This lab will introduce you to the process by which we record, or *burn*, CDs and DVDs. Rather than burning a disc full of your favorite tunes or photos, you'll be making the type of disc that a technician would have in his toolkit when troubleshooting a computer that won't boot.

✔ **Cross-Reference**

For additional information on burning CDs and DVDs, refer to the "Applications" section in Chapter 9 of *Mike Meyers' A+ Guide to Managing and Troubleshooting PCs, Vol. 2: PC Tech*.

Learning Objectives

In this lab, you'll use a third-party burning program to create bootable ISO images on CD-R discs.

At the end of this lab, you'll be able to

- Work with writable optical media and burning tools

- Create a bootable CD-R

Lab Materials and Setup

The materials you need for this lab are

- A working computer system with a CD-RW or DVD-RW drive installed

- Internet access (preferably a high-speed connection) for downloading

- A CD-burning application such as Nero Burning ROM or freeware CDBurnerXP

- Blank CD-R or CD-RW discs (more than one if possible)

Getting Down to Business

In Lab Manual Vol. 1: Essentials, Lab Exercise 9.02, you were asked to prep a number of newly donated PCs by preparing their hard drives for the installation of an operating system; you already partitioned and formatted the drives. To do that, you used an open-source utility called GParted. GParted is a Gnome Linux LiveCD with the Gnome Partition Editor application installed. Your instructor may have provided you the bootable CD, or you may have jumped ahead to this lab to make it yourself. In this lab you will burn the ISO image of the open-source, bootable LiveCD of Gnome Linux and the utility GParted.

Step 1   Ensure that you have CD/DVD-burning software that will allow you to burn ISO images. An ISO image is a complete copy of a CD, including all of the boot information in the boot record. Windows XP's built-in burning software is unable to write ISO images (at the time of this writing), so you'll need a third-party product such as Nero Burning ROM software. You can also try CDBurnerXP, an excellent freeware burning tool that supports the burning of ISO images; it's available at www.cdburnerxp.se.

Launch your browser and load the CDBurnerXP Web site.

Follow the instructions and run the installation. You now have all the tools necessary to burn ISO images (see Figure 9-4).

✔ **Hint**

Microsoft is constantly updating operating systems and applications, such as Internet Explorer and Windows Media Player, so don't forget to check occasionally to see if they have updated the built-in burning application with the ability to handle ISO images.

Step 2   Now visit the GParted Web site at http://gparted.sourceforge.net. Select Download and follow the instructions. You can download the full ISO, or download the .zip file to improve transfer times (remember you will have to expand the .zip file after it's on your system).

Step 3   Once you have the ISO image, open the tray on your CD/DVD drive and insert a blank writable disc. Close the tray and launch your CD/DVD-burning software. Navigate to the GParted ISO file, and follow the instructions to burn the ISO image on the disc. Most programs will eject the tray with the disc once the writing process is complete.

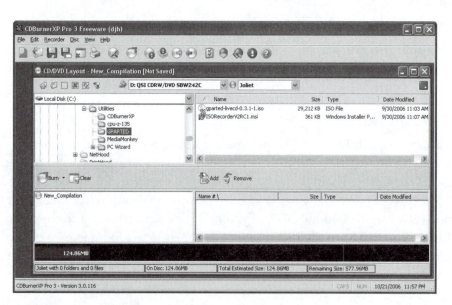

Figure 9-4 CDBurnerXP

Step 4   With the newly created disc in the drive and the tray closed, reboot the computer. If all has gone well, GParted will boot, detect your hard drives, and give you the option to partition and format these drives.

✖ Warning

Remember, any time you partition or format a hard disk, you will delete the data currently on that drive. Do not run GParted on the disk containing your operating system unless you have been instructed to delete it.

→ Try This: Ultimate Boot CD

Now that you have an understanding of why you might want to boot a computer from removable media—to perform low-level diagnostics, troubleshoot, or just prep the disk before installing an operating system—take a cruise over to www.ultimatebootcd.com.

You can download the ISO image of "The Ultimate Boot CD, UBCD," which has over 100 different freeware tools, all placed on a LiveCD. Use the method you learned in this exercise to burn the ISO image to a CD, boot a computer with the UBCD, and explore some of the tools. You might find that using some of the drive manufacturer's low-level formatting tools will bring a dead drive back to life.

Lab Analysis Test

1.   Jessica is a commercial artist and has been building a digital portfolio of her work for a number of years. She will save the final portfolio to a DVD+R as it is already over 4 GB of information; however, while she is compiling the works for the portfolio, she would like to have as much of her work on a thumb drive as possible. Conduct a Web search to address the latest capacities of USB flash drives.

2.   Ray is working with a new USB thumb drive that is not being recognized by the system. He goes to a computer that has Internet access and downloads the updated drivers, storing them on a floppy disk. He then returns to his computer, pops in the floppy disk, and starts the computer, only to have it report "NTLDR not found." What happened?

3.   Cecelia is a freelance Web designer who is delivering some files to a client. She sits down at a Windows XP system in the client's office and plugs in her trusty USB thumb drive, but nothing happens—Windows doesn't acknowledge the device at all. The thumb drive has been working perfectly well, as recently as this morning. What is most likely the reason that the USB drive won't connect with the client PC?

4. When Philip puts his CD-RW disc in the drive and copies files to and from it, he notices that the drive speeds up and slows down. Is this normal? What should he do to fix it?

5. Tad has been using a thumb drive to archive some of his favorite photos, and often is copying files back and forth between his laptop and thumb drive. Today, he noticed that a number of files that were saved during the last session are corrupt. What advice might you give Tad?

Key Terms Quiz

Use the following vocabulary terms to complete the following sentences. Not all terms will be used.

burn

CDBurnerXP

CD-ROM drive

CMOS

disc

DMA

DVD+R

Label

Nero

scratches

spiral

surface

UBCD

USB 1.0

USB 2.0

1. If you would like to perform a low-level format of your hard drive, a great tool would be the _____. It has a number of the manufacturer's low-level formatting utilities included.

2. When you record data on a CD-R, CD-RW, DVD+R, or DVD+RW, the term "_____ the disk" is commonly used.

3. A popular freeware program that supports the burning of ISO CDs is _____.

4. The _____ version of thumb drives supports a throughput of 480 Mbps.

5. The reflective aluminum layer of an optical disc can be damaged by _____.

Chapter 10
Working with the Command-Line Interface

Lab Exercises

Although the CompTIA A+ certification exams have dropped the requirements of working with the MS-DOS operating system, they do stipulate that PC technicians should know some of the basic commands and functions available at the command-line interface in all versions of Windows. Why? Because they still work, and good techs use the command line often. You'll need a solid understanding of several basic command-line commands and a few advanced tasks. Commands such as CD, COPY, and ATTRIB, as well as the tasks of starting and stopping services, editing files, and converting file systems, should be part of your PC tech arsenal.

If you have a system crash and are able to gain access to the computer using the Microsoft Recovery Console, you'll really need to know the proper commands for navigating around your drives, folders, and files, and launching utilities that will get your operating system up and running again. Also, when you start working with networks, the command-line interface on all Windows systems is invaluable.

✔ **Cross-Reference**

You will further explore the use of the Recovery Console in the lab exercises for Chapter 11, "Troubleshooting Windows." You will also have the opportunity to work with additional networking command-line utilities in the lab exercises for Chapter 16, "Maintaining and Troubleshooting Networks."

The command line can often provide a quicker way to accomplish a task than the graphical alternative. In cases where a virus, hard drive failure, or operating system problem prevents you from booting to Windows, you need to know how to get around with the command line. The following labs are designed to give you the chance to practice your basic command-line skills, so that when the need arises, the command line will be your friend.

> ✔ **Hint**
>
> As you have worked through the labs in these manuals, I have recommended often that you explore features, options, and components not specifically covered in the lab exercises. You have embarked on the journey to become a CompTIA A+ certified technician! Natural curiosity, enthusiasm, and determination will go a long way toward developing the understanding and experience you need to become a competent technician and pass the exams. These qualities are especially important when it comes to working with the command-line interface. As you navigate through the following labs, it is easy to take a left when you should have taken a right, and get lost in subdirectories, mistype a command, or delete a file you didn't want to. Don't let it discourage you.
>
> Making mistakes while learning is good, and learning from those mistakes is great! If you get lost, explore ways to get back to where you need to be—you're unlikely to hurt anything. If you really get lost, work with your instructor or a more experienced classmate to determine where you went astray, and then work through it again.

 **30** MINUTES

Lab Exercise 10.01: Configuring the Command-Line Window

Before you can use the command line, you need to know the basics: ways to access it, manipulate and customize the look of it within the graphical user interface (GUI), and close it down properly. This lab covers those basics.

Learning Objectives

In this lab, you'll practice opening, resizing, customizing, and closing a command-line window.

At the end of this lab, you'll be able to

- Open a command-line window from within the Windows operating system
- Resize the command-line window
- Customize the look of the command-line window
- Exit the command-line window

Lab Materials and Setup

The materials you need for this lab are

- A PC with Windows 2000 or Windows XP installed

Getting Down to Business

The first thing you'll need to do, obviously, is get to a command line. Spend the next several minutes becoming familiar with accessing the command-line window.

✔ Cross-Reference

For details on how to access the command-line interface, refer to the "Accessing the Command Line" section in Chapter 10 of *Mike Meyers' A+ Guide to Managing and Troubleshooting PCs, Vol. 2: PC Tech.*

Step 1 Turn on your system, and wait for the Windows desktop to appear. Then follow these steps:

a) Select Start | Run, and then type **CMD**.

b) Click OK to display a command-line window (see Figure 10-1).

Step 2 There are three ways to change the size of the command-line window for better viewing:

- Use the resize arrows along the edges of the windows (this will not work when the window is maximized).

- Use the minimize/maximize button in the upper-right corner of the window.

- Press ALT-ENTER to toggle between the full screen and a window.

Step 3 In Windows 2000, you should be looking at a black screen with your operating system information in the upper-left corner and a C prompt (C:\>) below. Windows XP will have a different prompt (C:\WINDOWS\Documents and Settings\username>). This just means that in Windows 2000, the command line opens as a default at the root of the C: drive, whereas Windows XP opens with the focus pointing to the user's personal area in the Documents and Settings folder.

To the right of the prompt, you'll see a flashing cursor indicating that it's waiting for your input. There's also a scroll bar along the right side of the window. Sometimes your command causes more information to be displayed than the window can hold, and it's really useful to be able to scroll back up and see what messages were displayed.

You'll now execute a few commands, for the purpose of exploring the scrolling issue. You will explore these commands further in later lab exercises. The Change Directory command (CD) lets

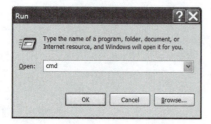

FIGURE 10-1 Opening the Windows XP command-line window

you change the focus of the working directory displayed in the command-line window. The Directory command (DIR) lists the file name, extension, file size (in bytes), and creation date/time of the files in the current folder.

You are going to change from the current working directory to a subdirectory with hundreds of files. Type **CD C:\WINDOWS\SYSTEM32** (C:\ is the root directory, WINDOWS is the system folder, and SYSTEM32 is where many of the system configuration and driver files are stored). You may have to use a different drive letter or system folder name to arrive at the SYSTEM32 directory.

Now type **DIR** and press ENTER. The SYSTEM32 folder contains over 1000 files, so the command-line window will not be able to display all of the information at once. If there's more than one screen's worth of information, it will keep scrolling out of sight until everything has been displayed. You can use the scroll bar to go back a few screens' worth—give it a try.

If you were actually trying to work with a few of the files in the folder, you're probably out of luck, as you can't scroll back more than a few screens. To address this problem, there's a command you can use that forces the information to be displayed one screenful at a time. Type **DIR /P** and then press ENTER. Adding the /P switch to the command tells it to pause after each screenful of text. Press SPACEBAR to display the next screenful. You can't go back if you're too quick with SPACEBAR, so take a good look at each screen! If you tire of paging through the screens, you can end the command by pressing CTRL-C.

Step 4   Just as with most applets in the Windows environment, if you right-click the title bar and select Properties, you can configure some of the features of the command-line window:

- **Options**   Configure the cursor size, command history, display options, and edit options.
- **Font**   Select from a limited set of command-line fonts and sizes.
- **Layout**   Set the screen buffer size and window size, and position the window on the monitor screen.
- **Colors**   Configure the color of screen text, screen background, pop-up text, and pop-up background.

Explore some of the settings you can change, and feel free to set up the command-line window to your personal taste. I grew up on early IBM computers, in the days when owning a color monitor meant that you had an electric green or bright orange character on a black monochrome screen. See if you can re-create this wonderful look!

Step 5   There are two common ways to close a command-line window:

- Click the X in the upper-right corner of the window. This method isn't recommended if the window is actively running a program. You should wait until you see the prompt before clicking the X.
- Type **EXIT** at the command line, and press ENTER. I prefer this method, because I can be sure the window is inactive when I quit.

 30 MINUTES

Lab Exercise 10.02: Navigating Basic Commands

Before you can really use the command line, you must know the basic commands needed to navigate around a drive to locate and modify files. In this lab exercise, you'll learn more basic command-line commands that you would need to know when troubleshooting your or your client's PC.

✔ **Hint**

For the most part, mistakes such as spelling a command or file name incorrectly won't be disastrous for you. It's possible to misspell just incorrectly enough to delete the wrong file, or something similar, especially if you're using wildcards (I'll get to those in a bit). Typically, though, if you misspell a command or file name, the command line won't know what you're asking it to do and therefore won't do anything, or won't know what file you're asking to work with, and will return an error message.

Learning Objectives

In this lab, you'll learn or review commands for directory and file management while using the command line.

At the end of this lab, you'll be able to

- Use commands to view, navigate, create, and delete directories using the command line
- Use commands to copy, move, rename, and delete files using the command line

Lab Materials and Setup

The materials you need for this lab are

- At least one working computer running Windows 2000 or Windows XP

✔ **Hint**

Other Windows versions will work just fine for this exercise, as long as you understand that the results may appear differently on your screen.

Getting Down to Business

Hundreds of commands and switches are available to you from the command-line interface. Although it is beyond the scope of these exercises to explore every possible command and its associated switches, you should spend the time in this lab exercise working with the specific ones that form the cornerstone of command-line navigation. These are the basic commands you'll use most often when working with the command line.

Step 1   Follow these steps:

   a)   Launch the command-line interface by typing **CMD** in the Run dialog box and either clicking OK or pressing ENTER.

   b)   When you first open the command-line window, your prompt might not be focused on the root directory. Because you want to focus on the root directory at this time, you must change directories before continuing.

The CD (Change Directory) command changes the directory the system is focused on. When you use the CD command, you must type the command followed by a space and then the name of the directory you want to view. This is true of all command-line commands. First, type the command followed by a space and then any options. Because you want to focus on the root of C: and the name of the root is the backslash (\), you'd type in the following and press ENTER (assuming that you're in the C: drive to begin with):

```
C:\Documents and Settings\username>CD \
```

Notice that the prompt has changed its focus to C:\> (see Figure 10-2).

Step 2   Probably the most frequently typed command is the request to display the contents of a directory (DIR). Because the command-line interface doesn't continually display everything the way a GUI does, you have to ask it to display specific information. The way you display the contents of a directory is to focus on the particular directory or subdirectory, and enter the command **DIR**.

Let's take a look at the contents of your root (C:\>) directory. You should already be focused there from the previous step in this exercise. Type **DIR** at the command prompt and press ENTER.

✔ **Hint**

From now on, when you see an instruction to type a command, you should assume that you should press ENTER afterward to complete the request (command). Otherwise, the command line will sit there, waiting patiently until the sun grows cold.

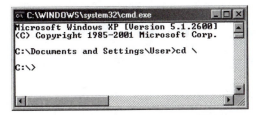

FIGURE 10-2 Changing the command-line focus

Now here's where it gets a little gray. Because I don't know what's in your root directory, there's no way to predict exactly what your C:\ contents will look like—but it's a good bet that *something* will be different from what I show you here! In theory at least, your display should be similar to Figure 10-3. Windows 2000 and XP will have the same basic look.

Notice that using the DIR command in any Windows operating system gives you the following information:

- File name

- File extension

- Date and time of creation

- Size in bytes

- Designation as either a directory (<DIR>) or a file

- The number of files in the directory

- The amount of free space on the drive

Look at your particular results and note the mixture of files, which display a size in bytes, and directories, which have the annotation <DIR> after their name. In the preceding examples, AVG7QT.DAT is a file of 12,288,463 bytes, and WINDOWS, Program Files, and Documents and Settings are all names of directories.

Note whether you see the following files or folders in your root (C:\>) directory (you won't see them all):

AUTOEXEC.BAT	Yes ___	No ___
CONFIG.SYS	Yes ___	No ___
WINNT	Yes ___	No ___

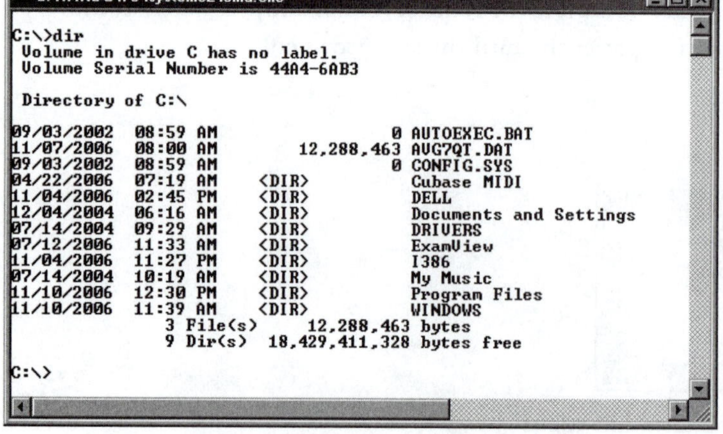

FIGURE 10-3 Viewing a sample Windows XP root directory

WINDOWS   Yes ____   No ____

Documents and Settings   Yes ____   No ____

Program Files   Yes ____   No ____

List the names of all the directories you see displayed in your root directory:

_____	_____
_____	_____
_____	_____
_____	_____
_____	_____
_____	_____

Step 3   The biggest challenge when working with the command prompt is remembering what exactly to type to achieve your goal. Learning the commands is one thing, but each command can have switches and options that modify it somewhat. Also, you may have noticed that the screen fills up and scrolls from top to bottom, making it difficult to view all the information you might need. Let's look at a command to clear the screen and another to provide assistance with how to use the commands.

Type the command **CLS**. What happened? _____

Type the command **DIR /?**. What happened? _____

The question mark (/?) is a standard help switch for most commands. Even though I've used these commands for decades, I still use the /? switch occasionally to remember what options are available for a specific command.

✔ **Hint**

Be careful not to confuse the backslash (\) and the forward slash (/). In a command-line world, the path uses the backslash and command switches use the forward slash.

At this point, a huge amount of help information is displayed (see Figure 10-4), so you may feel like you're in command overload! Take comfort in the fact that DIR is the most complex command. Other commands are more straightforward with their help. You don't need to know what all the switches are—just know how to use the help switch (/?) to find them! The main thing to learn is the syntax of the commands.

Everything in brackets ([ ]) is optional for the command. Notice that DIR is the only mandatory part in that command even though there are several optional switches and parameters. This is the same for all of the commands. The system will use defaults if you don't specify a switch or

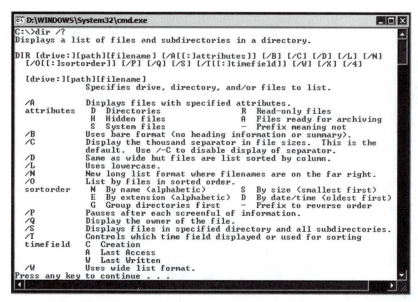

FIGURE 10-4 Viewing the syntax of the DIR command

optional parameter. It's the defaults that can cause problems if you're not careful when using these commands. Now follow these steps:

a) Put a known good disc with files in your CD-ROM drive and let it spin up and come to rest. Cancel any windows that automatically open and proceed to the next substep.

b) Type **DIR**, and examine the resulting list of files and folders. Did they change from the previous step? _____

Do you think it read the compact disc? Probably not, because your prompt is still focused on the root directory of the hard drive.

c) Type **DIR D:** (replace D: with the appropriate drive letter for your CD-ROM drive, if necessary) and examine the resulting list of files and folders. Did they change this time? Aha! The option of [drive:] was needed to change the focus of the DIR command to the CD-ROM drive.

The [drive:] option will work for any of the drive letters. Floppy diskettes, CDs, DVDs, Universal Serial Bus (USB) thumb drives, and Zip drives are all fair game as well. When you use this option, you can look at those other drives without switching from the directory you're in.

Step 4 Type **DIR /?** to look at two more optional switches: /P and /W. The /P switch is used when all the information will not fit on one screen, and /W is used to see a condensed listing of the directory.

Let's focus on a different directory. Remember, the CD command will let you change the directory you want to focus on:

a) Type **CD \WINDOWS**.

b) Type **CLS**.

c)   Type **DIR** at the command prompt. This shows way too much data for the screen to display all at once.

d)   Type **DIR /P** at the command prompt. This very useful switch causes the display to stop scrolling (pause) after each screen, waiting until you press the spacebar to show you more. In directories with lots of files, this is a lifesaver!

✔ **Hint**

If you want to stop a process that seems to be running forever, you can press CTRL-C. The process will end, and you'll get the prompt back.

e)   Now type **DIR /W** at the command prompt. This switch is convenient when you're simply looking to see if a particular file resides in a particular directory, because it shows a "wide" list with file names but no details.

f)   Now practice moving around in the command window. Right now you're focused on the WINDOWS directory. Go back to the root directory by typing **CD **. To change the focus to another directory, use the CD command as you've learned. Use the DIR command to see what directories you have available in your current folder.

g)   Try going to a subdirectory in another subdirectory and listing the contents. Look back at the list of directories you made previously and select one. Issue the CD command followed by a backslash (\) and the name of the target directory. For example, to switch to the Documents and Settings directory in the previous listing, type this:

```
C:\WINDOWS>CD \DOCUMENTS AND SETTINGS
```

Do this using several of the directory names you wrote down previously, and then type **DIR** to see what's there. Are there any subdirectories in this directory? Make a note of them.

_____   _____

_____   _____

_____   _____

✔ **Hint**

After you've changed the prompt focus many times, you may become confused about exactly where you are. You can always get to the root directory from any focus by typing **CD **.

Step 5   A normal Windows XP installation creates a Drivers directory, within a directory called System32, under the WINDOWS directory in the root of the C: drive. To go to the Drivers directory, you don't have to do the CD command three times unless you really want to. If you know the path, you can go directly to the subdirectory with one CD command.

Go to the Drivers subdirectory by typing this at the command prompt:

```
C:\>CD \WINDOWS\SYSTEM32\DRIVERS
```

Your prompt should now look like Figure 10-5.

Type **DIR** to see what's there.

One final navigation hint—you can change directories going back up toward the top level without returning directly to the root. If you want to go up a single directory level, you can type **CD** followed immediately by two periods (sometimes referred to as *CD dot dot*). For example, typing this takes you up one level to the System32 directory:

```
C:\>\WINDOWS\SYSTEM32\DRIVERS>CD..
C:\>\WINDOWS\SYSTEM32>
```

Do it again to go to the Windows directory:

```
C:\>\WINDOWS\SYSTEM32>CD..
C:\>\WINDOWS>
```

Type the command once more to arrive at the root directory:

```
C:\>\WINDOWS>CD..
C:\>
```

Take a minute and practice using the CD command. Go down a few levels on the directory tree, and then jump up a few, jump back to the root directory, and then jump down another path. Practice is the only way to get comfortable moving around in a command-prompt environment, and a good PC technician needs to be comfortable doing this.

Step 6 Sometimes a technician needs to make a directory to store files on the system. This could be a temporary directory for testing purposes, or maybe a place to store something more permanently (diagnostic reports, for example). In any case, it's important that you know how to create and remove a directory. The CompTIA A+ certification exams will test you on this. Follow these steps:

a)   Be sure you're in the root directory. If you aren't there, type **CD ** to return to the root directory, where you'll add a new top-level directory. Actually, you can make a directory anywhere in the file structure, but you don't want to lose track of where it is, so make your new directory in the root. Do this using the MD (Make Directory) command.

b)   Type **MD /?** to see how the command is structured and view the available options (see Figure 10-6).

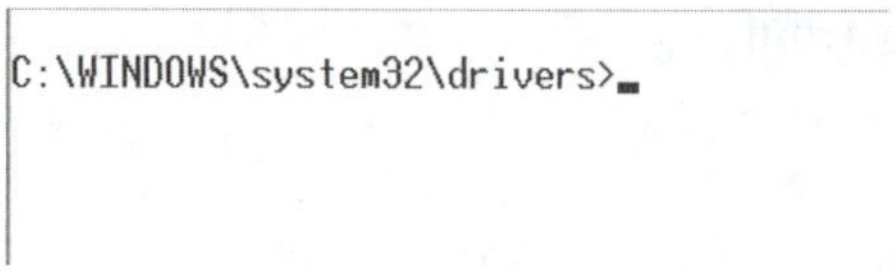

```
C:\WINDOWS\system32\drivers>_
```

FIGURE 10-5 Focusing on the Drivers subdirectory

```
C:\>md /?
Creates a directory.

MKDIR [drive:]path
MD [drive:]path
```

FIGURE 10-6 Using the MD command

c) At the command prompt, type the following:

    `C:\>MD CORVETTE`

d) When the command line just presents a fresh prompt, it means that everything worked correctly. But to verify that the directory was actually made, type **DIR** to see your new directory in the list. It's as simple as that!

✖ **Warning**

Be careful—the new directory will always be created wherever the prompt is focused when you issue the command, whether that's where you meant to put it or not.

---

e) Be sure you're in the root directory (type **CD**), and prepare to remove your new CORVETTE directory.

    Removing a directory requires the RD (Remove Directory) command and two conditions: First, the directory must be empty, and second, your system must not currently be focused on the directory about to be deleted.

f) Type this command:

    `C:\>RD CORVETTE`

    The directory has been deleted.

g) Type **DIR** to confirm that CORVETTE has been removed.

✔ **Hint**

Be *very* careful when you remove directories or delete files in the command line. It isn't as forgiving as the Windows GUI, which allows you to change your mind and "undelete" things. When you delete a file or directory using the command line, it's gone. If you make a mistake, there's nothing left to do but pout. So think carefully before you delete, and be sure you know *what* you're deleting before you do it—you'll save yourself a great deal of agony. Also pay attention to the directory you're currently focused on to ensure that you're in the correct one.

Step 7   Sometimes you know the name of the file you want to use, but you don't know the directory where it's located. In this case, working with files and directories can become quite tedious. To help you locate files more easily, here are some switches and wildcards you can use with the DIR command:

a)   Look again at the results of the DIR /? command, and find the /S switch. The /S switch will look for a file(s) in the specified (focus) directory and all subdirectories under that directory.

b)   Windows XP has a file named XCOPY.EXE somewhere on the drive. Locate the path to the XCOPY.EXE file using the /S switch.

c)   Start with your command prompt at the root directory (CD \).

d)   Type this command:

```
C:\>DIR XCOPY.EXE
```

If the file isn't in the root directory, nothing will be displayed.

e)   Now try the new switch you just learned about to search all subdirectories. Type this command:

```
C:\>DIR /S XCOPY.EXE
```

f)   On my system, the file shows up in two places: in the C:\WINDOWS\system32 directory and in the C:\WINDOWS\system 32\dllcache directory (see Figure 10-7).

Another way to look for a file is to use a *wildcard*. The most common wildcard is the asterisk character (*), which you can use in place of all or part of a file name to make a command act on more than one file at a time. Wildcards work with all commands that use file names.

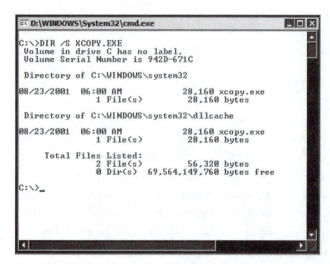

FIGURE 10-7 Locating the XCOPY.EXE file

The * wildcard replaces any number of letters before or after the dot in the file name. A good way to think of the * wildcard is "I don't care." Replace the part of the file name that you don't care about with *.

For example, if you want to locate all the README files on a hard drive and you don't care what the extension is, type the following:

```
C:\>DIR /S/P readme.*
```

The result is a list of all the README files on the hard drive. Notice that I used the /S switch to look in all the directories and the /P switch so I can view one screenful of results at a time (see Figure 10-8).

You can use the * wildcard for any number of characters. For example, not all companies use README.TXT as the help file name. Some use READ.ME, and others may use READ.TXT.

Because READ is common to all those variations, let's find all the files with READ in the file name. You should be prepared to see a long list of every file with READ in the name, not just the README files.

Type the following:

```
C:\>DIR /S/P *read*.*
```

Figure 10-9 shows the first screenful of results from my system. I found 104 files with READ somewhere in the file name. How many files and directories did you find with READ as part of the name?

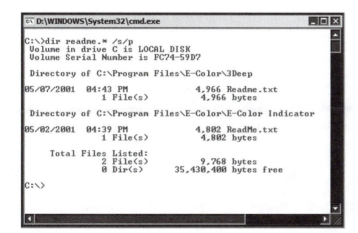

FIGURE 10-8 Using a wildcard to locate files

```
D:\WINDOWS\System32\cmd.exe - DIR /S/P *read*.*                        _ □ ×
 Volume in drive C is LOCAL DISK
 Volume Serial Number is FC74-59D7

 Directory of C:\Program Files\E-Color\3Deep

05/07/2001  04:43 PM               4,966 Readme.txt
05/07/2001  04:43 PM               4,966 ReadmeNT.txt
               2 File(s)           9,932 bytes

 Directory of C:\Program Files\E-Color\E-Color Indicator

05/02/2001  04:39 PM               4,802 ReadMe.txt
               1 File(s)           4,802 bytes

 Directory of C:\Work Files

10/20/2001  12:30 PM               6,895 Style Guide Proofreader's and Editor's Sy
mbols.htm
02/21/2003  01:02 PM    <DIR>            Style Guide Proofreader's and Editor's Sy
mbols_files
               1 File(s)           6,895 bytes

Press any key to continue . . . _
```

FIGURE 10-9 Using a wildcard to locate *READ*.* files

 30 MINUTES

Lab Exercise 10.03: Using Command-Line Tools

Commands such as TYPE, COPY, MOVE, RENAME, and DELETE are used for manipulating files, such as you would be doing while troubleshooting a client's PC. These are more of the commands that every working tech should know by heart.

Learning Objectives

In this lab, you'll use commands for file management.

At the end of this lab, you'll be able to

- View text (.TXT) documents from the command-line interface
- Rename files using the command-line interface
- Copy files using the command-line interface
- Move files using the command-line interface
- Delete files using the command-line interface

Lab Materials and Setup

The materials you need for this lab are

- At least one working computer running Windows 2000 or Windows XP

Getting Down to Business

You might refer to these as the "second-tier" commands. Once you've used commands such as DIR, MD, and CD to navigate and create folders, you can use the following commands to manipulate individual files.

Step 1   In Lab Exercise 12.02 of the Vol. 1: Essentials Lab Manual, you created a text document using Notepad that you could safely use to explore file commands in this chapter. You will now navigate to your My Documents folder and verify that the file is there and contains readable text:

✔ **Hint**

If for some reason you are having difficulty finding the original file created during your lab work in preparation for the CompTIA A+ Essentials (220-602) exam, you may re-create a small text file, name it Command Line Test.TXT, and save it to your My Documents folder.

a)   If you don't already have the command-line window open, get to a command prompt.

b)   Enter the following commands:

```
C:\>CD \Documents and Settings\%USERNAME%\My Documents
C:\Documents and Settings\%USERNAME%\My Documents\>DIR /P
```

✔ **Hint**

To locate the file you created and saved to My Documents, you should be logged on as the same user. The variable %USERNAME% (including the preceding and trailing percent signs) in the command-line syntax represents the user name you're currently using. Microsoft has assembled many variables that can be used in this manner, such as %SYSTEMROOT% to represent the system folder (usually named WINNT or WINDOWS). You may actually use the variable in the command-line syntax to have the system insert your user name (the folder where all of your personal settings and saved documents are) in the path. I have included a generic example of the use of this variable in Figure 10-10.

Do you see the file you created in the previous chapter's lab? (It should be called Command Line Test.TXT.) _____

FIGURE 10-10 Using an environment variable to insert the user name

Now you will use another command to verify that the file is a text file containing readable text. There are many ways to do this; you'll use one of the simplest methods. The TYPE command displays the contents of a text file, but doesn't allow you to edit or manipulate the text in any way.

   c)   Enter the following (carefully enter the line in the exact syntax as shown, including the quotation marks):

```
C:\Documents and Settings\%USERNAME%\My Documents\>TYPE "COMMAND LINE TEST.TXT"
```

You should see the text that you entered in Notepad during the creation of the file. All of the text should be displayed, although you may have to resize your command-line window to see all of it, and even then it won't be pretty.

The other thing you may have noticed is that to access the text file, you had to add quotation marks to the beginning and the end of the file name. This is because the command line only understands spaces as breaks between commands and operators or switches. Leave the quote marks out of the command line and run the **TYPE** command again. What happened?

_____

You should see something similar to the output in Figure 10-11.

You're going to use this file in the next few steps, and it will be easier to work with if its format conforms to the 8.3 rule. In the early days of MS-DOS, file names could only be eight characters long, with a three-character extension after the period. The three-character extension has remained throughout all versions of Microsoft operating systems, but you can now use up to 255 characters (with spaces) as the file name. To make this file easier to work with in the command line, you'll use the REN (Rename) command to change the file name.

   d)   Type the following command:

```
C:\Documents and Settings\%USERNAME%\My Documents\>REN "COMMAND LINE TEST.TXT"
CMDLNTST.TXT
```

   e)   Now confirm that this has worked by typing the following command:

```
C:\Documents and Settings\%USERNAME%\My Documents\>TYPE CMDLNTST.TXT
```

Great! Now you will be able to type the file name more quickly as you complete the rest of the exercise.

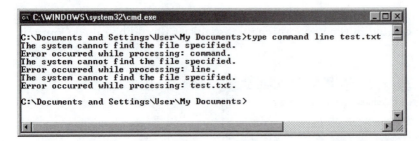

FIGURE 10-11 Results of running TYPE without using quotation marks

Step 2   At the command prompt, type **CD ** to change your focus to the root directory. You'll now create a new directory in the root called STUDY so that you can do some copying and moving. The only difference between copying and moving is that COPY leaves the original file in the same place (as a backup) with a duplicate made elsewhere, whereas the MOVE command relocates the original file to a new location with no backup available. They're otherwise similar, so once you've learned the COPY command, you've pretty much learned the MOVE command too! Follow these steps:

a)   Make a directory named STUDY by typing the following:

    C:\>MD STUDY

b)   Verify that the directory is there by using the DIR command.

Now follow these steps for copying your file named CMDLNTST.TXT to the new STUDY directory:

a)   Change the focus of the command prompt to the STUDY directory:

    C:\>CD STUDY

b)   Copy the CMDLNTST.TXT file to the STUDY directory:

    C:\STUDY>COPY "C:\DOCUMENTS AND SETTINGS\%USERNAME%\MY DOCUMENTS\CMDLNTST.TXT"
    C:\STUDY\CMDLNTST.TXT

Here, COPY is the command, C:\DOCUMENTS AND SETTINGS\%USERNAME%\ MY DOCUMENTS\CMDLNTST.TXT is the current location and name of the file (notice the use of the quotation marks and the %USERNAME% variable once again), and C:\STUDY\ CMDLNTST.TXT is the target location and name of the file.

The entire command and response will look similar to Figure 10-12.

c)   Run the DIR command to see if you copied the file. If the file isn't there, carefully repeat the previous steps or ask your instructor for help.

d)   Change your directory focus back to the My Documents folder (**CD \ DOCUMENTS AND SETTINGS\%USERNAME%\MY DOCUMENTS**) and run the DIR command to see if the original CMDLNTST.TXT file is still there.

```
C:\WINDOWS\system32\cmd.exe                                                    _ □ ×
C:\STUDY>COPY "C:\DOCUMENTS AND SETTINGS\%USERNAME%\MY DOCUMENTS\CMDLNTST.TXT" C:\STUDY\CMDLNTST.TXT
        1 file(s) copied.
C:\STUDY>
```

FIGURE 10-12 COPY command and response

✔ **Hint**

If you're already in the target directory, you don't need to include the target path in the command. My idea of copying or moving files is to start in the directory to which you want to copy the files. Then you can bring the files to where you are. Each time you copy or move a file, you can run the DIR command to see if it's actually there. The other way of sending a file to a directory can be troublesome if you're moving files, because you may accidentally send them to a wrong directory and waste time looking for them.

Another good use of the COPY command is to make a backup copy of a file and rename it at the same time, so that the two files can reside in the same directory.

   e)   To make a backup of the CMDLNTST.TXT text file, type the following command:

```
C:\STUDY\>copy CMDLNTST.TXT CMDLNTST.BAK
```

You now have three copies of the same file; you will clean these up in the last step.

Step 3   The last two commands you will work with in this lab exercise are the MOVE and DEL (Delete) commands. First, you will delete the copy of CMDLNTST.TXT that you copied into the STUDY folder in the last step. You will then move the file permanently from the My Documents folder to the STUDY folder. Follow these steps:

   a)   Change the focus of the command prompt to the STUDY directory:

```
C:\>CD STUDY
```

   b)   Delete the CMDLNTST.TXT file from the STUDY directory:

```
C:\STUDY\>DEL CMDLNTST.TXT
```

   c)   Run the DIR command to see if you deleted the file. If the file isn't there, you deleted it.

Now you will follow the steps to move the file from My Documents to the STUDY folder. You will then verify that the file is in the STUDY folder and no longer in the My Documents folder.

   a)   Make sure the focus of the command prompt is still the STUDY directory.

   b)   Move the CMDLNTST.TXT file to the STUDY directory:

```
c:\STUDY>MOVE "C:\DOCUMENTS AND SETTINGS\%USERNAME%\MY DOCUMENTS\CMDLNTST.TXT"
C:\STUDY\CMDLNTST.TXT
```

In this case, MOVE is the command, C:\DOCUMENTS AND SETTINGS\%USERNAME%\ MY DOCUMENTS\CMDLNTST.TXT is the current location and name of the file (notice the use of the quotation marks and the %USERNAME% variable once again), and C:\STUDY\CMDLNTST.TXT is the target location and name of the file.

   c)   Run the DIR command to see if you moved the file. If the file isn't there, repeat the previous steps or ask your instructor for help.

d) Change your directory focus back to the My Documents folder (**CD \
DOCUMENTS AND SETTINGS\%USERNAME%\MY DOCUMENTS**) and run
the DIR command to see if the original CMDLNTST.TXT file is still there. Do you see it?
_____ Why or why not? _____

You should now have two copies of the file in the STUDY directory, CMDLNTST.TXT and
CMDLNTST.BAK. The file should have been moved from the My Documents directory.

 1 HOUR

Lab Exercise 10.04: Advanced Command-Line Utilities

In Windows, you can perform many tasks either from the GUI or from the command-line window.
The CompTIA A+ certification exams want you to be comfortable with both methods to accomplish
these tasks. To practice your skills with the command-line versions of these tasks, work through the
following scenarios and steps to explore the BOOT.INI system file, the Print Spooler service, and the
New Technology File System (NTFS), all with the view from the command prompt.

Learning Objectives

In this lab, you'll work through three scenarios.

At the end of this lab, you'll be able to

- Work with the ATTRIB and EDIT utilities

- Start and stop services with the NET command

- Convert file systems

Lab Materials and Setup

The materials you need for this lab are

- At least one working computer running Windows XP

- A hard drive with at least 1 gigabyte (GB) of unallocated space, or a 1-GB or greater
  partition formatted with the FAT32 file system

✔ **Hint**

If the computers configured with multiple hard drives are still available from Lab
Exercise 8.07, "Implementing Software RAID 0 with Disk Management," you can convert
these back to basic disks and format them with FAT32 to use in Step 3 of this exercise.

Getting Down to Business

Working through commands as you have in the prior exercises is an excellent method to explore the commands and their usage, but it can seem a little sterile since the commands are isolated and out of context. The next few steps are built around scenarios common in the workplace, requiring you to perform tasks that incorporate both commands you have learned in prior exercises and new commands that will be introduced as needed.

Step 1 BOOT.INI is a file that the Windows 2000 and Windows XP operating systems use to locate the system files during the boot process. This is especially important if the computer has been configured to be a multi-boot computer capable of launching different operating systems. In the steps that follow, you will use the command-line text editor, EDIT, to modify the BOOT.INI system file. You'll have to change the status of the READ ONLY attribute using the ATTRIB command, and verify successful configuration using the System applet's Startup and Recovery settings.

    a)   Using your favorite method, launch the command prompt and change your focus to the root directory.

    b)   To open BOOT.INI using the command-line editor, type the following command:

        `c:\>EDIT BOOT.INI`

This launches the text editor, which displays the BOOT.INI text. Move your cursor down to the line that reads **timeout=30** and change it to **timeout=10**. What happens when you do this?

_____

Exit the command-line editor by pressing ALT-F and then pressing x (this is the keyboard shortcut for File | Exit).

    c)   To list the files and all of their attributes, use the ATTRIB command:

        `c:\>ATTRIB`

The BOOT.INI file is currently set with the attributes R (Read Only), H (Hidden), and S (System). You must change the attributes before you can modify the file. Type **ATTRIB /?** to see the available options for the ATTRIB command.

    d)   Now change the attributes for the BOOT.INI file so that you can edit it in the command-line text editor. Type the following command:

        `c:\>ATTRIB -R -H -S BOOT.INI`

This should remove the attributes from BOOT.INI. To verify the status of BOOT.INI, type **ATTRIB** at the command prompt. Did the previous ATTRIB command clear the attributes of the BOOT.INI file? _____

    e)   Launch the command-line editor again using the following command:

        `c:\>EDIT BOOT.INI`

Again move your cursor down to the line that reads **timeout=30** and change it to **timeout=10**. Save the file by pressing ALT-F and then pressing s (File | Save). Exit the command-line editor by pressing ALT-F and then pressing x (File | Exit).

f) Verify that you have modified the BOOT.INI file by following these steps:

- Access Control Panel.

- Open the System applet, and click the Advanced tab.

- Click the Settings button in the Startup and Recovery area.

The setting called *Time to display list of operating systems* should be changed from 30 seconds to 10 seconds (see Figure 10-13).

g) Now change the attributes for the BOOT.INI file again so that it's a read-only, hidden, system file. Type the following command:

```
c:\>ATTRIB +R +H +S BOOT.INI
```

This will keep the file safe from accidental or malicious deletion or modification until the next time you, the PC tech, need to edit it for different configurations.

Step 2 One recurring problem you will run into in the field is when one of the services in Windows stalls—in particular the Print Spooler. The Print Spooler is a holding area for print jobs, and it's especially important for network printers. If the print device runs out of paper while printing a document, you may have to stop and start the Print Spooler to allow the print device to receive jobs again. Typically, you just open the Computer Management console, select Services, and restart the service. However, there may be times when it is more convenient or just plain necessary to accomplish this task from the command-line interface.

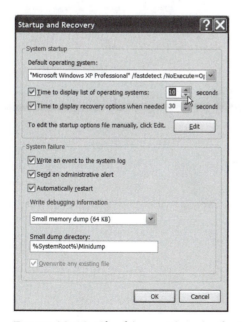

FIGURE 10-13 Checking settings in the Startup and Recovery window

FIGURE 10-14 Print Spooler properties

The following steps walk you through stopping and starting the Print Spooler from the command-line interface:

a)   Launch the Services console by opening Control Panel, launching the Administrative Tools applet, and double-clicking Services.

b)   Scroll down and highlight the Print Spooler, and then select Action | Properties. You should see that the Print Spooler is started and running (see Figure 10-14).

c)   Now launch the command-line interface and change the focus to the root directory.

d)   Type the following command at the prompt:

```
c:\>NET STOP SPOOLER
```

The command line should inform you that the Print Spooler service is stopping, and then that the Print Spooler service was stopped successfully (see Figure 10-15).

FIGURE 10-15 Stopping the Print Spooler service from the command-line interface

FIGURE 10-16 The Print Spooler Properties window

✔ **Cross-Reference**

You will explore the NET command-line utility in the lab exercises for Chapter 16, "Maintaining and Troubleshooting Networks." If you would like to explore the NET command while working on this lab, type **NET /?**.

---

e) Using ALT-TAB, change your focus to the Print Spooler Properties window you opened earlier. You should be able to confirm that the Print Spooler service has been stopped (see Figure 10-16).

f) Change the focus back to the command-line window, and type the following command at the prompt:

```
c:\>NET START SPOOLER
```

The command line should inform you that the Print Spooler service is starting, and then that the Print Spooler service was started successfully (see Figure 10-17).

FIGURE 10-17 Starting the Print Spooler service from the command-line interface

In the real-world scenario, your Print Spooler service would be restarted, and you should have a healthy, functioning print server once again. Now you just have to figure out where you stored the extra toner!

Step 3   Many of the legacy systems in the field started out as computers running Windows 98 and Windows 2000. Often, these systems' hard drives were partitioned and formatted with the FAT32 file system. As you upgrade these systems, you may want to leave the FAT32 file system intact until you verify that the upgrade has been successful. After successful completion of the upgrade, it is recommended that you convert the file system to NTFS. This is a nondestructive, one-way conversion! Once you switch to NTFS, you will have to delete the data and reformat the partition if you want to revert to FAT32.

In this step, you will create a FAT32 partition (unless you already have one from earlier labs) and then use the command-line utility called CONVERT to convert the partition to NTFS.

a)   Boot a computer system with at least 1 GB of unallocated hard drive space. If you have access to the system you used to explore Redundant Array of Independent Disks (RAID) 1 (striping), you can use the extra hard drives installed in the system.

b)   Launch the Disk Management console. From Control Panel, go into Administrative Tools and then select Computer Management.

c)   Click Disk Management.

d)   Right-click an area of unallocated space, and select New Volume from the drop-down menu.

e)   Follow the wizard instructions to create a FAT32 partition of at least 1 GB.

f)   Close the Disk Management console, and double-click My Computer. Create and save a text file to the new drive to verify that the drive is accessible. Right-click the drive, and select Properties; notice the tabs and file system (see Figure 10-18).

FIGURE 10-18 FAT32 partition properties

Now that you have a FAT32 partition, you can launch the command-line window and convert the file system from FAT32 to NTFS. You will then verify that the conversion was indeed nondestructive by opening the text file you created in step (f).

g) Launch the command-line window, and change the focus to the root directory using the **CD ** command.

h) Type the following command at the prompt (substitute the drive letter for your FAT32 partition):

```
c:\>CONVERT E: /FS:NTFS
```

Your results should look similar to Figure 10-19.

i) Exit the command-line window and double-click My Computer.

j) Right-click the drive that you just converted, and select Properties. Your drive should now be formatted with the NTFS file system. Notice the additional tabs for Security and Quota (see Figure 10-20).

k) Close the Properties window, and double-click the drive. The text document you created in step (f) during the setup should still be there and accessible.

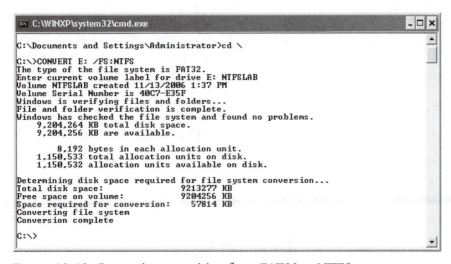

FIGURE 10-19 Converting a partition from FAT32 to NTFS

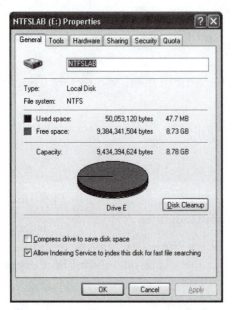

FIGURE 10-20 NTFS partition properties

Lab Analysis Test

1. Nate would like to make backup copies of all of his Word documents in the root directory. He types the following at the command prompt:

    `C:\>COPY A:\*.DOC`

    Will this command work? Why or why not? What will it do? Are there any limitations?

2. Which command(s) would you use to make a full copy of a file in the same directory under a different name?

3. The XCOPY.EXE file is in the SYSTEM32 directory, which is in the WINDOWS directory that's in the root directory of the primary hard drive. What's the complete command-line path to the file?

4. Explain the 8.3 rule. What does the 8 mean? How about the 3?

5. Thomas was messing around one day and deleted a file named CRITICAL.DLL from the SYSTEM32 directory. His friend gave him a copy on a floppy disk. What's the exact command he'd use to copy it back to the correct place?

Key Terms Quiz

Use the following vocabulary terms to complete the following sentences. Not all terms will be used.

CD

COPY

DEL

DIR

MD

RD

REN

/P

/W

/?

1.   The command to create a new directory is _____.

2.   The command used to create a duplicate file is _____.

3.   The _____ switch is used to get help about command syntax.

4.   When there are too many files to show on the screen while using the DIR command, add the _____ switch.

5.   For a listing of a directory's contents that displays only the file names, use the _____ command with the _____ switch.

Chapter 11
Maintaining Windows

Lab Exercises

The average layperson looks at a PC technician as a computer genius who sees almost any problem that takes place on a Windows PC and, through a few magic keystrokes, fixes all of their problems. As techs, we know that PC troubleshooting is a far more complex process that requires us to not only understand how Windows works, but also to appreciate and use many tools and utilities to diagnose the problem and make the repair.

The issues that come to light in these lab exercises include some of the more basic troubleshooting aspects of Windows. First, you'll work with log files to make sure you can see what's taking place on your system. Then you'll inspect the Advanced Options menu and the Recovery console, followed by some real-world startup issues common to many Windows PCs. Last, you'll go through the process of using the handy and powerful Windows System Restore tool.

 30 MINUTES

Lab Exercise 11.01: Examining and Configuring Log Files in Event Viewer

The Windows Event Viewer, available in Windows 2000 and Windows XP, is a valuable tool to anyone who maintains or troubleshoots these systems. It's mostly run as a standalone program, but it can also be added as a snap-in to the Microsoft Management Console (MMC).

Event Viewer monitors various log files and reveals things about the health of the operating system. This utility reports real-time statistics, but normally this data is only used with servers. Desktop computer users are less proactive and usually depend on the after-the-fact log files to help determine the cause of a problem.

Learning Objectives

You'll become familiar with using Event Viewer to analyze the different logs kept by the system.

At the end of this lab, you'll be able to

- Run the Event Viewer program

- Examine an event log entry

- Save the event log

Lab Materials and Setup

The materials you need for this lab are

- A working PC with Windows 2000/XP installed

Getting Down to Business

You can start Event Viewer from Control Panel by double-clicking the Administrative Tools applet. If you've added Event Viewer to your MMC, you can also access it there. For practice, you'll do this lab by accessing it the conventional way, but you should confirm that everything works the same through the MMC.

Step 1   Go to Control Panel and double-click the Administrative Tools icon. Then double-click the Event Viewer icon to start the applet. Event Viewer displays events from three log files: Application, Security, and System. (Applications may install more log files but concentrate on these three.) Figure 11-1 shows the contents of the system event log in Event Viewer.

Notice in Figure 11-1 that there are three kinds of log entries for the system and application logs: Information, Warning, and Error. The security event log shows two types of entries: Success Audit and Failure Audit. These types of events are only logged when auditing is turned on; again, this is normally done only on servers.

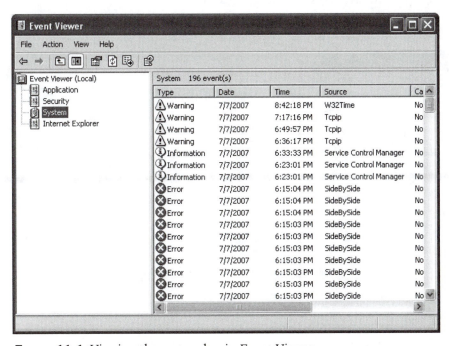

FIGURE 11-1 Viewing the system log in Event Viewer

Double-clicking any entry gives you details of the event.

Step 2   Follow these steps to change the size of a log file:

a)   In Event Viewer's left panel, right-click System Log and select Properties.

b)   Change the number in the Log Size box to **1024** (512 is the default), and select *Overwrite Events As Needed* (see Figure 11-2).

c)   Do this for all three event logs: Application, Security, and System.

d)   Sometimes the log can be completely full before you get a chance to look at the entries. Scrolling through all of the events can be a little boring and time-consuming, but you can fix that with filter settings. Click the Filter tab, and look at the filter settings (see Figure 11-3).

You can filter events based on type, source, category, ID, user, computer, and date. This only controls what Event Viewer displays; all the events information will still be logged to the file, so you can change your mind about filter settings.

e)   Click OK to close the Properties dialog box.

Step 3   To clear, archive, and open a log file, follow these steps:

a)   Clear the system log by right-clicking System Log and selecting Clear All Events (see Figure 11-4).

b)   When you're prompted to save the system log, click Yes.

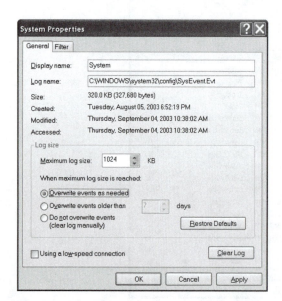

FIGURE 11-2 Changing the size of a log file

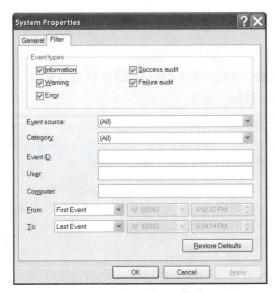

FIGURE 11-3 Setting Event Viewer's settings

c)   You can archive log files using different file names each time (recommended), and select a location other than the default. Give your file a name you can remember, and save it.

d)   To open a saved file, click the Action menu and select Open Log File. Select the file and log type (System, Application, or Security), and click Open.

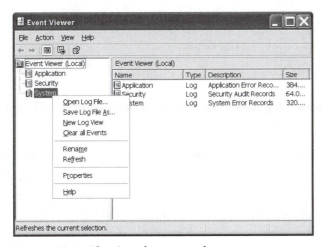

FIGURE 11-4 Clearing the system log

 45 MINUTES

Lab Exercise 11.02: Using the Advanced Options Menu and the Recovery Console

An errant upgrade or a poorly written driver can cause the system to lock up. Some software problems, such as corrupt registry files, will even prevent the system from booting. This means that you must be ready to use alternative methods to boot the system to make repairs or replace files.

Windows has several ways to boot, and these ways are as different as the operating systems themselves. A Safe Mode boot is available with all the Microsoft operating systems. There's also a nice recovery tool that comes with Windows 2000 and Windows XP known as the Recovery console.

Learning Objectives

You'll become familiar with alternative methods of booting a faulty system.

At the end of this lab, you'll be able to

- Boot to Windows' Advanced Options menu and enable Safe mode

- Install the Recovery console for Windows XP

- Repair the registry using the Recovery console

Lab Materials and Setup

The materials you need for this lab are

- A working PC with Windows 2000 or Windows XP installed (preferably a non-production system, as you will be corrupting and repairing the registry)

- The Windows 2000 or XP installation CD

Getting Down to Business

If your system won't boot normally because of some system problem, you need a way to gain access to the hard drive and your files to troubleshoot the problem. There are, happily enough, troubleshooting tools that give you access to these files if the normal boot process won't work. You'll begin this exercise with the first line of defense, the Advanced Options menu, and boot to Safe mode. You will then install and explore the Recovery console, eventually repairing the registry manually.

Step 1   Power up a computer running Windows 2000 Professional or Windows XP Professional and, when prompted, press the appropriate key or key combination to invoke the Windows Advanced Options menu on this system. Depending on your system, you will see a number of different boot options. Record the various modes and provide a small description for each:

_____

_____

_____

_____

_____

✔ **Cross-Reference**

For definitions of each of the boot modes, refer to the "Advanced Startup Options" in Chapter 11 of *Mike Meyers' A+ Guide to Managing and Troubleshooting PCs, Vol. 2: PC Tech.*

Step 2 Select Safe Mode and press ENTER.

The system will proceed to boot into the operating system, but it will inform you many times that it is running in Safe mode (see Figure 11-5).

Safe mode is often used when video settings have been changed and render the display unusable. In Safe mode, a standard video graphics array (VGA) driver is installed, and the minimal settings (16 colors, 640 × 480 resolution) are set. This enables you to revert to previous drivers, and/or correct the settings for the current display or monitor you are using. Complete the following steps to explore the display properties:

a) Right-click somewhere in the empty space of the desktop, and select Properties from the drop-down menu. The Display Properties dialog box appears.

b) Click the Settings tab, and note the display, color, and screen resolution settings. Record your settings here: _____

c) Click Cancel to close the Display Properties dialog box.

d) Click Start | Shut down.

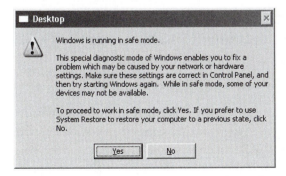

FIGURE 11-5 Windows running in Safe mode

Step 3   Next you will explore using the Repair menu item from the Windows installation CD to launch the Recovery console. (The following steps were completed using a Windows 2000 Professional installation.)

a)   Place the Windows installation CD into the tray, and then reboot the system from the CD. The installation program loads a number of files and then displays a screen with the following information:

```
Welcome to Setup
This portion of the Setup program prepares Microsoft
Windows 2000™ to run on your computer
     To set up Windows 2000 now, Press ENTER.
     To repair a Windows 2000 installation, press R.
     To quit Setup without installing Windows 2000, press F3.
```

b)   Because the operating system is already installed, press R to select the Repair function. The next screen offers two choices:

```
To repair a Windows 2000 installation by using
     the recovery console, press C.
To repair a Windows 2000 installation by using
     the emergency repair process, press R.
```

c)   Press C to open the Recovery console.

You'll now see a command-line interface asking which installation you want to access. If you have a dual-boot system, you'll have to choose an operating system; type its number from the list and press ENTER. Then type the administrator's password. This is the password for the first account created when you initially installed the operating system. You now have a command-line prompt from which to work.

✖ Warning

Be sure you know what you're doing here. You have access to files that you can add, change, rename, or delete. Only a small subset of the command prompt commands work here.

---

d)   To see a list of commands, type **help** and note the results.

e)   Type a command followed by **/?** to get an explanation of that command. You'll explore some of these commands later when you install the Windows XP Recovery console.

f)   Type **exit** to quit the Recovery console; the system will then reboot.

Step 4   Although you can run the Recovery console by booting directly to it from the Windows 2000 or XP installation CD, it's much more convenient to set it up as a startup option on your boot menu. In this step, you'll install the Windows XP Recovery console as a boot option. You can do the same thing using the same steps for Windows 2000 (see Figure 11-6).

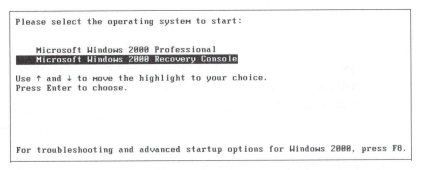

```
Please select the operating system to start:

    Microsoft Windows 2000 Professional
    Microsoft Windows 2000 Recovery Console

Use ↑ and ↓ to move the highlight to your choice.
Press Enter to choose.




For troubleshooting and advanced startup options for Windows 2000, press F8.
```

FIGURE 11-6 Installing the Windows 2000 Recovery console

✔ **Hint**

To install the Recovery console, you must have administrative rights on the computer.

a) Put your Windows XP (or Windows 2000) installation CD into the CD drive; if it autostarts, select Exit. You can also hold down SHIFT until the CD stops loading.

b) Select Start | Run.

c) In the Open box, type **D:\I386\WINNT32.EXE /CMDCONS** (where D is the drive letter for your CD drive).

d) A Windows Setup dialog box appears, which describes the Recovery console option. The system prompts you to confirm installation. Click Yes to start the installation procedure.

e) When the installation is complete (Figure 11-7), restart the computer. You will see a Microsoft Windows Recovery console entry on the boot menu.

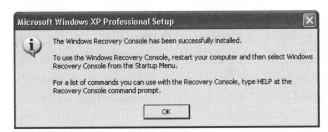

FIGURE 11-7 Completing the Recovery console installation

✔ Note

When you're installing the Recovery console, the CD you use must be the same version of Windows that was used for the system's main operating system installation. For example, if you used a Windows XP Service Pack 2 CD to install Windows on this system, you cannot use a pre–Service Pack 2 CD for this procedure.

It's wise to install the Recovery console on important servers and on critical workstations.

Step 5   Reboot your system, and at the boot menu screen, select the Recovery console. Watch for the boot menu; you have to be quick! Go directly to the command-line prompt (you'll need the administrator password).

To see a list of the commands, type **help** at the command prompt. Type a command followed by **/?** to get an explanation of the command use.

Several commands are worth mentioning; for the CompTIA A+ certification exams, you should know what the following commands do:

- **CHKDSK**   Checks the clusters and sectors of a disk (fixed or removable) and, if possible, repairs bad clusters or sectors

- **DISKPART**   The Windows 2000 equivalent to FDISK

- **EXIT**   Closes the Recovery console and restarts your computer

- **EXPAND**   Extracts copies of single files from the CAB files

- **FIXBOOT**   Writes a new partition table

- **FIXMBR**   Equivalent to FDISK /MBR

- **HELP**   Displays a Help screen

✔ Hint

Many techs resort to the Recovery console when a system fails to boot in the normal fashion (from the hard drive). Three of the commands, FIXBOOT, FIXMBR, and CHKDSK, are particularly important when it seems that the hard disk, the master boot record, or the system partition are missing, corrupt, or damaged. If you come across a system exhibiting these symptoms (and you will), follow good troubleshooting procedures, but remember that you have these tools available to you.

The files that make up the Recovery console reside on the system partition, making the Recovery console useless for a system partition crash. In such a situation, you would use the CD drive to access the Recovery console. The Recovery console shines in the business of manually restoring registries, stopping problem services, rebuilding partitions (other than the system partition), or using the EXPAND program to extract copies of corrupted files from a CD or floppy disk.

Step 6 As mentioned in the previous step, the Recovery console is excellent when you need to restore registry files. In the following steps, you will crash a system by deleting the SYSTEM folder, and then use the Recovery console to access the repair folder and recover the system.

✖ **Warning**

As mentioned in the equipment needs, you are going to purposefully delete/corrupt the SYSTEM folder of a working Windows XP Professional system. For this reason, the system you use must be a non-critical, non-production system. Don't risk your family's financial records or your 40-gigabyte (GB) photo archive—find another system to use for this exercise!

✔ **Cross-Reference**

The following steps use many components of Windows XP Professional and the Recovery console. To fully understand the files, folders, and registry components that are involved, be sure to read the "Registry" section in Chapter 11 of *Mike Meyers' A+ Guide to Managing and Troubleshooting PCs, Vol. 2: PC Tech*.

Microsoft has also gathered invaluable information in their Knowledge Base articles (a component of TechNet). The following lab steps incorporate valuable information from Knowledge Base articles 307545 and 309531. As previously mentioned, Web sites change over time, so if you don't find these exact articles, use your favorite search engine and locate similar articles related to the Recovery console and repairing the registry.

---

a) Some preparation may be required to complete the steps to corrupt and restore your registry folders. Open My Computer, select Tools | Folder Options, and click the View tab. Select *Show hidden files and folders*, clear *Hide extensions for known file types*, and select *Hide protected operating system files (Recommended)*. Click OK.

b) Boot to the Recovery console, and after logging on as the administrator, type the following commands at the prompt:

```
MD C:\%SYSTEMROOT%\TMP
COPY C:\%SYSTEMROOT%\SYSTEM32\CONFIG\SYSTEM
C:\%SYSTEMROOT%\TMP\SYSTEM.BAK
DELETE C:\%SYSTEMROOT%\SYSTEM32\CONFIG\SYSTEM
EXIT
```

c) At this point the Recovery console closes and Windows restarts. Allow Windows XP to boot normally. Did anything inhibit the normal loading and startup of Windows XP?

_____

d) Boot to the Recovery console once again, log on as administrator, and type the following commands at the prompt:

```
COPY C:\%SYSTEMROOT%\REPAIR\SYSTEM C:\%SYSTEMROOT%\SYSTE32\CONFIG\SYSTEM
EXIT
```

e) The Recovery console again closes and Windows reboots. Allow Windows XP to boot normally. Did Windows boot properly this time? _____

→ Try This: Create a Batch File to Restore a Corrupted Registry

Though floppy drives are becoming scarce, the use of Recovery console and some form of accessible, removable media will enable you to semi-automate the restoration of the critical registry folders. Create the following batch file and save it to a floppy disk.

1. Open a text editor, type the following lines of code exactly, and save your work as a text file (located on a floppy disk) called MyRegBak.txt.

MD TMP

COPY C:\%SYSTEMROOT%\SYSTEM32\CONFIG\SYSTEM C:\%SYSTEMROOT%\TMP\SYSTEM.BAK

COPY C:\%SYSTEMROOT%\SYSTEM32\CONFIG\SOFTWARE C:\%SYSTEMROOT%\TMP\SOFTWARE.BAK

COPY C:\%SYSTEMROOT%\SYSTEM32\CONFIG\SAM C:\%SYSTEMROOT%\TMP\SAM.BAK

COPY C:\%SYSTEMROOT%\SYSTEM32\CONFIG\SECURITY C:\%SYSTEMROOT%\TMP\SECURITY.BAK

COPY C:\%SYSTEMROOT%\SYSTEM32\CONFIG\DEFAULT C:\%SYSTEMROOT%\TMP\DEFAULT.BAK

DELETE C:\%SYSTEMROOT%\SYSTEM32\CONFIG\SYSTEM

DELETE C:\%SYSTEMROOT%\SYSTEM32\CONFIG\SOFTWARE

DELETE C:\%SYSTEMROOT%\SYSTEM32\CONFIG\SAM

DELETE C:\%SYSTEMROOT%\SYSTEM32\CONFIG\SECURITY

DELETE C:\%SYSTEMROOT%\SYSTEM32\CONFIG\DEFAULT

COPY C:\%SYSTEMROOT%\REPAIR\SYSTEM C:\%SYSTEMROOT%\SYSTEM32\CONFIG\SYSTEM

COPY C:\%SYSTEMROOT%\REPAIR\SOFTWARE C:\%SYSTEMROOT%\SYSTEM32\CONFIG\SOFTWARE

COPY C:\%SYSTEMROOT%\REPAIR\SAM C:\%SYSTEMROOT%\SYSTEM32\CONFIG\SAM

COPY C:\%SYSTEMROOT%\REPAIR\SECURITY C:\%SYSTEMROOT%\SYSTEM32\CONFIG\SECURITY

COPY C:\%SYSTEMROOT%\REPAIR\DEFAULT C:\%SYSTEMROOT%\SYSTEM32\CONFIG\DEFAULT

2. Place the floppy with your text file in the computer that needs restoration. Launch the Recovery console, locate the text file, and execute the following batch command to restore the registry to a working state:

C:\%SYSTEMROOT%\BATCH A:\MyRegBak.TXT

 30 MINUTES

Lab Exercise 11.03: Troubleshooting Startup Problems

When it comes to troubleshooting tools, Windows 2000 and Windows XP inherited the best of both the Windows NT and 9x operating system families. They have vintage tools such as the Last Known Good Configuration startup option for startup failures and the Task Manager for forcing errant programs to close. Both operating systems have the Recovery console. Each also has a completely revamped and improved version of Windows Help.

I'll leave the finer details of these tools for you to explore through Windows Help, the main textbook, and other labs. In this lab, you'll explore a simple tool known as the System Configuration utility. The System Configuration utility has been around for some time, having been introduced in Windows 98. It was never incorporated into Windows NT or 2000, but it is included in Windows XP.

Learning Objectives

You'll be reintroduced to some troubleshooting tips using a vintage tool with Windows XP.

At the end of this lab, you'll be able to

- Use the System Configuration utility to perform diagnostic startups

Lab Materials and Setup

The materials you need for this lab are

- A working Windows XP system

Getting Down to Business

Many systems have way too many startup options enabled. This isn't only a source of boot problems; it can also slow down the boot process and hog random access memory (RAM) from programs that need it. If Windows XP experiences failures during startup, consider using the System Configuration utility to discover and fix the problem.

Step 1   Select Start | Run, type **msconfig**, and then press ENTER.

The System Configuration Utility opens (Figure 11-8).

Notice that on the General tab, you can select Diagnostic Startup. This is useful if you have just added new hardware that's causing intermittent problems, because it enables you to boot with only basic devices.

The Selective Startup feature is also nice; it lets you bypass some configuration files to see which one contains the errors that are causing problems.

Notice the SYSTEM.INI and WIN.INI tabs, which provide settings that enable you to change the load sequence of your drivers and edit the entries when you find an error.

Step 2   The BOOT.INI tab is powerful (see Figure 11-9) and goes well beyond the CompTIA A+ certification exam requirements, but there are a couple options you should know about.

One important option for troubleshooting is to create a log of what transpired during the boot process. On the BOOT.INI tab, you can enable a BOOTLOG to be created each time the system boots.

If you're troubleshooting a problem and you need to start in the Safe mode every time, instead of pressing F8, you can enable the /SAFEBOOT option.

Step 3   One item that I find useful is under the Services tab. Microsoft has many services that you can disable during bootup if you believe they're causing problems. The Hide All Microsoft Services option, when enabled, only displays those services you've installed—like my video adapter (NVIDIA) driver in Figure 11-10.

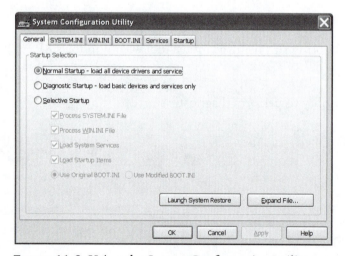

FIGURE 11-8 Using the System Configuration utility

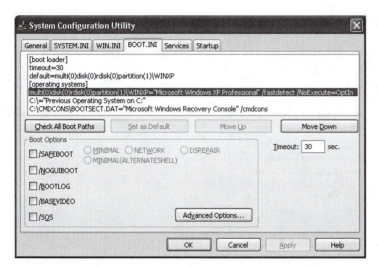

FIGURE 11-9 The BOOT.INI tab

Step 4 The Startup tab is perhaps the most useful. You can enable or disable any of the Terminate and Stay Resident (TSR) programs that are installed. This is a good place to look if some unexplained program is trying to load every time you boot, even though you thought you'd uninstalled it.

Notice in Figure 11-11 that one program on the list doesn't have a name. I'm kind of suspicious about what this program might be doing! If you find questionable entries in your Startup tab listing, you should fire up a browser and do some research to see whether they're harmful.

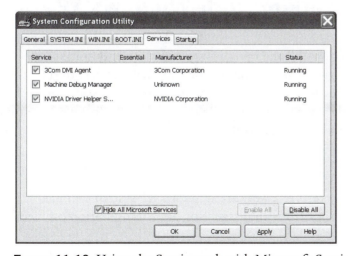

FIGURE 11-10 Using the Services tab with Microsoft Services hidden

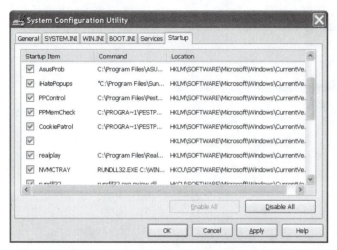

FIGURE 11-11 Checking your startup programs

✔ **Hint**

You can also run the System Configuration utility in Safe mode. If you're having problems, you can boot to Safe mode and then use this utility to identify the source of the problem.

 **30** MINUTES

Lab Exercise 11.04: Working with Windows XP System Restore

The prior labs dealt with upgrading Windows XP and optimizing device drivers. In some cases, installing a service pack or updating a device driver can cause problems, in which case the best thing you can do is to put the system back to the state it was in before you started. You've already worked with Safe mode and the Recovery console when the system will not boot; this lab focuses on restoring the system to a previously working state when you can still access the system.

Learning Objectives

The successful technician knows how to restore a working Windows XP system that has encountered problems beyond those associated with installation and configuration problems.

At the end of this lab, you'll be able to

• Manually create a restore point in Windows XP

• Restore a Windows XP system to a restore point

Lab Materials and Setup

The materials you need for this lab are

- A working PC with Windows XP installed

Getting Down to Business

Windows XP has a great utility to help you restore your system after a botched program or driver installation. It watches for any system changes and basically records them in a diary. To restore a system to a previous state, you can just open the diary and point to a date and time to which you want to return.

Step 1   In this step, you'll manually create a restore point in Windows XP. The operating system automatically creates restore points each day, as well as any time you install an application, update a driver, or add a piece of hardware. You also have the option to create your own restore points whenever you want and give them unique names that are meaningful to you. You might decide to create a restore point before tweaking a bunch of settings in the Display applet, for example, and name the restore point "VideoBack" in case your changes should have a dire effect on your video display.

a)   To create a restore point, select Start | (All) Programs | Accessories | System Tools | System Restore to open the System Restore utility (see Figure 11-12).

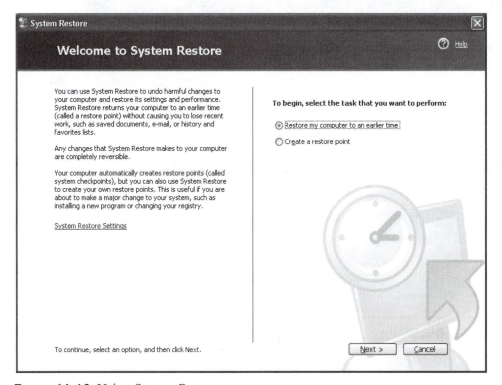

FIGURE 11-12 Using System Restore

b) At the Welcome screen, choose *Create a restore point* on the right side of the screen, and click Next.

c) Type **My Test Restore Point** and then click Create.

d) The system takes some time building the restore file information and then displays a confirmation screen (see Figure 11-13). Click Close to exit the System Restore utility.

You're done! That was easy, wasn't it?

Step 2 To restore the system to an earlier time, return to the System Restore utility, but this time, select *Restore my computer to an earlier time*.

When you click the Next button, the Select a Restore Point screen displays, with a calendar and a listing of the most recent restore points (see Figure 11-14). Based on your knowledge of when your system started having problems, select a restore point and follow the prompts to complete the restore operation.

System Restore is pretty powerful. Even if you crash hard and can only boot to Safe mode, you can still run the System Restore utility to recover your system. It sure beats the alternative!

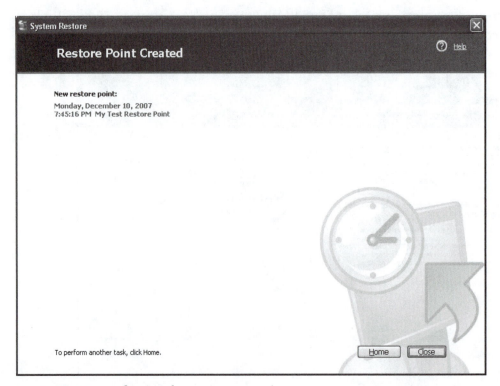

FIGURE 11-13 Confirming the new restore point

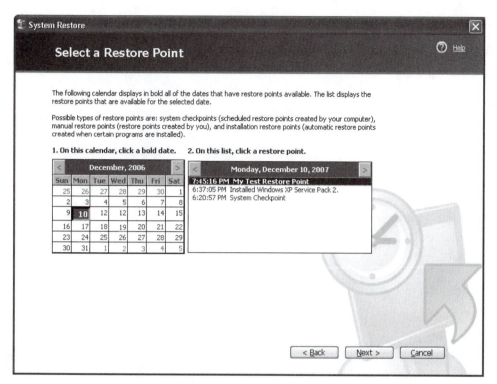

FIGURE 11-14 Choosing a restore point

Lab Analysis Test

1. Tim is a user who feels he's really a programmer at heart—he always seems to be opening the registry with REGEDIT and changing settings directly in it. Today, it doesn't go so well, and he ends up with the Blue Screen of Death (BSoD). What can Tim use to get back to a working system?

2. Laurie has been given six computers in various stages of disrepair. Not one of the systems will boot, even though they are Windows 2000 and XP systems. A friend gives her some floppy disks labeled "ERD" and "ASR," and recommends that she boot the computers using these floppies. When she tries it, the computers display the message *Non-System disk or disk error, replace and press any key when ready*. Why?

3. William has been running his Windows XP system for a few days and notices a small yellow shield in the system tray/notification area. He calls you to ask what it might be.

Key Terms Quiz

Use the following vocabulary terms to complete the following sentences. Not all terms will be used.

ASR

automatic updates

driver signing

ERD

Event Viewer

MSCONFIG

Recovery console

service packs

System Restore

WHQL

1. The _____ can be added as a boot menu option.

2. The _____ provides three log files—System, Security, and Application—to assist with the troubleshooting of a Windows operating system.

3. The process of returning a device driver to its previous version is called driver _____ .

Chapter 12

Installing and Troubleshooting Video

Lab Exercises

Few components affect the PC user like the video system, the primary output for the PC. As you know from the textbook, the video system has two main hardware components—monitor and display adapter—that work together to produce the image on your screen. Both components must be installed and configured properly in Windows, or your viewing pleasure will be seriously compromised. Good techs know how to do video right!

In this set of labs, you'll install a display adapter, hook up a monitor, load video drivers, and configure Windows for optimal viewing. You'll then run through some of the typical troubleshooting issues that techs face when dealing with video.

✖ **Warning**

It is critical to understand that only *trained* monitor technicians should remove the cover of a video monitor (or a television set, for that matter). The inside of a traditional monitor might look similar to the interior of a PC, with printed circuit boards and related components, but there's a big difference: No PC has voltages up to 50,000 volts or more inside, but most cathode ray tube (CRT) monitors *do*. So be sure to get one thing clear—casually opening a monitor and snooping around has the potential to become harmful to you and the monitor—and in cases of extreme carelessness, it can even be deadly! Even when the power is disconnected, certain components (capacitors) still retain substantial levels of voltage for an extended period of time. Capacitors work like batteries. Yes, they can maintain 50,000 volts! If you inadvertently short one of the capacitors, a large discharge will occur into the monitor circuits, destroying them. If you're touching the metal frame, you could fry yourself—to death. Given this risk, certain aspects of monitor repair fall outside the necessary skill set for a standard PC support person, and definitely outside the CompTIA A+ certification exam domains. Make sure you understand the problems you can fix safely and the ones you need to hand over to a qualified electronics repair shop.

 30 MINUTES

Lab Exercise 12.01: Installing Video

Your office staff's computers need a serious video upgrade. Some of the PCs have tiny 14-inch CRT monitors that simply have to go, while others have decent 17-inch and 19-inch CRTs that have a year or two of life left in them. Your boss has bought new AGP and PCI video cards and some liquid crystal display (LCD) monitors to replace the older CRTs. You're tasked with installing the cards, loading drivers, and setting everything up in Windows.

✔ **Cross-Reference**

For the details of CRT versus LCD monitors, refer to the "CRT Monitors" and "LCD Monitors" sections in Chapter 12 of *Mike Meyers' A+ Guide to Managing and Troubleshooting PCs, Vol. 2: PC Tech.*

Learning Objectives

At the end of this lab, you'll be able to

- Identify the make and model of a video card
- Install a video display adapter card
- Check the basic input/output system (BIOS) for proper video settings
- Adjust the monitor for the proper display
- Optimize the video settings in Windows

Lab Materials and Setup

The materials you need for this lab are

- A working PC with Windows 2000 or Windows XP installed
- A working monitor (access to both a CRT and an LCD monitor is recommended)
- A working computer system with access to the Internet

✔ **Hint**

Classrooms that have a variety of different monitor types and video display adapter cards are a plus.

Getting Down to Business

To begin this lab, you'll become familiar with the video components in your system. You'll then step through the proper installation and configuration of a video adapter.

✖ Warning

Some versions of Microsoft Windows operating systems have problems when you make changes to the video display adapters, even when you're simply removing and reinstalling the same card into a different slot. If you perform this lab on a test computer, you should have no real problem if things go wrong. If you're using your primary PC to do the lab, however, make certain you have current drivers available for your video card, or a source to get drivers if necessary.

Step 1 Shut down your system properly and unplug the power cable from the system unit and the wall. Remove the cover from the PC to expose the expansion buses.

   a) Find your video display adapter card (the one to which the monitor is attached). What type of video display adapter is installed: PCI, AGP, or PCIe? _____

✔ Hint

Many laptop computers and some low- to mid-level desktop systems include display adapters integrated right into the electronics of the motherboard. On desktop systems with this configuration, the 15-pin connector will appear in line with the PS/2 and universal serial bus (USB) ports. If your system uses this type of display adapter, the overall performance of the system may suffer because the display typically "steals" 32 to 64 megabytes (MB) of system random access memory (RAM) to serve as video RAM. Not only is this a small amount of video RAM for today's PC applications, it also lowers the total amount of system RAM available for the system. Laptops are usually designed around this limitation, but if your desktop system is of this type, you can increase the performance (and usually the video quality) by installing a display adapter card and disabling the onboard video in the BIOS. Typically, you can also balance between video and system performance by selecting how much memory is allocated to the onboard video in BIOS.

   b) Detach the monitor's cable from the video card.

   Using good electrostatic discharge (ESD) avoidance procedures, remove the screw that holds the card in place, put it a secure location, and then remove your video display adapter card (see Figure 12-1). Examine it closely to answer the following questions. Be careful not to touch the expansion slot contacts on the card!

   c) Look for a name or model number on the adapter's circuit board or chipset.

   Who is the manufacturer, or what is the model number? Write it down. (Note that for this lab's scenario, you'd actually be looking up the information for the new video cards, not the ones already installed—*those* will most likely be donated to charity!)

   _____

FIGURE 12-1 This video card has a cooling fan for the Graphics
Processing Unit (GPU) and eight onboard RAM chips.

Be sure to write down as much information as you can collect from the display adapter for
a later assignment.

d) Reinsert the video card into the same slot, and make sure it is properly seated. Reattach
    the monitor cable and test your system with the case still open to see if it works. This
    could save you the frustration that results when you close the case, fire up the system, and
    get a video error. (Not that I've ever done that!)

✔ **Hint**

AGP and PCIe cards can be a little tricky. They must be seated perfectly or they will not
work. Many of these types of cards use slots with locking levers—if you were observant
when you removed the card initially, you'll know what you have to do now for proper
physical installation.

e) Boot your system and open your favorite browser to search the Web.

Conduct your search using the information you've gathered about the manufacturer and
model number of your card.

Can you find the specifications for your display adapter? _____

What is the highest resolution you can achieve with your video adapter according to these
specifications? _____

How much memory is available? _____

What type of memory is used? _____

Does the adapter support SLI or CrossFire? _____

Does the adapter have any features that are unusual or unfamiliar to you?
_____

Step 2   Reboot your system and press the proper key sequence to enter the complementary metal-oxide semiconductor (CMOS) setup utility. Depending on the BIOS manufacturer and version, there can be as many as five or more video-related settings. My lab system has ten settings directly related to video or the AGP slot. Complete each of these questions based on your specific BIOS. Some of the names of the sections will undoubtedly differ from the ones presented here. Search around a bit and you'll find video options in your CMOS.

On the Standard CMOS Setup or similar screen, how many choices are there for video, and how is your video set? _____

On the Chipset Features Setup or similar screen, what is the value for your Video RAM Cacheable setting? _____ Are there any AGP-specific settings? _____ Are there any settings for the amount of RAM the onboard adapter will use? _____

On the Power Management Setup or similar screen, do you have settings to control how the monitor and video adapter will react when not in use for a period of time? What are your settings? _____

On the Integrated Peripherals or similar screen, do you have an Init Display First setting? What are the choices? _____ What does your setting say? _____ Know that when this setting is wrong, the monitor display might not work.

Step 3   You'll now examine a monitor and see what external controls it has. If you're not in a computer lab, you can go to your local computer store and examine a wide variety of monitors.

Figures 12-2 and 12-3 show the control buttons for adjusting the display attributes for an LCD and a CRT monitor, respectively. Both of these have the controls on the front of the monitor, but some have the controls behind a door under the front of the monitor screen, and others may have them on the back.

A monitor can have quite a few adjustable features. How many of the following can you adjust on your LCD monitor?

Brightness   _____

Contrast   _____

Clock   _____

H-position   _____

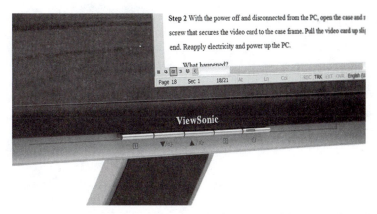

FIGURE 12-2 An LCD monitor with front-panel buttons for adjustments

V-position   _____

Color temperature   _____

Auto balance   _____

Sharpness   _____

Gamma   _____

Signal select (for LCDs with both VGA and DVI inputs)   _____

Full screen   _____

Language   _____

FIGURE 12-3 Front controls on a CRT monitor

How many of these can you adjust on your CRT monitor?

Brightness   _____

Contrast   _____

Color saturation   _____

Vertical size   _____

Vertical position   _____

Horizontal size   _____

Horizontal position   _____

Pincushioning (for adjusting displays that are narrow
in the middle but flare out at the top and bottom)   _____

Keystoning (for adjusting displays that are narrow at
the top but flare out at the bottom)   _____

Degauss (for adjusting displays that have become fuzzy
due to electromagnetic interference)   _____

Play with the controls of your monitor or a test monitor. If the current settings use percentages, write down the settings before doing any adjustments. Then follow these steps:

a)   Change the settings such as color and sizing. Don't be shy!

b)   Put the settings back as close as possible to their original positions.

c)   Optimize the screen for clarity and position.

Step 4   The hardware is set up properly and the BIOS settings should be correct, so now you need to configure and optimize the Windows settings that determine your video display characteristics. To do this, you need to use the Display applet.

✔ Hint

This lab simulates a working PC that you upgrade with new hardware and drivers. All the steps can work just as well for installing a video card into a new system, although the pace of that installation would differ. In a new system, you would physically install the video card, let Windows use generic VGA drivers until you make sure you can boot properly, and only then install the drivers for the video card. Finally, you'd go to the Display applet and optimize the video card settings. Windows XP is fairly good at finding a suitable driver the first time around, but you should still understand how to locate and update drivers for your video card.

Choose your favorite way to navigate to the Display applet, then click the Settings tab. This tab displays the monitor settings, such as those shown in Figure 12-4.

✖ **Warning**

You're going to make changes to the look and feel of Windows. Making some of these changes can result in frustrating and time-consuming problems. Use a test computer, if you have one available. If you must use your own computer, write down all your display settings before you make any changes.

Each video display adapter manufacturer has different options for its cards. By clicking the Advanced button, you can access more information about the display adapter. You may see a choice for setting the refresh rate, as well as other features. Look through the settings on the Advanced dialog box, and see what your display adapter manufacturer provides. Remember that the video adapter "pushes" the monitor. If you set the refresh too high, it can cause problems, and in the case of older CRTs may even damage your monitor.

Write down your display's current resolution, color depth, and refresh rate.

Close the Advanced dialog box (if you selected it), but leave the Display Properties dialog box open.

Make some changes to the background and colors on your screen. You'll find these options on the Background and Appearance tabs, respectively. Be sure to note the original settings so you can change things back when you're done.

FIGURE 12-4 The Display Properties dialog box's Settings tab

✔ **Hint**

The setting changes suggested in this step are perfectly safe and easy to undo.

Change the desktop background to something you might like better, such as Autumn or Bliss. Then try the following:

- Experiment with color combinations.

- Make some changes to the displayed fonts and menu bars.

- Add a screen saver, or change the one you currently have. You'll find these options on the Screen Saver tab. Play with the settings.

- Experiment with changing the colors and resolution of your display.

Can your machine run in 16-bit color? _____

How about 24-bit color? _____

Can you run 800 × 600 resolution? _____

Can you run 1024 × 768 resolution? _____

Can you run 1280 × 960 resolution? _____

Do you have any other options? _____

Click the Advanced button again, and experiment with changing the refresh rate (see Figure 12-5).

FIGURE 12-5 A typical refresh setting under Display Properties

✔ **Hint**

Because of the way that LCD monitors work, the refresh rate setting doesn't really apply to them. As a general rule, LCD monitors display a stable, flicker-free image at 60 hertz (Hz). There are no visible differences between 85 Hz and 60 Hz.

Can you make specific numeric changes? _____

Are the Optimal and Adapter Default settings the only choices you have?

_____

✔ **Hint**

The refresh rate is not an option on all video adapters. This setting may be in a different location, or not on your system at all.

Make sure you return all the settings to their original values, and then close the Display Properties dialog box.

Check the drivers for your video card and monitor. Are they "standard" drivers, or are they specific to your hardware? Follow these steps:

a) Go to the Device Manager, locate your display adapter, right-click, and select Properties.

b) Locate your driver information.

c) Can you identify the version number(s) of your video drivers? Write them down.

d) Go online and find the manufacturer's Web site.

e) Check to see if newer drivers are available. If so, download and install them. (Do this on a test computer first. Get comfortable with the whole process before you do this on your personal computer.)

How did this affect your computer?

✔ **Hint**

New drivers will sometimes fail to work properly, thereby crippling your PC. Windows XP has the Driver Rollback feature that enables you to go back to a driver that worked correctly in case this should happen.

Step 5   One more place to look for video settings is the Power Management Control Panel applet. Take a look at any power management settings you may have.

Go to Control Panel and double-click the Power Management or Power Options applet, if you have one.

Click the arrow next to the drop-down list to see what power management schemes are available.

Which one do you have running? _____

How long is the period of inactivity before your monitor shuts off?

_____

Close the applet and Control Panel.

 30 MINUTES

Lab Exercise 12.02: Troubleshooting Video

Video troubleshooting really boils down to two distinct questions. First, are the physical video components installed and configured properly, as discussed in Lab Exercise 12.01? Second, do the current video display adapter and central processing unit (CPU) support the software technologies you're trying to use? (Or have you loaded that killer game and completely overwhelmed your video subsystem?) In this lab exercise, you'll create connectivity problems to simulate real-world installation problems, and use the DirectX Diagnostic tool to analyze your system.

Learning Objectives

At the end of this lab, you'll be able to

- Recognize and fix typical video installation and connectivity problems
- Use the Microsoft DirectX Diagnostic tool to analyze and test the graphic display attributes of a PC system

Lab Materials and Setup

The materials you need for this lab are

- A working PC with Windows 2000 or Windows XP installed
- Any version of the Microsoft DirectX Diagnostic tool installed

Getting Down to Business

If you went through Lab Exercise 12.01 and had typical results—video card not seated properly, forgetting to plug things in all the way, and so on—you can probably skip Steps 1 and 2 of this lab. If you had a perfect reinstall, on the other hand, then definitely do all of the steps!

Step 1   Loosen the screws that hold the monitor data cable securely to the video card. With the system fully powered up and in Windows—and being gentle with your hardware—partially disconnect the monitor cable.

What happened to the screen? _____

With many monitors, a loose cable results in a seriously degraded display. Colors fade out or a single color disappears, or the display may appear grainy or snowy, for example. If you run into these symptoms in the field, check your connectivity!

Connect the monitor cable and tighten the restraining screws to resume normal operation.

Step 2   With the power off and disconnected from the PC, open the case and remove the screw that secures the video card to the case frame. Pull the video card up slightly on one end. Reapply electricity and power up the PC.

What happened? _____

You might have to run through this a couple of times to get the desired effect, which is a seemingly dead PC and some beeping from the system speaker. That long-short-short beep code is pretty universally recognizable as the PC's cry for help: "Hey! My video card isn't seated properly!"

With the power off and disconnected, reseat your video card, reinstall the restraining screw, and power up your PC to resume normal operation.

Step 3   Access the Microsoft DirectX Diagnostic tool using these steps:

a)   Select Start | All Programs | Accessories | System Tools | System Information.

b)   Select Tools | DirectX Diagnostic tool (see Figure 12-6).

✔ **Hint**

Many technicians prefer to use the command line because it can save a lot of time. If you're one of them, try this: Select Start | Run, then type **dxdiag** and click OK.

Step 4   Select the Display tab (see Figure 12-7).

What is the name of your display adapter? _____

How much total memory is on the adapter? _____

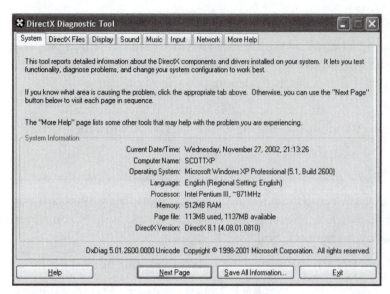

FIGURE 12-6 Using the DirectX Diagnostic tool

What is the current display mode? _____

What is the drive name and version? _____

Does it display a driver version date? _____

Should you look for a more current driver? _____

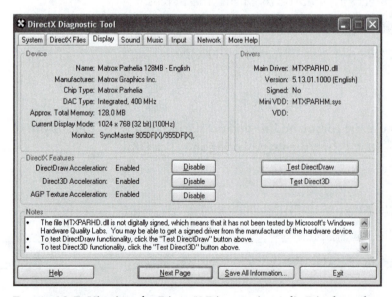

FIGURE 12-7 Viewing the DirectX Diagnostic tool's Display tab

Step 5   Check out the Notes box at the bottom of the Display tab, and read the information provided. This is where you can find out about any conflicts or problem areas.

Do you show any conflicting information? If so, what's the problem? _____

_____

Step 6   Select and test the DirectDraw feature, and follow the instructions.

Did the test complete correctly? _____

Step 7   Select and test the Direct3D feature, and follow the instructions.

Did the test complete correctly? _____

Step 8   Some programs run very slowly or not at all unless Microsoft DirectDraw or Direct3D hardware acceleration is available. On the Display tab, look in the DirectX Features section to see whether DirectDraw, Direct3D, or AGP texture acceleration is set to Not Available or Disabled.

You may need to enable these items or adjust your graphics acceleration, as described in the following steps. You might also consider upgrading your hardware if necessary to improve performance.

   a)   Go to Control Panel.

   b)   Open the Display applet, and select the Settings tab.

   c)   Click Advanced, and select the Troubleshoot tab.

   d)   Move the Hardware Acceleration slider to Full.

✔ **Hint**

If you're looking at a Windows 2000 system, the tab under the Advanced options for hardware acceleration is called Performance or Troubleshooting.

Lab Analysis Test

1.   If you remove an AGP video display adapter and replace it with a PCI video display adapter, what must you do to be sure the Windows desktop will display properly?

2.   Your nephew Brian visited and used your computer last night, and this morning your monitor is dead. What should you do first, second, and third?

3.   What can happen if the refresh rate for a CRT is set too high?

4.   Teresa installed a new game, but she is frustrated because it responds too slowly. What might she check?

5.   Taylor installed a new video display adapter, but the best setting he can adjust it to is 800 × 600 resolution with 256 colors. What must he do to make it go higher?

Key Terms Quiz

Use the following vocabulary terms to complete the following sentences. Not all terms will be used.

color depth

degauss

Direct3D

DirectX Diagnostic

Display applet

hardware acceleration

Init display first

keystoning

pincushioning

refresh rate

resolution

1. Martin has just installed a really cool 3-D game called *FEAR*. It is running horribly slow, so you suggest he checks to make sure _____ acceleration is enabled in the DirectX Diagnostic tool.

2. Erin's monitor was set to 640 × 480, a very low _____.

3. When you display a bright white background, your CRT monitor has areas that appear shaded or dim. You use the _____ option from the monitor menu options to correct the image.

4. Clair is attempting to adjust her monitor for the most symmetrical alignment possible. She uses the _____ and _____ adjustments and is able to produce a beautiful, symmetrical, rectangular screen image.

5. _____ can offer excellent visuals in games and not bog down the system.

Chapter 13
Sound and Multimedia

Lab Exercises

You have been hired on as an entry-level tech for a public school district. Your first day on the job, the technology manager asks how familiar you are with recording, storing, and playback of audio files on computer systems. It turns out that the sociology department wants the students to be able to record audio documentaries on current events, store the files on the network, and produce podcasts of the documentaries. Demonstrating your enthusiasm, you respond that you are somewhat familiar with sound and will tackle the project. You are tasked with researching the sound card, building the prototype system, and providing some basic audio recording and storage training to the sociology instructors.

As a competent PC tech, you need to understand not just the tasks of installing the physical sound card and associated drivers, but also the applications that take advantage of the PCs' sound capabilities. As such, the CompTIA A+ certification exams expect you to know about sound cards and their workings. The following lab exercises will introduce you to sound card hardware and drivers, as well as the basic use of some of the popular Windows audio applications.

 30 MINUTES

Lab Exercise 13.01: Installing Sound

The first task on the agenda is to do a little research on sound cards and choose a few that meet the needs of this project. There are a number of different sound chips, and the "card" can be anything from the on-board sound capability of a mid-priced system to professional multichannel (input/output) devices used in recording studios. After you assemble a few candidates, you will select a sound card and then install, configure, and test that card. For the purpose of completing this lab, it is perfectly acceptable to use any working card, or an on-board sound device if that's what you have available.

Learning Objectives

This lab teaches you the basics of installing and configuring a sound card.

At the end of this lab, you'll be able to

- Identify features of sound cards

- Remove and install a sound card and associated devices (speakers and microphone)

- Configure a sound card

Lab Materials and Setup

The materials you need for this lab are

- A working computer system running Windows 2000 or Windows XP

- A removable sound card, microphone, and speakers properly installed and functioning (the sound drivers must either be part of the operating system in use or be available on CD or diskette)

✖ Warning

Different versions of Windows handle the drivers differently, to say the least. You should have a current driver disc or diskette for your sound card handy, just in case Windows decides it cannot remember your sound card when you go to reinstall!

Getting Down to Business

This lab will step you through removing, researching specifications for, installing, and configuring a sound card.

Step 1   Begin by examining the configuration and resources currently being used by the sound card. Turn on your computer and boot to Windows, and then open the Device Manager (Figure 13-1).

✔ Hint

There are several ways to access the Device Manager. If you need a memory jog, review Pathing in Chapter 12 in *Mike Meyers' A+ Guide to Managing and Troubleshooting PCs, Vol. 1: Essentials.*

Now follow these steps:

a)   Click the plus sign (+) next to *Sound, video and game controllers.*

b)   Highlight the sound card icon.

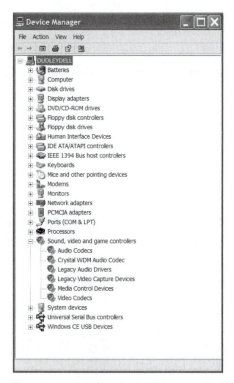

FIGURE 13-1 The Device Manager in Windows XP

✔ **Hint**

The name of the sound card icon differs according to the type of sound card you have installed. A Creative Labs SoundBlaster Live! card, for example, has the entry listed as "Creative SB Live! Series (WDM)." Try them all if it's not obvious at first glance which is the appropriate icon.

---

c) Right-click and select Properties.

d) Click the Resources tab.

Verify which resources the sound device is using, and confirm that there are no conflicts.

Which interrupt request (IRQ) is listed? _____

What direct memory access (DMA) channels are listed, if any? _____

What input/output (I/O) addresses are listed? _____

e) Now click the Driver tab, and record all the available information about the driver that is currently installed.

Step 2 Take a moment and look up the specifications of your current sound card. Identify the following:

Resolution _____

Sampling rate _____

Dynamic range _____

Signal-to-noise ratio _____

Now see if you can find this information on some other cards—try M-AUDIO Revolution 5.1, Creative SoundBlaster X-Fi, SoundMAX Integrated Digital Audio, and Voyetra Turtle Beach.

Step 3 Now that you've seen what resources are currently being used, and some of the relevant specifications, the next step is to practice removing and reinstalling the sound card.

✔ **Hint**

This lab assumes that you have a removable sound card, not onboard sound. If all you have to work with is a system with onboard sound, go into the CMOS setup utility and turn off the onboard sound. Make what observations you can and resume the exercise with Step 4. When the time comes in the second half of Step 4 to reinstall the sound card, just go back into CMOS and enable the onboard sound again.

---

a) Close the Device Manager and shut down your system properly. Unplug the power cord.

b) Remove the case cover from your system and locate the sound card (see Figure 13-2).

FIGURE 13-2 A typical sound card

What type of slot does the card use? _____

c)   Disconnect any cables that are attached to the sound card (both internal and external), take out the screw that secures the sound card to the case, and then carefully remove the card. Make sure you're properly grounded before you touch the card!

What sort of internal connectors does the card have? _____

What sort of external connectors does it have? _____

Does the card have jumpers? What are they used for? Again, look on the Internet for the answers. Find the name of the card manufacturer and search that company's Web site for information on your specific model. This information is also available in the documentation for the card, if you still have it around. _____

_____

What is the brand name of the sound-processing chip?

_____

Is the name on the chip different from the name of the manufacturer of the card? (For example, the chip might have *ESS* printed on it, while the board is marked *Creative Labs*.)

_____

Describe the cables you disconnected when you removed the sound card.

_____

Does the card have an IDE interface? If so, you have a really old card. How would the IDE interface be used? _____

✔ Hint

In old systems that had only one IDE controller on the motherboard, how were CD-ROM drives connected when you had two hard drives in the system?

Step 4   With the card out of your system, turn on the computer and let it boot to the Windows desktop. Then go to the Device Manager and see if your sound card is still listed.

Did Windows automatically remove the device when the card was removed?

_____

If the sound card is still listed, highlight its icon, right-click, and select Uninstall. (Am I sure? Yes, I'm sure!)

Save your changes and shut your system off properly.

The next steps will confirm that the device has been removed:

a)   Reboot your system, go to the Device Manager, and confirm that the sound device is no longer listed.

b)   Shut down your system and disconnect the power cord. Insert the sound card in the slot where you originally found it, secure the card to the case using the screw you removed, and reconnect all the cables.

c)   Reboot the system. When Plug and Play (PnP) kicks in, your system should recognize that you have added a card.

Windows will now locate the software drivers for the new hardware you installed. In fact, unless you uninstalled them, the drivers should still be on your system.

Step 5   Return to the Device Manager and repeat Step 1 to verify what resources the sound card is now using and confirm that there are no conflicts.

What IRQ is listed now? _____

What DMA channels are listed, if any? _____

What I/O addresses are listed? _____

Are the settings the same as in Step 1 before you removed the card? _____

Go to the Drivers tab and confirm that Windows installed the same drivers in the system. If necessary, use the driver diskette or CD to reinstall the correct drivers.

Step 6   To confirm that sound is working properly, start by ensuring that the speakers are powered and connected, and that the volume is set at a comfortable level.

Make sure your speakers are plugged into the proper jack on the sound card.

Is the speaker pair plugged into a working alternating current (AC) outlet, or does it have good batteries? _____

Is there a volume adjustment knob on your speakers? _____

If you have a volume knob, adjust it to the middle position, and then access Control Panel.

Now place a Volume icon in the taskbar's system tray/notification area so that volume adjustments will be more convenient. Follow the procedure that matches your operating system.

•   In Windows 2000, open the Sounds and Multimedia Control Panel applet, and select the *Show volume control on the taskbar* check box.

•   In Windows XP, open the Sounds and Audio Devices Control Panel applet, and select the *Place volume icon in the taskbar* check box.

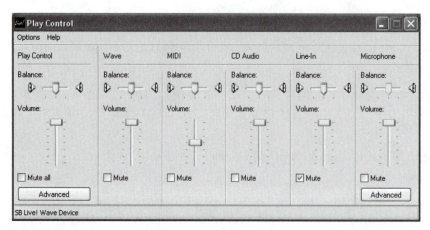

FIGURE 13-3 Setting the volume controls

Once you have the Volume icon in the taskbar, double-click it to open the volume controls and then follow these steps:

a)   Check to be sure that the *Mute all* option is not selected (see Figure 13-3).

b)   Select Options | Properties.

c)   Select the volume controls that you want to control.

d)   Click OK to close the Properties window.

e)   Now adjust all the sliders to the center position.

You now have a good starting point to play sounds. Once you have ensured that the speakers are successfully putting out sound, you can go back and customize the levels to your liking.

Step 7   Test the speakers, and adjust the sound volume to a comfortable audible level. A good tool to use to test your sound card is the DirectX Diagnostic tool. Click Start | Run and type **dxdiag** to launch the DirectX Diagnostic tool (see Figure 13-4).

a)   Click the Sound tab, and examine the information displayed about your sound card and drivers.

b)   Click the Test DirectSound button. This steps you through a series of tests to confirm the operation of your sound system.

c)   Now switch to the Music tab, and click the Test DirectMusic button. This tests whether your system supports the DirectMusic component of DirectX.

Step 8   You've learned to remove, install, and configure a sound card. You've also learned how to test the various parts of the sound system. Now it's time to talk about troubleshooting.

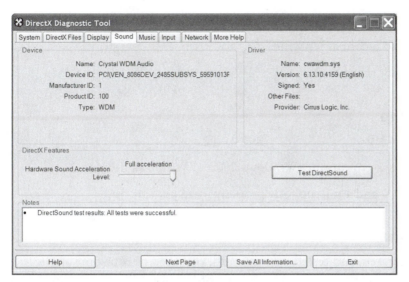

FIGURE 13-4 Using the DirectX Diagnostic tool

Your sound system is working, but your speakers sound a little rough. Are they "blown" out because they were overdriven with poor adjustments? You can go to this Web site and test the response of your speakers at different frequencies:

www.eminent-tech.com/music/multimediatest.html

These tests will help you confirm whether your speakers can still handle all the frequencies they are designed to handle.

 **30 MINUTES**

Lab Exercise 13.02: Recording Sound

With the sound card installed, configured, and tested, it's time to get the project really rolling with recorded sound. It is expected that each student's documentary will last from eight to ten minutes and will encompass typical current events. Each student has a microphone, sound card, and speakers. What you want to do is get the speech recorded digitally, maybe add some music, and choose the audio quality based on the expected delivery method.

Learning Objectives

The purpose of this lab exercise is to guide you in the recording of sound.

At the end of this lab, you'll be able to

- Use the microphone to record a .WAV file

- Fine-tune the quality of the recording

Lab Materials and Setup

The materials you need for this lab are

- A working computer system running Windows 2000 or Windows XP

- A sound card, speakers, and a microphone properly installed

Getting Down to Business

Once you have installed, configured, and tested a sound card, you need to run some applications to see if this is going to work. This lab steps you through recording sound into the computer and saving the recording as a .WAV or .MP3 sound file.

Step 1   To check your system's ability to capture audio so that you can record the documentaries, you will use the Windows Sound Recorder. Make sure your microphone is plugged into the proper connector before you proceed.

Access the Sound Recorder by selecting Start | All Programs | Accessories | Entertainment | Sound Recorder. What you have now is similar to an audio cassette player. The buttons are the same—Record, Play, Fast Forward, Rewind, and Stop—but they're labeled with icons instead of words (see Figure 13-5).

Step 2   You will now explore three different levels of recording. When working with digital audio files, the balance between sound quality and sound file size is driven by the project. If you were recording a project for a CD, you would want the highest quality. For streaming audio and podcast audio, the .MP3 file format is probably acceptable. Telephone quality, while achieving small file size, is not considered production quality.

a)   To set the recording quality, select File | Properties and then click the Convert Now button. In the Sound Selection dialog box, click the Name drop-down menu and select CD Quality. Click OK and then OK again to return to the Sound Recorder window.

FIGURE 13-5 Using the Windows Sound Recorder

b)   Click the red Record button and start talking into the microphone. Watch the graph to see that your voice is being recorded. If nothing seems to be happening, check your microphone connections.

c)   Record a full 60 seconds of CD-quality audio, then click Stop (the button with a square icon, next to Record). To hear your recording, click Play (the single right arrow).

d)   To discover how much space this sound file uses, click File | Properties and observe the file's data size. Record the file size here: _____

e)   Create a subfolder named **podcast** in your My Music folder (under My Documents) and save the sound file as CDQUALITY.WAV in the podcast folder.

✔ **Hint**

As you've probably figured out, our scenario for the social studies department would require a more sophisticated digital audio recording application. One minute is not going to be a lengthy documentary! The Sound Recorder is a good application to demonstrate the steps required to record audio, and you could use it to set up custom sound files to play during events. An example would be the infamous sound file that announces: "You've got mail." If you would like to explore digital audio recording and playback further, you can find and download the open-source program called Audacity at http://audacity .sourceforge.net.

Step 3   Telephone quality is low-resolution and frequency response, meaning that it will probably sound muffled and dull. Follow these steps to convert the CD-quality sound file to a telephone-quality sound file:

a)   Select File | Properties, click Convert Now, and change the Name setting to Telephone Quality. Click OK and then OK again to return to the Sound Recorder window.

b)   Now check out the data size of the file and record it here: _____ Has the size of the sound file changed? How does it sound?

c)   Save the sound file in the podcast folder as TELEPHONEQUALITY.WAV.

Step 4   Finally, you will explore saving a recording as an MPEG Layer-3 (MP3) sound file. This is probably the best balance between audio quality and file size.

a)   Launch Sound Recorder and open the CDQUALITY.WAV file.

b)   To set the recording quality to the MP3 format, select File | Properties, and then click Convert Now. In the Sound Selection dialog box, click the Format drop-down list, select MPEG Layer-3, and then click OK.

    c)   Note the file's data size and record it here: _____ Has the size of the sound file changed? How does it sound?

    d)   Open the podcast folder, and save the sound file as MP3QUALITY.MP3.

 Hint

In the Sound Selection dialog box, you can also set more specific attributes for an MP3 file; just click the Attributes drop-down list after selecting MPEG Layer-3 and you'll see a number of options to fine-tune the quality of your recording.

 **30** MINUTES

Lab Exercise 13.03: Exploring Windows Media Player

Now that you have successfully recorded the project, you will have to look at some of the methods used to play the files and create an archive of the documentary on CD. The Windows environment has used Windows Media Player since the introduction of version 6.1 in 1998. You can always download the latest version of Windows Media Player from Microsoft's Web site. In this exercise you will learn some of the basic navigation steps for using Windows Media Player, and burn your recordings to an audio CD.

 Hint

The audio standard for the Apple Macintosh environment is QuickTime.

Learning Objectives

This lab exercise will help you learn the steps to navigate and play audio files, and then burn an audio CD using Windows Media Player.

At the end of this lab, you'll be able to

- Open and play sound files of various formats

- Navigate Windows Media Player

- Burn a CD of your recording

Lab Materials and Setup

The materials you need for this lab are

- A working computer system running Windows 2000 or Windows XP

- A properly installed sound card, speakers, and a microphone

- Windows Media Player 9 or newer (WMP11 is used in the lab exercise)

- A commercially produced music CD of your choice

- A blank CD-R or CD-RW

Getting Down to Business

Once you've recorded the sound and saved it as a .WAV or .MP3 sound file, you'll need a method to audition the finished product and package the sound file for distribution. You may want to make an MP3 file for portable players or streaming audio over the Internet, or you may want to distribute high-quality audio CDs.

✔ **Hint**

There are a number of paths you could take to accomplish the playback of your recordings and archive them to a CD. This lab exercise steps you through one method that explores some of the features of Windows Media Player 11. Some of the steps, windows, and icons may look different depending on the version of Windows Media Player you use. You can download Windows Media Player 11 from Microsoft to follow along exactly with the steps in the lab.

Step 1 Launch Windows Media Player and then follow these steps:

a) If you have installed Windows Media Player 11, right-click the main menu, and select Show Classic Menus. This displays the traditional menu bar with File, View, Play, Tools, and Help (see Figure 13-6).

b) Click the Now Playing tab. To open the three files you created in the previous lab (TELEPHONEQUALITY.WAV, MP3QUALITY.MP3, and CDQUALITY.WAV), select File | Open, and then click Look in. Use the drop-down menu to locate the podcast folder and files. Click the first file, then hold down the CTRL key while you click each of the two remaining two files. Drag the three selected files to the Now Playing playlist. The first sound file should start to play automatically and display the file name in the pane on the right.

FIGURE 13-6 Windows Media Player 11

c) While listening to the podcast, click File | Save Now Playing List As, and save the list as PODCAST.WPL. This organizes your files into a named list for ease of use.

d) Now click the Burn tab, and then click Burn 'podcast' in the Burn List pane on the right side of the Windows Media Player window.

e) Insert a blank CD-R or CD-RW into an optical-media drive on your system with recording capabilities, and then click the Start Burn button.

f) Wait while the podcast audio file is burned to the CD-R/RW disc, completing the task of archiving your recordings.

Step 2 While you have Windows Media Player open, explore the other options available to you as you work with sound files. One of the most popular uses of the computer when it comes to working with audio is to convert your CDs to MP3 sound files for use on portable MP3 players. Complete the following steps to calculate how many CDs you could fit onto a 2-gigabyte (GB) MP3 player.

a) Insert a music CD into the CD/DVD-ROM drive.

b) Right-click Rip and select More Options. This opens the Options dialog box for Windows Media Player, with the Rip Music tab selected.

c) Under Rip Settings, click the Format drop-down list, and select WAV (Lossless). Use the information at the bottom of the dialog box to calculate the number of CDs that would fit onto a 2-GB MP3 player at this resolution. _____

d) Now click the Format drop-down list again and select MP3. Experiment with the *Audio quality* slider (which ranges from 128 kilobits per second [Kbps] to 320 Kbps), and calculate the number of CDs that would fit onto a 2-GB MP3 player at various quality settings. _____

Lab Analysis Test

1. Suddenly and for no apparent reason, the speaker icon no longer shows up in the taskbar/notification area. Where would you check to be sure it is enabled?

2. John replaced his motherboard with one that has built-in sound. He still wants to use his Creative Labs Audigy sound card. What must he do to prevent conflicts?

3. Theresa has been using her system for a long time to visit with friends in chat rooms. Lately her friends are complaining that her sound quality is getting worse. What should she check first?

4. Karl is not getting any sound from his speakers. What three things should he check?

5. John complains about annoying sounds when he opens and closes certain programs and sometimes when he clicks his mouse. He asks you if you can make them go away. Can you?

Key Terms Quiz

Use the following vocabulary terms to complete the following sentences. Not all terms will be used.

aux

compression

line-in

.MID

.MP3

sound card

sound file

Sound Recorder

speaker

.WAV

1. Joe wants to record himself singing the '50s classic "Hound Dog" to honor the birthday of Elvis Presley. He plugs a microphone into his sound card and opens _____, the recording software that comes with Windows.

2. By default, Windows Sound Recorder saves audio recordings as _____ files.

3. Joshua is the keyboard player for a local band. He records some of the band's songs into a sequencer using Musical Instrument Digital Interface (MIDI). When he looks for the files on the computer, he can only find files with the _____ extension.

4. The MP3 format is popular because of the _____ scheme it uses.

5. The most common sound file format for portable sound players today is _____

Chapter 14
Portable Computers

Lab Exercises

Working on the hardware side of portable computing devices used to be the realm of only highly specialized technicians. As portable computing devices become increasingly common and the technology inside becomes more modular, frontline general technicians (think CompTIA A+ certified technicians here) increasingly get the call to upgrade and repair these devices.

Most portable computers (PCs, not PDAs) have parts that a user can easily replace. You can swap out a fading battery for a newer one, for example, or add a second battery in place of a CD-RW drive for long airplane trips. Lurking beneath access panels on the underside or below the keyboard on some models are hardware components such as RAM, a hard drive, a network card, and a modem—just like laptop batteries, these units can be easily accessed and replaced by a technician. Some laptops even have panels for replacing the video card and CPU.

In this series of labs, you'll explore the hardware of current portable computing devices. First, you'll use the Internet to research the upgrades available for portable computing devices so you can provide proper recommendations to employers and clients. Then, you'll open a laptop and gut it like a rainbow trout—removing and replacing RAM, the most common of all hardware upgrades.

> **✖ Warning**
>
> I want to caution you that completely disassembling a laptop can be like trying to wrestle a bear. Even seasoned technicians pause before removing the dozens of screws involved in replacing broken screens or damaged system boards. These types of repairs require patience and finesse, as you disassemble and reassemble delicate plastic coverings and connect and disconnect fragile wiring harnesses. Troubleshooting damaged laptops is beyond the scope of this lab manual. The lab exercises here focus on the more accessible upgrades, as outlined in the CompTIA A+ 220-602 (IT Technician) objectives.

 **30** MINUTES

Lab Exercise 14.01: Researching Laptop Upgrade Paths

Your boss just sent word that one of your most important clients wants to extend the life of their sales force's laptop computers by upgrading rather than replacing. You've been asked to provide an upgrade track for your client. This requires you to research the laptops used by the company to determine which upgrades you can make, and to verify that the laptops themselves are not so old that the cost to upgrade them outweighs the cost of new laptops with new technology. You have to determine whether you can add RAM, replace the hard drives, replace the aging batteries, or add docking stations to provide extra functions when the salespeople are at the home office. Get to work!

Learning Objectives

Given the manufacturer and model number of a notebook computer, you'll figure out how to upgrade your client's computers.

At the end of this lab, you'll be able to

- Determine the replacement price of a battery

- Determine memory upgrades, including the quantity and type of RAM

- Determine hard drive upgrades, including the capacity and price of a hard drive

Lab Materials and Setup

The materials you need for this lab are

- A working PC with Internet access

Getting Down to Business

Limber up your surfing fingers, because you're about to spend some time on the Web. Researching information about hardware and software is something technicians do all the time. The better you are at it, the better you are at your job!

When you're searching for replacement and upgrade parts and information, always take a look at the device manufacturer's Web site. Most major PC manufacturers, such as Dell and IBM (Lenovo has purchased IBM's personal computer line, so IBM laptops are now supported by Lenovo), have comprehensive product specification sheets available to the public on their sites. You can even order replacement parts directly from them! A popular tactic for researching upgrades is to grab the upgrade specs from the manufacturer's site and then search the Internet for the best prices. Not only are you doing your job well, but you'll be saving your company money, too!

In the following steps, you'll navigate the tumultuous seas of the Internet in a quest to find the Golden Fleece of laptop battery, memory, and hard drive upgrades.

Step 1   Fire up your Web browser, and surf over to the device manufacturer's Web site. Try www.dell.com. If you can't locate that site, try www.batteries-store.com to get information about battery upgrades. If that site isn't available, do a Google search (www.google.com) for "laptop battery." Many sites sell every laptop battery imaginable. The goal of this exercise is to become familiar with using the Internet to identify parts, confirm the specifications, and purchase replacement batteries. Once you reach a suitable Web site, answer the following questions:

- You need replacement batteries for several Dell Inspiron 8600 PCs. What's the vendor's part number and price for this battery?

- What's the voltage, current, and/or power capacity of the battery?

✔ **Hint**

Just like any other electrical power source, batteries are rated according to voltage (9.6 V, for instance), current capacity (2600 milliamps per hour, or mAh), and sometimes power capacity (72 watts per hour, or WHr). When purchasing laptop batteries from third-party vendors (that is, vendors other than the laptop manufacturer), make sure to buy a battery that matches the voltage recommended by the manufacturer. Depending on the type of battery (nickel-cadmium (Ni-CD), nickel metal hydride (Ni-MH), or lithium ion (Li-Ion)), the current or power capacity of replacement batteries may be greater than the original battery. This is not a problem—increased current/power capacity means longer run times for your portable PC.

Step 2   Search the manufacturer's Web site for information on memory. If that isn't available, browse to www.kahlon.com to check RAM prices and availability. If the site isn't available, perform a Google search to find other Web sites that sell "laptop memory." Then answer the following questions.

Your client has ten Dell Inspiron 8600s with 256 megabytes (MB) of RAM. How much RAM can you install? How many sticks of RAM will it take to upgrade this computer to a respectable 1 gigabyte (GB) of memory, and how much will it cost?

Step 3   Stay where you landed in your search for memory upgrades. Do they have replacement hard drives available as well? If not, try www.kahlon.com, but now research possible hard drive upgrades for the five IBM ThinkPads the client owns. Answer this question:

The client's five IBM ThinkPad T41 Pentium M 2374 PCs have 20-GB hard drives and 512 MB of RAM. How much will it cost to upgrade each ThinkPad to an 80-GB hard drive and 1 GB of RAM?

 **30** MINUTES

Lab Exercise 14.02: Replacing and Upgrading RAM

Your client settled on the RAM upgrades as the first step for making their laptops more usable, and you get tagged as the person to remove the old RAM and install the new. Upgrading RAM is the most common technician-performed upgrade on portable PCs and something you're likely to run into in the real world.

Learning Objectives

In this lab, you'll learn essential skills for upgrading portable PCs.

At the end of this lab, you'll be able to

- Access the RAM panel in a laptop

- Remove RAM in a laptop

- Install RAM properly in a laptop

Lab Materials and Setup

The materials you need for this lab are

- A working portable computer (one with modern SO DIMM or DDR SO DIMM modules is preferable)

- A tiny Phillips-head screwdriver

✖ Warning

Opening a portable computer can result in a nonfunctional portable computer. Don't use the instructor's primary work laptop for this exercise!

Getting Down to Business

You're about to open the sensitive inner portions of a portable computer, but before you do, it's a great idea to refresh your memory about avoiding electrostatic discharge (ESD). The inside of a laptop looks different from the inside of a desktop or tower case, but the contents are just as sensitive to static electricity. Watch out!

Step 1   Using your handy screwdriver or other handy tool, open the access panel for the RAM. Every portable PC offers a different way to access the RAM, so I can't give you explicit directions here. Most often, you'll find a removable plate on the bottom of the laptop secured with a tiny Phillips-head screw. Some laptops require you to remove the keyboard, unscrew a heat spreader, and then access the RAM. Figure 14-1 shows a typical panel, accessible from the underside of the laptop.

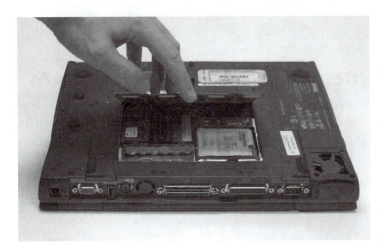

FIGURE 14-1 Opening the access panel to find RAM

Step 2 Once you have the panel open, push outward on the restraining clips on the RAM stick(s). This will cause the RAM to pop up partially (see Figure 14-2).

Step 3 Remove the RAM gently, gripping only at the non-contact edges. Place the stick(s) on an anti-static pad or in an anti-static bag.

Step 4 Install the replacement RAM into the laptop, reversing the process of removal. Place the stick(s) at an angle into the RAM slots and push firmly. Once the contacts have disappeared, press the body of the RAM into the restraining clips.

FIGURE 14-2 Releasing the RAM

If you don't have new RAM to install, simply install the RAM you removed in Step 3. This gives you the opportunity to practice!

Step 5   Replace the access panel.

Step 6   Power on the laptop to confirm that the new RAM is recognized and functioning properly.

Lab Analysis Test

1. Bill wants to upgrade his memory from 256 MB to the maximum amount of RAM his notebook can take. He has an IBM T43 notebook. How much RAM does he need to buy?

2. Mary has a desktop computer system that has an 80-GB hard drive. She has all but abandoned the desktop system for her shiny new laptop, but is disappointed with the 30-GB hard disk on her laptop system. She requests that you remove the hard disk from her desktop system and install it in the laptop. Will this work?

3. Maanit often travels cross-country and even back and forth to India on occasion. He uses his laptop to watch DVDs for hours on end, usually on battery power. Lately, the battery seems to run out of juice well before the battery specifications indicate. What could possibly cause this recent development? Are there any recommendations you would make to Maanit to improve his laptop's performance?

4. During your research earlier in these exercises, which did you discover to be the most expensive— hard drives, memory, or batteries? Which component was the most inexpensive to replace?

5. Many new laptop computers are being marketed as portable "multimedia" workstations, with high-performance graphics and sound. These components typically require more power and, therefore, will require extended battery life or additional batteries to remain portable multimedia workstations. Research and document some of the new trends in laptop batteries. What are some of the figures for operation times?

Key Terms Quiz

Use the following vocabulary terms to complete the following sentences. Not all terms will be used.

ACPI

battery

current

hard drive

hibernate

lithium ion (Li-Ion)

memory

nickel-cadmium (Ni-CD)

nickel metal hydride (Ni-MH)

notebook

personal digital assistant (PDA)

power capacity

Power Meter

Power Options

Power Scheme

SO DIMM

standby

1. When upgrading memory on a laptop, a small outline package was created to make the space the actual stick of memory occupied much smaller. This is referred to as _____ memory.

2. One of the first technologies used for laptop batteries was _____. These types of batteries had a nagging condition known as "battery memory." If you did not let them occasionally drain completely, they would not hold a charge for as long as specified.

3. The battery, _____, and _____ are all upgradeable laptop components.

4. Replacing a battery where the _____ or _____ of the replacement battery is greater than the original battery will increase the run time of the portable PC.

5. The latest development in batteries, the _____, provides as much as twice the life of the former technology and is completely immune to memory problems.

Chapter 15

Maintaining and Troubleshooting Printers

Lab Exercises

As you explored in the lab exercises in Chapter 17, "Understanding Printers," in *Mike Meyers' A+ Guide to Managing and Troubleshooting PCs, Vol. 1: Essentials*, printers continue to be a major part of the day-to-day working environment, and PC technicians will have to understand the operation of several types of printers and be able to keep them in good working order.

This chapter's labs will build on the scenario in which your boss walks into your office and tells you that there are five printers on their way to you—two impact printers using legacy parallel ports, two universal serial bus (USB) inkjet printers, and an HP LaserJet laser printer using a Jet Direct network interface. You need to install them so that they're accessible by anyone who needs them, and make sure they work properly. You'll then look at some of the maintenance issues that are required to keep the printers up and running and some of the techniques to follow when they stop.

 30 MINUTES

Lab Exercise 15.01: Installing a Printer

The key to a successful printer installation is having the correct software drivers and understanding how the printer will interface with the computer. You'll certainly need the drivers when you install those five printers, and you'll also have to configure the printers you are installing to use parallel, USB, and network interfaces. A common practice in multiple-user environments—companies considered to be Small Office/ Home Office (SOHO)—is to use a printer with its own network interface card (NIC), so that computers from anywhere in the network can print directly to the printer through the network interface.

Learning Objectives

In this lab, you'll install a printer, first as a directly connected device and then as a network device. You will then explore and change its settings.

At the end of this lab, you'll be able to

- Recognize the variations in key features of laser printers
- Install a laser printer in Windows

- Change laser printer settings in Windows

- Configure a Transmission Control Protocol/Internet Protocol (TCP/IP) port for a network printer

Lab Materials and Setup

The materials you need for this lab are

- A working computer with Windows 2000/XP installed

- An inkjet or laser printer for installation (or you can skip Step 1)

- A print device with a network interface card (optional)

Getting Down to Business

These days, installing a printer is a fairly straightforward task. This is good, because you'll probably do your fair share of it as a computer technician.

Step 1 If you have an actual print device, start here. (If you don't, skip to Step 2.)

Connect the printer to your system via a parallel or USB port, turn on the printer, and then turn on the PC. As the boot sequence progresses, the plug and play feature will locate the printer and install it for you. Follow the instructions on the screen.

✔ **Hint**

Here's the twist. If your printer is older than your operating system, the operating system should install the printer drivers with little interaction on your part. If the printer is newer than your operating system, you'll need to have the driver CD or disk handy, because the system will stop and ask you for it.

Step 2 If you don't have a print device, start here:

a) Access the Printer applet.

b) For Windows 2000, select Start | Settings | Printers. For Windows XP, select Start | Printers and Faxes.

c) Click the Add Printer icon. A wizard should appear. Click Next to proceed.

d) You want to install a printer attached to your PC, so select the *Local printer attached to this computer* option (see Figure 15-1).

e) Follow the steps through the Add Printer Wizard by selecting LPT1 and then a printer from the list of printers or your driver CD.

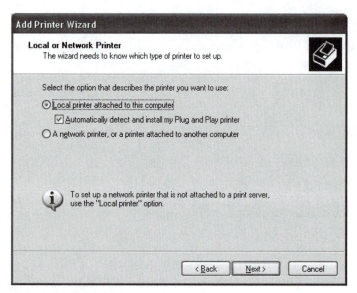

FIGURE 15-1 Installing a local printer

✖ Warning

If you weren't able to install an actual print device for this exercise, don't print a test page. You'll receive some interesting messages if you do.

Once you've installed the printer, open the Printers folder in Control Panel, right-click the new printer's icon, and select Properties.

You'll see the various tabs and options, depending on your printer. I used the Epson Stylus PHOTO 870 ESC/P 2 from the built-in drivers list. Check each of your tabs to see the information available and the features you can change:

- **General**   Description, preferences, and print test

- **Sharing**   To share or not to share; that is the question (this is covered in Chapter 16, "Local Area Networking")

- **Ports**   Additional ports to assign the printer

- **Advanced**   Spooling, separator page, and print defaults

- **Color Management**   Automatic or manual

- **Security**   Permissions

- **Utilities**   Nozzle Check, Head Cleaning, and Print Head Alignment

✔ **Hint**

You should know how to navigate all the previous steps for all the different Windows versions (Windows 2000/XP) for the CompTIA A+ certification exams.

Step 3 In the following steps, you will set up a TCP/IP printer interface port for a Hewlett Packard LaserJet printer with a Jet Direct network interface card. If you have access to a printer with a network interface, or your classroom is equipped with one, please use the IP address or printer name of the printer when configuring the port. This will allow you to actually test the installation.

   a) Open the Printer & Faxes folder by choosing Start | Settings | Printers & Faxes, and then launch the Add Printer Wizard.

   b) Select *Local printer attached to this computer* (note the information balloon at the bottom of the dialog box, shown in Figure 15-1), and clear the *Automatically detect and install my Plug and Play printer* check box. Click Next.

   c) Click the *Create a new port* option, and select Standard TCP/IP Port from the drop-down menu.

   d) This launches the Add Standard TCP/IP Printer Port Wizard (see Figure 15-2). Click Next.

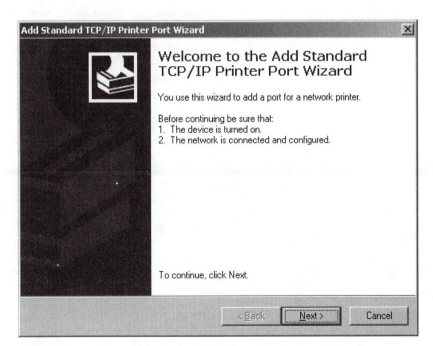

FIGURE 15-2 The Add Standard TCP/IP Printer Port Wizard

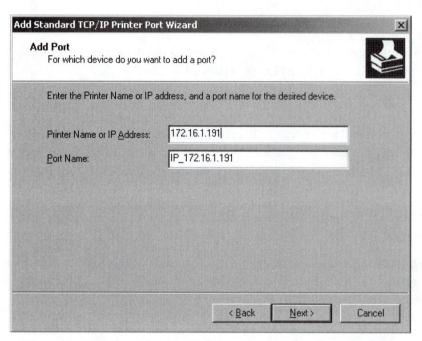

FIGURE 15-3 The TCP/IP address and port name of a Jet Direct printer

e) In the Add Port dialog box, enter the IP address of the network printer. The printer wizard automatically creates the port name (see Figure 15-3). Click Next.

f) If the IP address is fictitious, for the purpose of completing the lab steps, the Add Standard TCP/IP Printer Port Wizard will be unable to identify the printing device. In the Device Type dialog box, click the Standard drop-down menu, and select Hewlett Packard Jet Direct (see Figure 15-4). Click Next.

g) Review the port characteristics, and click Finish (see Figure 15-5).

h) You will now follow the steps through the Add Printer Wizard by selecting a printer from the list of printers or your driver CD, as you did when directly connecting to the printer in Step 2.

✖ **Warning**

Again, if you are unable to install an actual print device for this exercise, don't print a test page. You'll receive some interesting messages if you do.

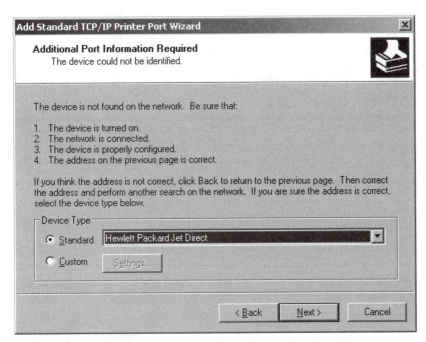

FIGURE 15-4 Selecting the Standard Hewlett Packard Jet Direct device type

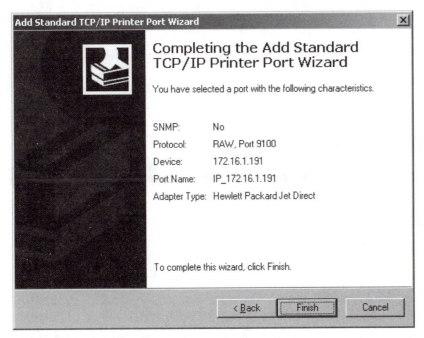

FIGURE 15-5 Port characteristics

 **30** MINUTES

Lab Exercise 15.02: Maintaining and Troubleshooting Printers

It is estimated that technicians, especially working for the help desk or desktop support group for a small to medium-sized organization, spend approximately 30 percent of their time on printer issues. If you think about it, of all of the components used in computing technology, printers have the highest percentage of moving parts. Moving parts tend to need maintenance more than static components or they wear out and break.

Printers also like to be finicky and stop printing, usually resulting in a phone call from the client to the help desk for quick resolution. The following exercises will help you develop some understanding of laser printer and inkjet printer maintenance, and what steps to take when they stop printing!

Learning Objectives

In this lab, you'll research laser printer maintenance kits, clean dirty inkjet nozzles, and troubleshoot a failed print job.

At the end of this lab, you'll be able to

- Select a proper maintenance kit for various laser printers

- Clean and verify operation of inkjet nozzles

- Manage print jobs in Windows

- Restart a stalled print spooler

Lab Materials and Setup

The materials you need for this lab are

- A working computer with Windows 2000/XP installed

- A connection to the Internet

- Access to an inkjet printer

Getting Down to Business

The following exercises will round out your activities as you finish with the rollout of the five new printers in your office. You will want to get your Internet connection fired up again and research the maintenance kit available for your laser printer. Then you'll check the print-head nozzles of the inkjet printers and run the cleaning routine, if necessary. Finally, you should prepare for any print errors so that you can correct them quickly and efficiently.

Step 1 Laser printers are, by design, highly precise machines. They typically move thousands of sheets of paper per month through the printing mechanism, placing 1200 to 1600 dots per inch (DPI) of toner on each page. As such, toner cartridges need to be replaced from time to time, and parts that wear out need to be refurbished. Most manufacturers offer a maintenance kit for the printer to assist in the upkeep of the printer when these common parts age or fail. It would be a good idea to have a maintenance kit on hand for each model of laser printer in your organization.

✔ **Hint**

Most of the current manufacturers of laser printers—Hewlett Packard, Lexmark, Kyocera, Canon, and so forth—offer some form of maintenance kit for their printers. You should be able to conduct an Internet search using your favorite search engine to uncover available kits, their contents, and competitive pricing. Don't be surprised to find the maintenance kits somewhat costly, though they should still be only a fraction of the cost of replacing the printer.

Select a laser printer make and model, and perform an Internet search to identify the appropriate maintenance kit, its contents, and the average cost of the kit. Use this information to fill in the following items:

Printer Model: _____

Maintenance Kit: _____

Contents: _____

_____

_____

Price: _____

Step 2 Though you have just installed new inkjet printers, if the printer sits idle for an extended period of time (a few weeks or months), or if the ink cartridges have been replaced, you may need to check the print quality and clean the nozzles. The following steps were performed on an Epson Stylus PHOTO 890, but are similar to the steps required on Hewlett Packard and Lexmark inkjet printers. Consult the manual for specific instructions.

✖ **Warning**

The nozzle-cleaning process uses a fair amount of the expensive ink. If you are working on a personal inkjet printer or one in the classroom, after printing the nozzle check page, run the nozzle cleaning process only if required.

a) Open the Printer & Faxes folder (choose Start | Settings | Printers & Faxes), and highlight your inkjet printer.

b) Right-click the printer and select Properties.

c) Click the Printing Preferences button (see Figure 15-6).

d) Select the Utility tab (Figure 15-7), and click Nozzle Check. This will print a test pattern using the cyan, yellow, magenta, and black ink nozzles.

e) If the printout is not clear, or if there are dropouts (missing parts of characters or completely missing characters), select Head Cleaning to clear the nozzles, and return to the Nozzle Check utility to verify performance.

Step 3 When you are called upon to troubleshoot a failed print job, you should follow a logical step-by-step process to make sure that no obvious, possibly simple failure has occurred. If the power cord has been kicked out or the paper tray is open, it would use valuable time to troubleshoot the network connectivity or the printer driver. Once you know the print device is online and ready and there are no paper jams or mechanical errors, then it might be time to open the Print Manager and attempt to restart the document.

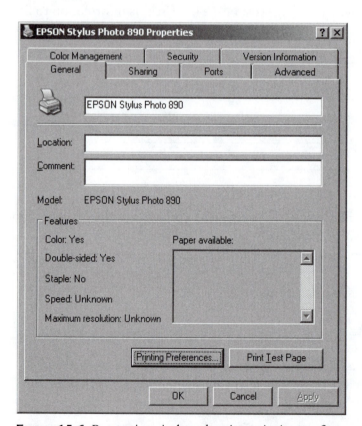

FIGURE 15-6 Properties window showing printing preferences

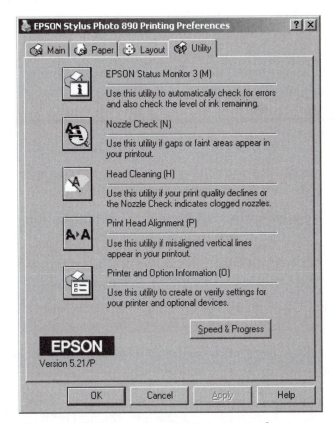

FIGURE 15-7   Utility tab under Printing Preferences

The following steps are meant to be a rough guideline to troubleshoot and diagnose a failed print job:

a)   First, check the physical print device:

- Is the printer plugged in, and is the power turned on?

- Is the printer out of paper, or is there a paper jam?

- Is the toner low, or in need of replacement?

- Are there any error messages on the printer's liquid crystal display (LCD) readout or are error indicator lights flashing?

- Is the printer online and ready to print?

If all of these areas are examined and everything appears to be in working condition, then you may have a problem with the connectivity between the computer and the printer, or there may be problems with the document or drivers.

b)   Make sure that the connections between the computer and the printer are in good condition and securely fastened. These may be USB, IEEE 1284 bi-directional parallel, or unshielded twisted pair (UTP) using RJ-45 connectors.

> ✔ **Hint**
>
> To create a failed print job, disconnect the printer cable, shut the power off on the printer, or open the printer paper tray. If you do not have a physical printer, install a printer, following the steps in Lab Exercise 15.01. Send a print job to the printer; the printer icon should appear in the system tray and indicate that the print job has failed. Then continue with Step 3.

c)   After checking all of the physical components, you should try to resend the document. Open the Print Manager by clicking the icon in the system tray/notification area.

In the Print Manager, select the failed print job by highlighting the job with *Error* in the status column (see Figure 15-8).

Select Documents | Restart. If you are creating the printer problem, the printer icon in the system tray/notification area indicates that the print job has failed once again.

d)   Highlight the document once again, and then select Documents | Cancel to delete the print request.

If this were a real scenario, you would verify that the print drivers were installed and are the correct drivers for the operating system. You would then perform Step 4 to see if the problem is related to the print spooler.

Step 4   If the print device is online and ready, there are no paper jams or mechanical errors, and restarting the document is of no help, you can check to see if the print spooler is stalled. The print spooler is a holding area for print jobs and is especially important for network printers. If the print device runs out of paper while printing a document, you may have to stop and start the print spooler before the print device will receive jobs again.

In Chapter 10, "Working with the Command-Line Interface," you accomplished this task using the command line. Now you will use the Services snap-in for the Microsoft Management Console (MMC) to do the same thing, only more quickly and in a graphical user interface (GUI).

a)   Launch the Services console by opening Administrative Tools in Control Panel and then double-clicking Services.

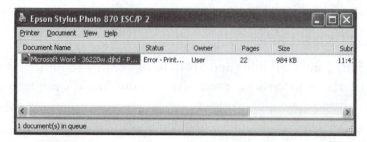

FIGURE 15-8   Print Manager showing Error status on a Word file

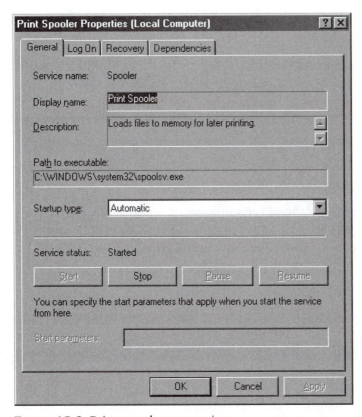

FIGURE 15-9 Print spooler properties

b) Scroll down and highlight the print spooler. Select Action | Properties. You should see that the print spooler is started and running (see Figure 15-9).

c) Click the Stop button. The print spooler indicates that it has stopped.

d) Click the Start button. The print spooler indicates that it has started.

e) Alternatively, you can highlight the print spooler and select Action | Restart. You'll see a message stating that the print spooler is stopping, and then another message indicating that the print spooler is starting.

In the real-world scenario, your print spooler service would be restarted, and you should have a healthy, functioning print server once again.

Lab Analysis Test

1. Patrick and Erik are having a small disagreement. Patrick says that printers can use a number of different interfaces, while Erik says that there are only two: parallel and USB. Who is correct? List the interfaces you are aware of and a typical use of each one.

2. Theresa is using Windows XP and just purchased a printer from a friend. When she installs it using the original driver CD that came with the printer, it won't install properly. Why?

3. Danyelle has just joined a large organization as a level II tech and is tasked with the evaluation of all of the laser printers in use. The business managers are concerned that all of the units will need to be replaced because of frequent paper jams and poor print quality. Danyelle makes her recommendations, and is actually awarded a bonus for saving the company money. What is her recommendation?

4. Brandon has sent a document to the printer, but the document never actually prints. Where can Brandon check to see the status of the document?

5. Sam has an inkjet printer that she has not used for a number of months. She prints a test page to see how the print quality has held up, and is disappointed to see that there are malformed characters and dropouts all over the page. What might be the problem?

Key Terms Quiz

Use the following vocabulary terms to complete the following sentences. Not all terms will be used.

DMA

dots per inch (DPI)

ECP

IEEE 1284

impact

inkjet

Jet Direct

laser

pages per month

parallel port

primary corona

print spooler

TCP/IP port

toner

transfer corona

USB port

1. When connecting a printer directly to your system unit, most printers connect via a(n) _____ or _____.

2. To use a printer that's attached to the network with its own NIC, you must configure a(n) _____.

3. A file created on a computer that holds and queues print jobs is know as the _____.

4. A popular network interface card used directly with Hewlett Packard LaserJet printers is the _____ card.

5. The print quality of a laser printer is usually stated in _____. High-resolution printers are usually between 1200 to 1600 _____.

Chapter 16
Local Area Networking

Lab Exercises

A competent PC technician is called upon to be a network guru, answering connectivity questions and making recommendations on the best price/performance considerations for homes and businesses. This happens frequently, especially in smaller companies that can't afford to hire multiple people to support both the network *and* the PCs. The CompTIA A+ certification exams reflect these changing roles of the PC technician and include many questions related to computer networking.

In this chapter's labs, you'll imagine that you've been hired to work for a small company that has made the decision to upgrade the network in their office. You'll need to have a working understanding of network hardware and network operating system issues, as well as some good troubleshooting tools for when things don't work quite right.

 **30** MINUTES

Lab Exercise 16.01: Sharing Resources

With the network all set up properly, the next thing to do is decide how you want to share resources. You can share any folder or other resource. Floppy drives, optical drives, Zip drives, and hard drives can all be shared.

Learning Objectives

In this lab, you'll set up file sharing for others to access information from their system.

At the end of this lab, you'll be able to

- Enable and configure shared directories and other resources

Lab Materials and Setup

The materials you need for this lab are

- A PC system that's properly configured for local area network (LAN) access using Windows 2000/XP

Hint

The exercise is written for Windows XP with notes for how to share using Windows 2000. For the CompTIA A+ certification exams, you should know how to share resources with any Windows operating system.

Getting Down to Business

Sharing a folder is one of the most important skills you can gain in a networked Windows world. This is where all of the cabling, NICs, and installed protocols finally pay off!

Step 1   Open My Computer, double-click the C: drive, and create a new folder on it. Name it Shared. Right-click the Shared folder icon to see the folder options, and select Sharing. This will open the Shared Properties dialog box (see Figure 16-1).

Hint

If the Sharing tab isn't there, it's probably because you forgot to enable the File and Printer Sharing option in the Networking applet. Go back and do that.

FIGURE 16-1 The Shared Properties dialog box's Sharing tab in Windows XP

> ✔ **Hint**
>
> If you're running Windows XP Home Edition or Windows XP Professional Edition in a workgroup environment, the Shared Properties dialog box is much simpler. It contains Share/Do Not Share buttons and a space to provide a share name.

Step 2 Try sharing and un-sharing the folder. Note that the share name and permissions are grayed out when you select Do Not Share This Folder. Share the folder again, change the share name, and look at the various levels of permissions: Full Control, Change, and Read.

Step 3 When you're done, click OK to close the dialog box.

 **30** MINUTES

Lab Exercise 16.02: Testing Your LAN Connections

There are tools available that will help you test and troubleshoot your new network. The textbook covers using these tools in detail. Some of these tools are beneficial to you now as a CompTIA A+ certified technician and are covered on the CompTIA A+ certification exams. This lab exercise lets you practice several key network troubleshooting tools on Windows 2000 and Windows XP operating systems.

Learning Objectives

In this exercise, you'll be introduced to troubleshooting tools for determining proper installation of the network components. These tools are covered in order of importance. First verify the local settings before trying to access other systems on the same LAN, and then test the Internet connectivity.

At the end of this lab, you'll be able to

- Use the IPCONFIG command to determine local network settings
- Use the NET CONFIG command to check the local system name and who is logged on as a user
- Use the PING command to test the local Transmission Control Protocol/Internet Protocol (TCP/IP) software and adapter
- Use the NET VIEW command to check for other computers on the network
- Use the PING command with switches to test connecting to other computers
- Use the NSLOOKUP command to translate IP addresses and domain names
- Use the TRACERT command to check the path to other computers

Lab Materials and Setup

The materials you need for this lab are

- A PC system that's properly configured for network access using Windows 2000/XP

- Access to the Internet

✔ **Hint**

The commands vary slightly, depending on the operating system you use. You should practice with both operating systems if possible. Test the LAN first by accessing another computer on the network using My Network Places and Computers Near Me.

Getting Down to Business

A PC technician should be familiar with several networking tools, both for his or her own good and because they're covered on the CompTIA A+ certification exams. You'll begin by looking at IPCONFIG.

✔ **Hint**

Since you have already used the IPCONFIG /ALL command, run through the steps again, either on your own system or on a different lab computer. Ask the instructor if any different networks or system configurations are available to explore.

Step 1   You have already examined IPCONFIG in the previous course. You'll now use the IPCONFIG command again to determine local network settings. As you have already learned, checking the automatic TCP/IP settings given to you by a Dynamic Host Configuration Protocol (DHCP) server and verifying your manual settings is easy: Just open a command-line window, type **IPCONFIG /ALL**, and press ENTER. The details of your local network connection appear on the screen.

Does the display contain the settings that were automatically assigned by the DHCP server or the ones you entered manually? _____

Record your settings here:

IP address _____

Subnet mask _____

Default gateway _____

DNS _____

✔ **Hint**

If you have a system in a peer-to-peer network (no servers) and there are no routers installed, you won't see information about gateways and Domain Name Service (DNS). What may appear are Windows Internet Naming Service (WINS) settings. More of this would be covered in the coursework for the CompTIA Network+ certification.

Leave the command prompt window open; you'll use it throughout the rest of this exercise.

Step 2 You'll now use the NET CONFIG command to check the local system name and to see who is logged on as a user. To confirm the computer name and discover who is currently logged on, you'll again use the command line.

Type **NET CONFIG WORKSTATION** at the command prompt, and press ENTER. You'll see how the identification is set up for your local PC. There's a lot of information listed, but you're only interested in a couple of items (see Figure 16-2).

How are these listed?

Computer name _____

User name _____

Workstation domain (workgroup) _____

Software version _____

Step 3 You'll now use the PING command to test the local TCP/IP software and adapter.

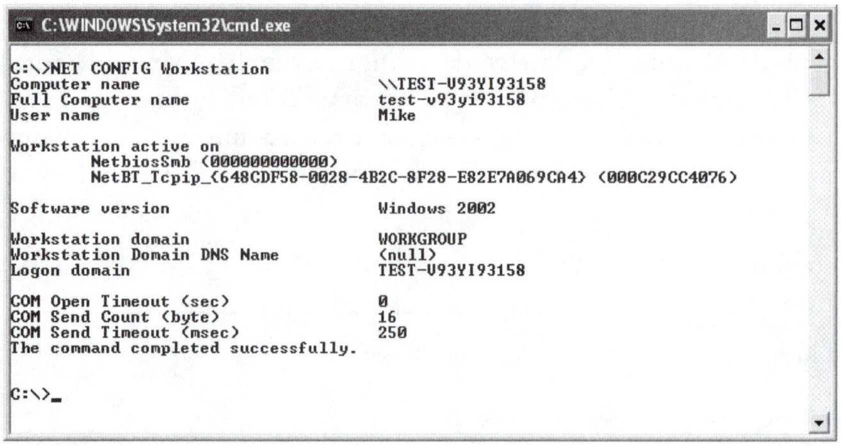

```
C:\WINDOWS\System32\cmd.exe                                         _ □ ×

C:\>NET CONFIG Workstation
Computer name                          \\TEST-U93YI93158
Full Computer name                     test-v93yi93158
User name                              Mike

Workstation active on
        NetbiosSmb (000000000000)
        NetBT_Tcpip_{648CDF58-0028-4B2C-8F28-E82E7A069CA4} (000C29CC4076)

Software version                       Windows 2002

Workstation domain                     WORKGROUP
Workstation Domain DNS Name            (null)
Logon domain                           TEST-U93YI93158

COM Open Timeout (sec)                 0
COM Send Count (byte)                  16
COM Send Timeout (msec)                250
The command completed successfully.

C:\>_
```

FIGURE 16-2 Using the NET CONFIG WORKSTATION command in Windows XP

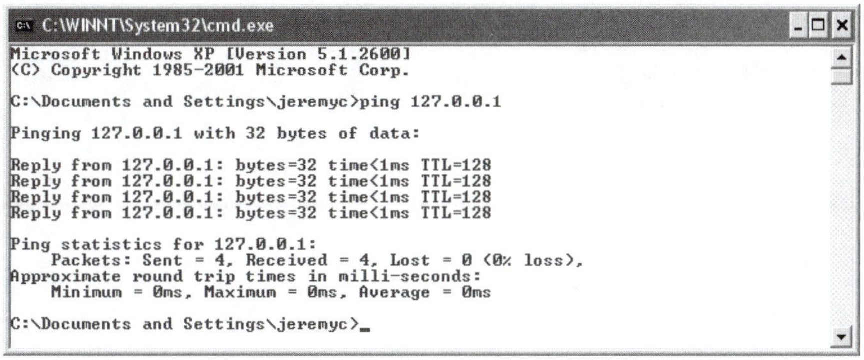

```
C:\WINNT\System32\cmd.exe                                    _ □ x

Microsoft Windows XP [Version 5.1.2600]
(C) Copyright 1985-2001 Microsoft Corp.

C:\Documents and Settings\jeremyc>ping 127.0.0.1

Pinging 127.0.0.1 with 32 bytes of data:

Reply from 127.0.0.1: bytes=32 time<1ms TTL=128
Reply from 127.0.0.1: bytes=32 time<1ms TTL=128
Reply from 127.0.0.1: bytes=32 time<1ms TTL=128
Reply from 127.0.0.1: bytes=32 time<1ms TTL=128

Ping statistics for 127.0.0.1:
    Packets: Sent = 4, Received = 4, Lost = 0 (0% loss),
Approximate round trip times in milli-seconds:
    Minimum = 0ms, Maximum = 0ms, Average = 0ms

C:\Documents and Settings\jeremyc>_
```

FIGURE 16-3 A successful PING test

At the command line prompt, type **PING 127.0.0.1** (including the periods) and press ENTER. This is known as the LOOPBACK or LOCALHOST address and will test the TCP/IP software and the internal part of the local network card. Look at Figure 16-3 to see a successful test. If you don't see the test results, there are serious problems with the software. Reinstall your network drivers, and reconfigure the TCP/IP settings.

Step 4   You'll now use the NET VIEW command to check for other computers on the network.

Can you see anyone else on the network that will prove your network card can transmit and receive data?

At the command line prompt, type **NET VIEW** and press ENTER. You'll see what other computers are on the network by a listing of their computer names (see Figure 16-4).

Step 5   Now you'll use the PING command to test your ability to connect to other computers on the network.

Okay, so now you can actually get the IP address and names of other systems on the local area network, but can you actually communicate with them?

At the command line prompt, type **PING *computer name***, where *computer name* is another PC on the network you found in Step 4, and press ENTER. The results will look the same as when you used PING to see your own computer, but with the other computer's IP address (see Figure 16-5).

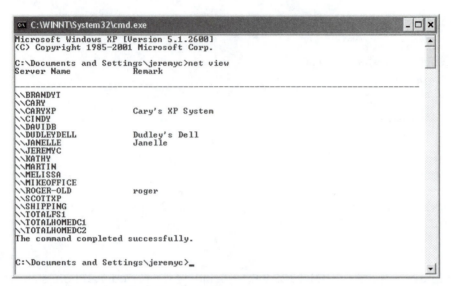

FIGURE 16-4 Using the NET VIEW command

Be sure to put a space between the PING command and the computer name. If you get errors, use the NET VIEW command again to be certain of the computer name's spelling. If the DNS is down, you can adjust by pinging the other computer's IP address instead of its name.

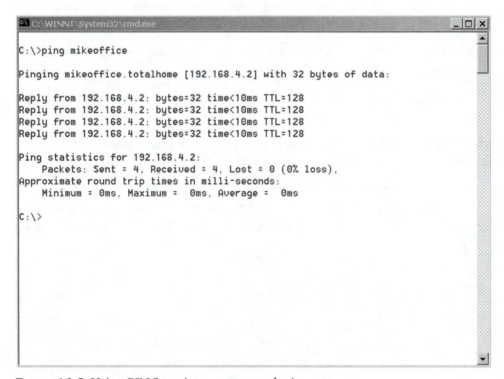

FIGURE 16-5 Using PING to view a computer by its name

→ **Try This: PING Switches**

The humble PING command is one of the most frequently used troubleshooting tools for TCP/IP. As you saw in Step 5, you can actually use PING to test whether DNS is working. If you do not receive a response from the computer using its HOST name, but you do receive a response when using the IP address, this points to a problem with DNS.

PING also has a number of switches that add to the functionality of the command. If you need to explore the switches, type the following at the command prompt:

```
c:\>PING /?
```

This will list all of the available switches and their functions. The following combination is typically used for a connection that seems to intermittently drop packets. You would run the command indefinitely and increase the packet size to overload the connection. Type the following command:

```
c:\>PING -t -l 65000 computername
```

To stop the continuous PING, press CTRL-C to break the program.

Step 6 You'll now use the NSLOOKUP command to translate an Internet domain name to an IP address or an IP address to an Internet domain name.

This is a good command for finding out the IP addresses of Web sites. Why do I want this, you ask? Well, when you use a Uniform Resource Locator (URL) in your browser, it has to be translated somewhere to an IP address. This slows down your access time. If you know the IP address and type that into the address of your Internet browser, the site will pop up faster. Follow these steps:

a)   Type **NSLOOKUP microsoft.com**, and then press ENTER.

What's the IP address(es) of www.microsoft.com?

_____

Try www.totalsem.com. What's the IP address(es)?

_____

b)   Now enter the IP address you got when you did a lookup for www.microsoft.com. If you get a different result, it could be that a Web site is being hosted by someone other than the original domain you looked up.

Step 7 You'll now use the TRACERT command to check the path to other computers or Web sites on the Internet.

This command will show you where the bottlenecks are in the Internet. The TRACERT command will list the time it takes to get from your PC to the Web site or other system you're accessing. Follow these steps:

a) Type **TRACERT maxtor.com**, and then press ENTER.

Was it successful? _____

How many hops did it take? _____

What's the IP address of the first hop? _____

b) Use the NSLOOKUP command with the IP address of the first hop to see where your first server is located. For example, type **NSLOOKUP 207.46.130.108**, and then press ENTER.

Go ahead—have fun with this! Part of the learning process with PCs is to dive in and tackle a subject that you're not completely familiar with. As long as you remember to write down any information you want to change before you change it, you can enjoy exploring the amazing world of computers and still have a recovery point.

Lab Analysis Test

1. Which command-line tools would you most likely turn to for diagnosing DNS problems? How would you use them?

2. The NET command is one of the oldest command-line commands available for use. Give some examples of scenarios where you would turn to this command.

Key Terms Quiz

Use the following vocabulary terms to complete the following sentences. Not all terms will be used.

Device Manager

hub

Network Connections applet

NET VIEW

NSLOOKUP

NIC

PING

PING -l

PING -t

RJ-45

router

switch

UTP

wireless

1. An excellent tool for determining who is currently logged on to the network is the _____NET VIEW_____ command.

2. To find out whether a computer can accept a large packet of data, you would use the _____ping -l_____ command.

3. Use the _____NS lookup_____ command to determine if a particular IP address is a DNS server.

Chapter 17
The Internet

Lab Exercises

The Internet is a complex system of communication that allows computers, in-business networks, mobile computers, and home PCs to share information worldwide. Today we even have cell phones, personal digital assistants (PDAs), and other personal devices that can connect to the Internet for accessing e-mail, downloading MP3s, and doing other tasks.

Connecting to the Internet requires three pieces in place and functioning: a modem, a wire, and an Internet service provider (ISP). The device referred to as a modem can be of various technologies. The use of 56 kilobits per second (Kbps) dial-up modems and integrated services digital network (ISDN) modems is rapidly declining due to slow access speeds and high cost. Much more common today are high-speed, or *broadband*, Internet connections, using digital subscriber line (DSL) and cable modem technologies.

The wire used to connect to the Internet can be a phone line (this is, in fact, what DSL and ISDN services use) or a coaxial cable. Corporate environments typically use dedicated T1 or T3 connections, or something even zippier. The ISP provides access to the worldwide network that makes up the Internet.

Because nearly everyone wants access to the Internet, implementing and troubleshooting Internet connectivity is a PC technician's bread and butter. The CompTIA A+ certification exams recognize this and test you on the details of installing and configuring a connection to the Internet. It may be a legacy dial-up analog modem used to connect to an ISP through a phone line or a broadband cable modem using the local cable company as the provider. This heightened usage brings with it a new task for the PC technician: security! Since most computers are now communicating with the world through the Internet, the exposure to malicious intruders and programs has greatly increased. Two components that go hand-in-hand with the Internet are firewalls and wireless network security. You'll explore the configuration of these two components here. This chapter's labs start by going through the properties of the current wide area network (WAN) connection technologies and then take you through the steps needed to perform the installation and configuration of these technologies. You'll also explore the configuration of the Windows Internet Connection Sharing and Firewall, explore a browser, and configure wireless security.

✔ **Cross-Reference**

Computer security is such an important component of a PC technicians training that the topic receives its own chapters in both the textbook and the lab manual. Refer to Chapter 18, "Computer Security," in *Mike Meyers' A+ Guide to Managing and Troubleshooting PCs, Vol. 2: PC Tech.*

 30 MINUTES

Lab Exercise 17.01: Identifying Internet Connectivity Properties

A new client has signed up with your firm, requesting that you evaluate their current Internet connectivity and recommend the best upgrade path for their 12-person office (six desktop PCs and two laptops). Your first job is to assess what method they are currently using to connect to the Internet and what methods are available in their location and then make a recommendation for upgrades, if necessary.

Learning Objectives

This lab tests basic assessment skills. Every technician should be able to go into a situation and quickly understand the state of the technology in question—in this case, an Internet connection. Plus, you should feel comfortable telling your clients about any concerns with aging technology and confidently recommend upgrade paths to higher performance technology.

At the end of this lab, you'll be able to

- Verify the Internet connectivity method

- Check the properties of the connection

- Perform an Internet search to learn about the performance of various connectivity methods

Lab Materials and Setup

The materials you need for this lab are

- A working computer running Windows 2000/XP, with some form of Internet connection

- Internet connectivity to perform your research

Getting Down to Business

First, you will visually inspect your computer and its surroundings for the method used to connect to the Internet. Then you will run an Internet utility to determine the speed of your connection and appropriate upgrade paths.

Step 1   Look at the back of your computer. Is there a phone cable (RJ-11) plugged in? This could indicate that this computer is using an analog modem for the Internet connection. Are there any universal serial bus (USB) or network (RJ-45) cables plugged into the system? Trace the wires. Do they connect to a cable modem or DSL modem? This could be your connectivity method. Is there a network patch cable plugged into the network interface card (NIC)? You may be connecting to the Internet through the corporate local area network (LAN). Are you on a laptop with wireless connectivity? You could have access to the Internet through a wireless access point (WAP) connected to a cable or DSL modem.

These are the possibilities a technician is faced with today, so the more you can explore the various methods of connectivity, the better your familiarity when you walk into the client's home or office and attempt to configure or repair their Internet connection. Examine the physical components that constitute the method your system uses to connect to the Internet and then record the details of the hardware/connectivity type. Figure 17-1 depicts a typical PC using a wired LAN patch cable to connect to a broadband cable modem.

Step 2   Once you have determined the connectivity method, boot your system and launch your Internet browser (I'm currently using Internet Explorer 7). Now surf over to the c|net Web site at www.cnet.com. This is an excellent tech Web site with many tools, applications, and forums for PC and network information. Click the Reviews tab, and look for the Internet Access hyperlink. Click the link and scroll down to the Bandwidth Meter speed test. Click the link and follow the onscreen directions.

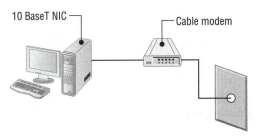

FIGURE 17-1 A PC and cable modem Internet connection

What is the speed of your connection?

Step 3 Using the table provided by the c|net Bandwidth Meter, fill in the approximate data transfer speeds of the various Internet connection types:

Dial-up 56 Kbps Modem _____

DSL _____

Cable _____

T1 _____

T3 _____

Step 4 Based on the results of the analysis of your client's Internet connection method and performance, are there any recommendations you would make to improve the performance of the connection?

 **30 MINUTES**

Lab Exercise 17.02: Installing and Configuring an Internet Connection

You determine that the client is currently using dial-up networking through analog modems to access the Internet. Though this is probably acceptable for occasionally connecting to the Internet, these folks have a business to run! You decide to recommend either high-speed DSL or cable. You explain to the client that unlike the analog modem they're currently using, the other methods use a standard NIC and an external device to interface between the DSL or cable lines. Ironically, this device is usually referred to as a DSL or cable *modem*. You will evaluate the current PCs and select one that will act as the interface to the Internet. If required, you'll add a Peripheral Component Interconnect (PCI) network interface card, connect the DSL or cable interface, and then configure the interface in Windows.

Learning Objectives

Installing DSL or cable high-speed Internet access requires four steps. First, you should verify whether your system is already equipped with a NIC, either integrated into the motherboard or as a PCI card, and if not, physically install such a device. Second, verify that this device is operating properly and has the latest drivers installed. Third, connect the DSL transceiver or the cable modem. Finally, configure the proper settings required by the ISP.

At the end of this lab, you'll be able to

- Install a network interface card (if not already present)

- Verify proper operation, and install or update the drivers

- Install the DSL transceiver or cable modem

- Configure the connection in Windows

✔ Cross-Reference

Refer to the "Digital Subscriber Lines (DSL)" and "Cable" sections in Chapter 17 of *Mike Meyers' A+ Guide to Managing and Troubleshooting PC's, Vol. 2: PC Tech* for help installing and configuring NICs. It's a good idea to have the textbook handy while you progress through this lab.

Lab Materials and Setup

The materials you need for this lab are

- A PC system with or without a NIC

- A PCI NIC

- Access to the proper driver software (either built-in Windows drivers or a separate CD)

- A copy of the Windows CD (may be needed, depending on the system)

Getting Down to Business

Break out your trusty screwdriver and anti-static wrist strap. It's time to install a NIC!

✔ Hint

You can omit Steps 1–3 if the system is already equipped with a network interface card, as most systems are today. The steps are included here for completeness. You will be asked to install a second NIC in Lab Exercise 17.04, "Implementing Windows Internet Connection Sharing (ICS)," so if you have that second NIC handy, go ahead and install it now.

Step 1 Make sure the PC is off and unplugged. Take proper electrostatic discharge (ESD) precautions, and remove the cover of the PC. Choose any free PCI slot to install the NIC. Remove the back plate if one exists.

Step 2 Plug the NIC into the PCI slot (see Figure 17-2). Physically inserting the NIC into the PC is the easiest part of the task. Take care to avoid touching the pins or any of the chips on the NIC. Once the card is inserted, secure it by putting the proper screw through the metal tab of the card and screwing it to the case. Put the cover back on and restart your computer.

Step 3 Now that you have physically installed the NIC, the next step will depend on your operating system. When you restart your computer, if you're running Windows 2000, the operating system will recognize that you've added new hardware and launch the Found New Hardware Wizard. Windows XP goes one step better—when you install a plug and play (PnP) device, the drivers are most likely already part of the operating system, so they'll be installed automatically. This all occurs with no user intervention. The operating system reports success installing the new device with a small balloon from the system tray.

✔ **Hint**

Every Windows operating system has a good selection of network interface drivers built in at the time of release, but your driver may not be one of them. For example, if the NIC you're installing was manufactured after the release of software you're using, the drivers may not be part of the operating system and will need to be installed or updated.

FIGURE 17-2 Inserting a PCI NIC

The following is the Found New Hardware Wizard driver installation process in Windows 2000:

a) As Windows boots, it displays the Found New Hardware Wizard screen (see Figure 17-3).

b) Click Next to continue. Select the option that directs Windows to search for a suitable driver for the new device (see Figure 17-4). If the driver is on a floppy disk or CD, select that as the search location, insert the media for the driver before continuing, and then click Next.

✔ **Hint**

A popular trick is to copy the drivers from the CD onto the PC's hard drive and then install them from there. That way, if you ever need the drivers again, you won't need to rummage around for the driver CD. You need to know exactly where you store the drivers, though, because you'll be asked to locate them during the install process. You could create a Drivers folder at the root of the C: drive to serve as a central repository for drivers. Remember, drivers are constantly being updated by manufacturers. Check the manufacturer's Web site before using the driver CD.

c) The wizard will search the drivers built into Windows and then the location you specified for the file(s), and will (you hope) report that it found the appropriate driver. Click Next. If prompted, you may also need to insert your Windows CD. When the wizard is finished, it'll prompt you a final time. Click the Finish button, and reboot your system. The new NIC and drivers are now properly installed.

If Windows doesn't detect the driver right away, you'll need to do a little extra work. Network interface manufacturers bundle drivers for multiple operating systems on the driver CD, so you

Welcome to the Found New Hardware Wizard

This wizard helps you install a device driver for a hardware device.

To continue, click Next.

< Back | Next > | Cancel

FIGURE 17-3 Using the Found New Hardware Wizard

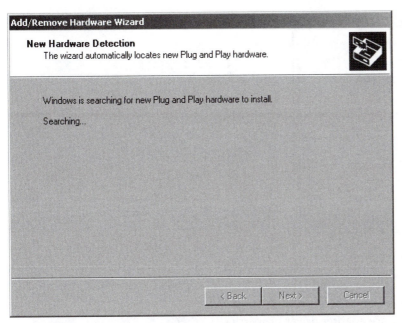

FIGURE 17-4 Completing installation by locating a suitable device driver

often need to navigate to the appropriate folder for your operating system before Windows will find the driver. In other words, look for a folder with a name like WIN2K or WIN2000 when installing modem drivers on a computer running Windows 2000. Other manufacturers package the driver into an installation routine. Check the CD for a SETUP.EXE file, and run it if you find it.

Step 4   Now that the drivers are installed, you should confirm the NIC properties and verify what drivers are installed. The following steps were completed in Windows XP, but they are similar in Windows 2000:

a)   In Classic view, select Start | Settings | Control Panel and double-click Network Connections.

b)   Right-click the Local Area Connection (note: if this is the second network interface, choose Local Area Connection 2) and click Properties. In the Local Area Connection Properties dialog box, click the Configure button next to the network interface adapter (on my system it is a SiS 900-Based Fast Ethernet Adapter).

c)   In the network interface adapter Properties dialog box, click the Driver tab (see Figure 17-5).

Record all the information provided about the driver you installed.

Step 5   Now examine the physical device that has been provided by your ISP to connect the computer to the Internet. If the device is a DSL transceiver, it will typically have an RJ-45 Ethernet connection to connect to the NIC of the computer, an RJ-11 connector to connect to the telephone wall jack, and some sort of power adapter. If the device is a cable modem, it will typically have an RJ-45 Ethernet connection to connect to the NIC of the computer, an F-connector to attach to the cable, and some sort of power adapter (refer to Figure 17-1). Both interfaces may provide a USB connection, but for the purposes of the lab exercise, this will not be used.

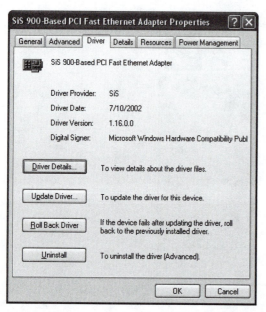

FIGURE 17-5　Network interface adapter driver properties

✔ **Hint**

If you are in a classroom lab environment, you may not have access to the actual DSL transceiver or cable modem. Follow the instructor's directions to connect the computer to the Internet. You should conduct an Internet search or make a trip to the local technology store to explore the specifications of common DSL and cable interfaces. For the most part, going through the full configuration of the actual connection is beyond the scope of this book, but you should at least know where to go to follow instructions from your ISP; that's the purpose of these last steps.

Connect the interface device following the instructions provided with the device or by your ISP. The layout and configuration of the device may differ somewhat from device to device, but you should be able to confirm that the device is working properly by observing the various indicator lights on the device.

Step 6　To finish this installation and gain high-speed access to the Internet, you will most likely have to follow specific directions from your Internet service provider to configure Windows to communicate through the DSL or cable device. Windows also provides a generic wizard to configure this communication. The following steps walk you through this generic configuration:

a)　Select Start | Settings | Network Connections, and click Create a New Connection in the Network Tasks pane to launch the New Connections Wizard.

b)　To continue, click Next and select *Connect to the Internet.* Click Next.

c)　Choose *Set up my connection manually* and click Next.

d) Choose *Connect using a broadband connection that is always on* and click Next.

e) In the Completing the New Connection Wizard window, click *Learn more about broadband connections*. Record some of the pertinent information related to your installation.

f) Click the Finish button.

If you have followed the steps (and actually have installed a DSL or cable interface), you should now have high-speed access to the Internet.

 **30** MINUTES

Lab Exercise 17.03: Exploring Windows Firewall

Your client is pleased with how the rollout of the office's Internet connection upgrade is progressing. They have been surfing around a little, and are impressed with the speed at which the Web sites are loading. You explain that you must now configure a firewall to protect them from outside intrusion through the high-speed connection. Microsoft's Windows XP Service Pack 2 offers a competent built-in firewall. In this lab, you will enable Windows Firewall and explore some of the services (ports) that you can allow or block.

Learning Objectives

Completing the following steps, you will explore the Windows Firewall and associated TCP and User Datagram Protocol (UDP) service ports.

At the end of this lab, you'll be able to

- Enable the Windows Firewall

- Identify various protocols and associated service ports

✔ **Cross-Reference**

To further explore the Windows Firewall, refer to "The Windows XP Internet Connection Firewall" in Chapter 17 of *Mike Meyers' A+ Guide to Managing and Troubleshooting PC's, Vol. 2: PC Tech.*

Lab Materials and Setup

The materials you need for this lab are

- A working computer running Windows XP

- A computer actually connected to the Internet (optional)

Getting Down to Business

Enabling the firewall is as simple as a few clicks of the mouse and verifying that you can communicate with the trusted sites that you prefer. Windows Firewall is practically self-configuring, but if you want to allow access to Web servers or e-mail servers in your organization, you will have to open some TCP ports. The CompTIA A+ certification exams will expect you to know some of these "well-known-ports," so you'll explore them in the Windows Firewall.

✔ Hint

If you are configuring a single computer for Internet access, you will want to implement the Windows Firewall on it to protect it from malicious intrusion. However, if you are configuring computers as part of a local area network, and using a proxy server or Internet Connection Sharing (as you will in the next lab exercise), you will only want to configure a firewall on the computer that connects directly to the Internet. Assume the computer in this lab is the one connected to the Internet.

Step 1 Open the Local Area Connection Properties dialog box by clicking Start | Settings | Network Connections. Right-click the Local Area Connections icon of the external connection (the one connected to the Internet), and then select Properties from the drop-down menu. Click the Advanced tab, and then click the Settings button in the Windows Firewall box (see Figure 17-6).

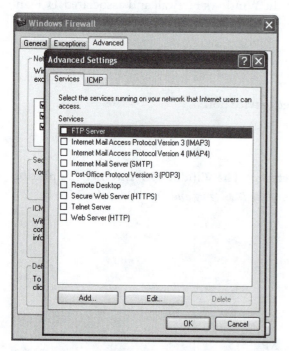

FIGURE 17-6 The Windows Firewall Properties screen

Step 2 Select Enable to protect the PC from unwanted access through the Internet connection.

Step 3 Now select the Advanced tab of the Windows Firewall dialog box, and select the Settings button for the Network Connection Settings (see Figure 17-7).

Step 4 This opens the Advanced Settings dialog box, where you can allow various services to pass through the Internet connection and access dedicated servers on your internal network. For instance, if you have a File Transfer Protocol (FTP) server that you have technicians update from the field, you will want to enable external communication by allowing TCP service port 21 to pass through the firewall (see Figure 17-8).

Using the Edit button, identify the service ports for the following protocols (I have completed the first one for you, see Figure 17-9):

1. File Transfer Protocol (FTP Server) _____**TCP Port 21**_____

2. Internet Mail Access Protocol Version 4 (IMAP4)_____

3. Simple Mail Transfer Protocol (SMTP)_____

4. Post-Office Protocol Version 3 (POP3)_____

5. Secure Socket Layer (HTTPS) _____

6. Hypertext Transfer Protocol (HTTP)_____

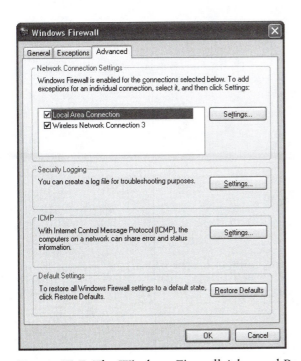

FIGURE 17-7 The Windows Firewall Advanced Properties screen

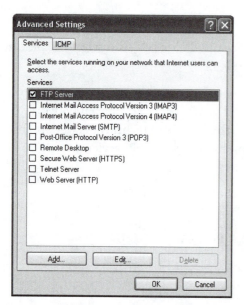

FIGURE 17-8 Allowing FTP traffic to pass through the firewall

Step 5   To complete this lab, check with your instructor to obtain the proper configuration of the firewall to allow the completion of further labs. You will probably disable the Internet Connection Firewall for normal classroom use.

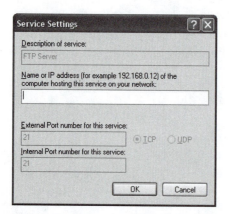

FIGURE 17-9 Service settings showing the TCP port number for the FTP server

 **30** MINUTES

Lab Exercise 17.04: Implementing Windows Internet Connection Sharing (ICS)

Now that the main PC is secure from external threats and attacks, it's time to configure this computer so that all of the PCs can take advantage of the secure Internet connection. Welcome to Internet Connection Sharing (ICS)! With ICS, you will be able to set up a small LAN that allows all the client computers to access the Internet through the ICS host computer (this PC).

Learning Objectives

In this lab, you will implement the steps to use ICS. It will take some extra hardware to actually test the configuration, but you can still learn the basic concepts through the configuration exercise.

At the end of this lab, you'll be able to

- Configure ICS

✔ **Cross-Reference**

To further explore ICS, refer to "Internet Connection Sharing" in Chapter 17 of *Mike Meyers' CompTIA A+ Guide: PC Technician*.

Lab Materials and Setup

The materials you need for this lab are

- A working computer running Windows 2000/XP
- An additional network interface card for the ICS host computer
- A network hub or switch
- A second computer running Windows 2000/XP to be configured as the client
- A computer actually connected to the Internet (optional)

Getting Down to Business

ICS allows a small workgroup of computers to connect to the Internet through one of the workgroup computers acting as an ICS host computer. There are a few items that need to be configured on the ICS host computer and on the client computers. The host will have two communication devices installed (in this case, two network interface cards [NICs]). The network will need a hub or a switch to allow multiple computers to communicate. Finally, the client computers will have to be configured to obtain their TCP/IP settings automatically.

Step 1 To use ICS, you will need two communication devices installed in the computer: either a modem connected to the Internet and an NIC connected to the internal network, or an NIC connected to a broadband interface and an NIC connected to the internal network. (If you need to install a second NIC to facilitate this lab exercise, perform Lab Exercise 17.02, Steps 1–3.)

Step 2 Open the Network Connections applet, and select the internal Local Area Connection. Select Properties, and then click the Advanced tab (see Figure 17-10).

Step 3 Select the *Allow other network users to connect through this computer's Internet connection* check box.

Step 4 Click the Settings button to view additional services that Internet users can access (if they are not blocked by the firewall).

Step 5 Click OK. A hand icon (representing sharing) should appear under the Local Area Connection that has just been configured with ICS (see Figure 17-11).

Step 6 Alternatively, if you have a second computer and a hub, you can test the ICS feature by following these steps:

a) Verify that the ICS host computer is capable of communicating with the Internet. Connect the external Local Area Connection NIC to the broadband interface (DSL or cable).

b) Power up the hub or switch, and connect the internal interface from the ICS host computer to the hub.

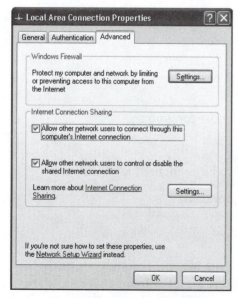

Figure 17-10 The Advanced tab of the Local Area Connection Properties dialog box showing Internet Connection Sharing

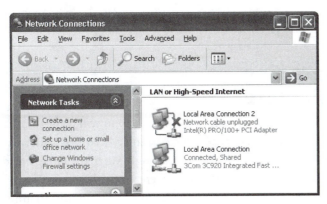

FIGURE 17-11 A shared Local Area Connection

c) Connect the network interface card of the client PC to the hub or switch.

d) Open the Network Connections applet of the client PC, select the Local Area Connection, and open the Properties dialog box. Highlight the Internet Protocol (TCP/IP) Properties, and verify that *Obtain an IP address automatically* and *Obtain DNS server address automatically* are selected (see Figure 17-12).

Launch Internet Explorer on the client computer; verify that the connection is set up to use the LAN connection. Type **www.comptia.org** in the address line and press ENTER. If there are any problems, shut down both computers, and check all of the connections. Boot the ICS host computer first (allow all of the services to start), and then boot the client computer.

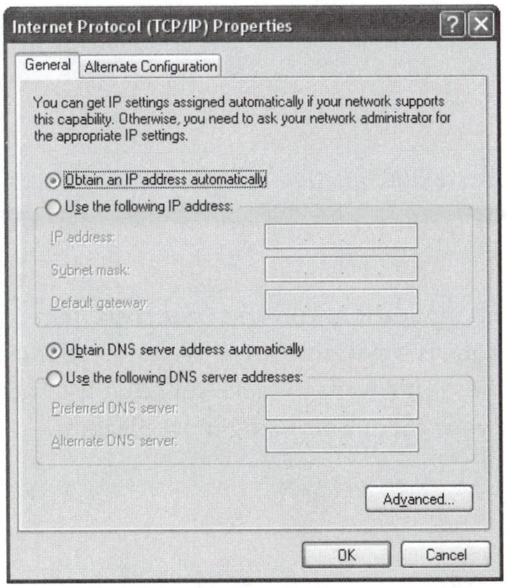

FIGURE 17-12 Internet Protocol (TCP/IP) properties

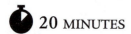 **20** MINUTES

Lab Exercise 17.05: Upgrading and Tweaking Internet Explorer

Now that you have improved and protected your client's Internet connectivity, you will want to make sure that the method they use to interact with the Internet is the most current. Microsoft's Internet Explorer is probably the most popular Internet browser in use today, although Mozilla's Firefox also has a strong following. The following steps will help you upgrade your client to the latest version of Internet Explorer (version 7 as of this writing) and introduce you to some of the configuration areas that you should be aware of.

Learning Objectives

When it comes to applications—and this includes Internet Explorer—the computer technician is looked to as the Master or Mistress of All Things Computer. For this reason, a knowledge and awareness of applications, in addition to learning and practicing your craft as an IT technician, will enhance your reputation as an expert. In this lab, you'll briefly explore the upkeep of a networking application.

At the end of this lab, you'll be able to

- Evaluate and upgrade the Internet Explorer application

- Fine-tune Internet Explorer settings

Lab Materials and Setup

The materials you need for this lab are

- A working computer running Windows XP Service Pack 2

- Internet access, preferably high-speed to facilitate downloads

Getting Down to Business

Internet Explorer is currently the most popular browser application. You and your client may launch Internet search engines such as Google or Yahoo!, visit manufacturers' Web sites to research, and, in some cases, purchase new hardware and software. You'll want to make sure that Internet Explorer is up to date and working efficiently to make your client's browsing more pleasant.

✖ Warning

The following lab steps have you update Internet Explorer and change some of the configuration settings. A prerequisite is to upgrade Windows XP to Service Pack 2. If you are performing these labs on a personal computer, evaluate the requirements for Internet Explorer 7 before upgrading. If you are in an instructor-led class or performing these operations on computers in your organization, verify that you have permission to perform the upgrades.

Step 1 Fire up your current browser and navigate to the Microsoft Windows Internet Explorer page (www.microsoft.com/windows/ie/default.mspx as of this writing). Examine the new features and requirements (click About Internet Explorer 7). Will Internet Explorer 7 work with all versions of Windows?

Verify that your system and operating system meet the requirements, and then download Internet Explorer 7.

Step 2 Open the Internet Options dialog box, and examine the General tab (see Figure 17-13).

Explore some of the features of the Home page (you may now have multiple pages available with the click of a tab), Browsing history, and Tabs sections.

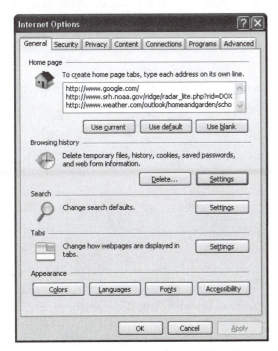

FIGURE 17-13 The General tab of the Internet Options dialog box in Internet Explorer 7

Step 3 Click the Content tab, and click the Settings button under the AutoComplete section. Notice the items that can be selected to AutoComplete. I like to disable the User Names and Passwords fields on forms.

Step 4 Click the Advanced tab, and explore the many settings that can be configured to modify how the browser deals with components and content. Navigate down to the Security heading, and locate *Empty Temporary Internet Files Folder when browser is closed*. I like to enable this setting.

Explore some of the other tabs available in Internet Options, and experiment with the different items you can configure. Microsoft has done a good job of setting the browser up with default settings that will work in most installations, but as the expert, you will want to be familiar with customizing the browser.

 30 MINUTES

Lab Exercise 17.06: Configuring Wireless Security

As mentioned in the first lab exercise, your client has two laptop computers. They would like to keep the laptops as mobile as possible, so they have asked you to install a wireless access point (WAP) in the office. The actual installation is almost simple enough that the office personnel could handle it; however, you know how vulnerable wireless networks are to unauthorized access. You agree to install the WAP, but you insist on securing the network to protect the business.

Learning Objectives

This lab exercise will use a LINKSYS wireless router to walk you through the steps to properly secure a wireless network. All of the principles developed here can be applied to most of the wireless routers of the other manufactures.

At the end of this lab, you'll be able to

- Configure router administration security
- Secure wireless access
- Protect data traveling over wireless networks using encryption

✔ **Cross-Reference**

To further explore wireless networking technology, visit the following Web sites:

www.3com.com   www.belkin.com

www.intellinet-network.com   www.linksys.com

www.netgear.com

Lab Materials and Setup

The materials you need for this lab are

- A working computer running Windows 2000 or XP

- A wireless router or wireless access point

Getting Down to Business

You're going to spend the next 30 minutes configuring wireless security that will protect the client and its employees, the company's confidential data, and the company itself. That will be 30 minutes well spent!

✔ **Hint**

The steps in this lab are written for a router that is in the factory-default condition. If the router has been in use or is part of the lab equipment in a classroom environment, ensure that the default settings are restored. Most wireless routers/WAPs have a reset button to clear all configuration information and return them to factory-default settings.

Step 1   Connect to the wireless router using a network patch cable (RJ-45 connectors, Cat5e UTP). Power up the router and boot the PC into Windows.

Step 2   Launch Internet Explorer (or the browser of your choice), and enter the IP address of the router's administration page. (LINKSYS usually uses 192.168.1.1; Intellinet usually uses 192.168.2.1.) Consult the documentation that came with the router for your specific model's IP address.

Step 3   Enter the default administrator name and password; many devices use **admin** for both the user name and password (for LINKSYS devices, leave the user name blank). This will bring you to the main administration page (the Welcome screen appears in LINKSYS). You will now configure the three important areas of administration, access, and encryption.

Step 4   Begin with securing the administration of the router by configuring the following components:

a)   Change the name of the router (this is accomplished on the Welcome screen of the LINKSYS router).

b)   Change the administrative password; the administrative user name is usually permanently set (check the device's documentation if necessary).

c)   If applicable, disable remote administration. You will not be able to configure the wireless router while wireless, but nobody else will be able to either!

Step 5   Now you'll secure access, allowing only the users you want to gain access to the wireless network. Normally, the first two steps are sufficient; the third step requires some additional information during configuration.

a)   Change the Service Set Identifier (SSID) of the router; this is the name of your wireless local area network. Many times, this is left to the default, allowing access to anyone who is familiar with wireless networking practices.

b)   Disable SSID broadcast. Your client will have to configure the laptops or share the SSID with the employees, but passersby will not have free Internet access.

c)   Allow access only to PCs with specific media access control (MAC) addresses. These can be manually entered for the computers you are allowing, or you may choose them from a list of computers currently allowed access.

Step 6   Finally, you will secure your client's data with encryption. There are three levels of encryption: Wired Equivalent Privacy (WEP) and two types of Wi-Fi Protected Access (WPA and WPA2).

WEP is the least secure of the three types of data encryption, but should be used if WPA or WPA2 is not supported. WPA is better and will provide a higher level of security than WEP, but the most secure is WPA2.

WPA2 is fairly new, but older routers are receiving firmware upgrades to enable them to take advantage of the highest data encryption. WPA2 uses a pre-shared key (PSK) methodology and allows complex passkeys of letters, numbers, and special characters to secure the data. It is recommended that passkeys be much longer than the traditional six to eight characters recommended for user passwords.

Though not directly related to wireless security, most wireless routers come with robust, built-in firewalls. The wireless router firewall will protect your client's network and systems from malicious attempts to procure their data.

Using security in the administration of a wireless router, access to the wireless network, and encryption of the data being transmitted through the air will at least deter all but the most aggressive threats and attacks. Stay alert for any change in activity on your systems.

Lab Analysis Test

1.   Tanner wants to configure his wireless network so that if Andrew just happens by with a laptop and a wireless card, he will not be able to gain access to the network without Tanner's approval. What component(s) does Tanner need to configure?

2.   Brandon is using his school's computer to do some research for a term paper. He attempts to surf to a Web site he has found on Google, only to receive an *Access Denied* message from the browser. What could cause this to happen?

3. Andrew has configured his four-computer network to use Internet Connection Sharing. He has double-checked the ICS host computer, and it can access the Internet. All of the physical connections between the computers and the switch seem to be in good shape. Yet, he still cannot access the Internet from a client computer. What might he have missed?

4. Mary has stated that when she used the c|net bandwidth meter, she achieved Internet transfer speeds around 7.5 megabytes per second (Mbps). What type of Internet access do you think Mary has? *CABLE*

5. Cindy is installing a high-speed connection to the Internet. What are the four components she will need to verify and have on hand?

Key Terms Quiz

Use the following vocabulary terms to complete the following sentences. Not all terms will be used.

analog

dial-up

digital

drivers

HTTP

ICS

ISP

PnP

POP3

RJ-11

RJ-45

SSID

transceiver

Windows Firewall

1. When connecting to the Internet using a high-speed digital subscriber line, the DSL *transceiver* is often referred to as a *DSL modem*.

2. The protocol that is synonymous with the World Wide Web is _*HTTP*_.

3. If the NIC isn't detected by _____, run the Add New Hardware Wizard.

4. Every wireless network has a network name that all of the computers accessing it must configure. This network name is known as a(n) _____.

5. The slowest means of accessing the Internet still in use today is _____.

Chapter 18
Computer Security

Lab Exercises

Computer security is paramount to protecting your client/company's business, finances, and in some cases, even life! In the following exercises, you will create a secure environment by configuring a Windows XP system properly with users, groups, logon methods, password policies, and complexity rules. Finally, you will clean a client's computer that has come to you with various malicious programs installed. You will do this by installing and running Lavasoft's Ad-Aware, PepiMK's Spybot Search & Destroy, and ALWIL's Avast! Antivirus software.

✔ **Note**

Due to the tremendous overlap in content on the CompTIA A+ certification exams, the Computer Security Labs for the Essentials exam (220-601) are the same as in the IT Technician (220-602) Lab book.

 **20** MINUTES

Lab Exercise 18.01: Users, Logon, and Simple File Sharing

User accounts are a powerful and necessary function used by Windows to provide security. While organizations with large networks usually take advantage of user accounts, standalone systems often fail to take advantage of them. In this exercise, you will configure user accounts for a standalone Windows XP Professional system.

By default, Windows XP uses simple file sharing unless you are on a Windows XP system configured as a member of a Windows domain, or unless you explicitly turn off simple file sharing. Windows XP also provides two different logon methods: the classic logon prompt and the Welcome screen. This lab will show both methods and help you determine when to use each method.

Learning Objectives

At the end of this lab, you'll be able to

- Create, modify, and delete local user accounts with Windows XP Professional

- Disable and enable simple file sharing in Windows XP Professional

- Modify logon and logoff options with Windows XP Professional

Lab Materials and Setup

The materials you need for this lab are

- A Windows XP Professional PC with the C: drive formatted as New Technology File System (NTFS). Configure the system as a member of the TEST workgroup with simple file sharing and the Welcome screen logon disabled.

- Access to the local administrator password.

Getting Down to Business

Step 1   Timmy and Fred are sharing a Windows XP system. They want to configure the system so that each user's personal information is hidden from the other, yet they also want to share some folders. Begin by logging on to the computer using the local administrator account. Use Task Manager to confirm you are logged on as the local administrator, as shown in Figure 18-1.

Step 2   Go into Control Panel and open the Users Account applet. Create a new account called FRED and make FRED a limited user. Create a second account called TIMMY and also make this account a limited user. After you create the accounts, give each account a password using the Change an Account option. Make sure to remember the passwords for these accounts!

Step 3   Log off the system and log on with the TIMMY account. Create a folder on the desktop called Timmy. Right-click this folder and select Sharing and Security.

Note that the dialog box tells you the only way to share the Timmy folder is to place it in the Shared Documents folder. Open the Shared Documents folder by clicking the Shared Documents link in the dialog box (see Figure 18-2), and drag the Timmy folder into the Shared Documents folder.

✖ Warning

Ignore the *Make this folder private* check box for this lab. If you select this, you are encrypting the folder. If you encrypt the folder, no one—not even the local administrator—will be able to access this folder or anything in it.

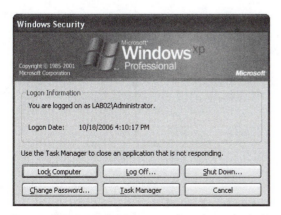

FIGURE 18-1 Task Manager showing administrator logged on

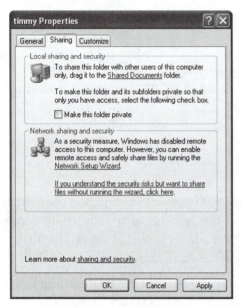

FIGURE 18-2 Folder properties

Step 4   Log off Windows and then log on with the FRED account. Open My Computer to see the Shared Documents and Fred's Documents folders, as shown in Figure 18-3. Open the Timmy folder in Shared Documents. Can the FRED account create a folder called Fred inside the Timmy folder?

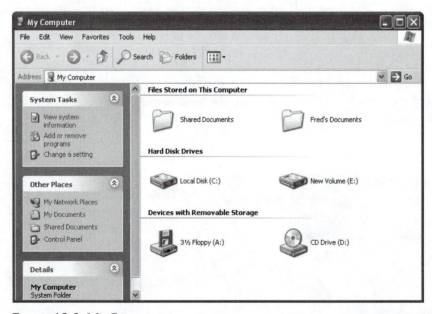

FIGURE 18-3 My Computer

Step 5   Still using the FRED account, close all open windows and reopen My Computer. This time open Local Disk (C:) and then the Documents and Settings folder. You should now see the Timmy folder as well as the Fred, All Users, and Administrator folders. Which of these folders can the FRED account open? What error does Windows display on some folders when the FRED account tries to open the folder? Why can't the FRED account open all of them?

Step 6   Log off and log back on with the administrator account. Once again, navigate to the C:\Documents and Settings folder. Which of these folders can the administrator account open? After answering this question, delete all the folders created for this lab.

Step 7   While still logged on as administrator, open My Computer and select Tools | Folder Options. Click the View tab and scroll down until you see the *Use simple file sharing* check box (Figure 18-4). Clear this box to turn off simple file sharing.

Step 8   Up to this point, you've been using the classic Windows logon prompt, so let's now change this. While still logged on as administrator, go to User Accounts in Control Panel, select *Change the way users log on and off*, and then select the *Use the Welcome screen* check box, as shown in Figure 18-5.

Step 9   Practice logging on and off your TIMMY, FRED, and administrator accounts. Compare the Welcome screen to the classic logon screen—why would Microsoft provide two totally different ways for you to log on to a system? Write down your answer, comparing the features of both logon methods. Here's a hint that will help with a part of your answer: You cannot use the Welcome screen on a system that is a member of a domain—why would Microsoft create this limitation?

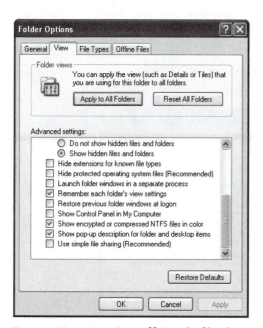

FIGURE 18-4 Turning off simple file sharing

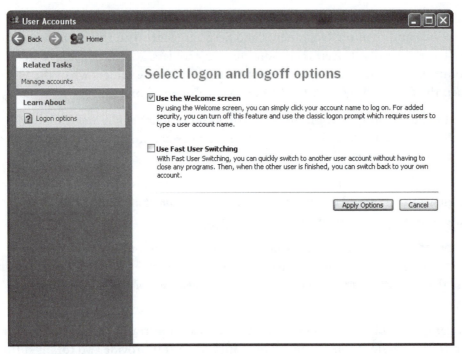

FIGURE 18-5 Enabling the Welcome logon screen

Step 10 Log on as administrator. Once again go to User Accounts in Control Panel and select *Change the way users log on and off*. This time select the *Use Fast User Switching* check box, as shown in Figure 18-6.

Fast User Switching becomes obvious once you try logging off. Instead of returning to the Welcome screen, what options do you see? What are the benefits of Fast User Switching? Come up with a work environment where Fast User Switching would be beneficial.

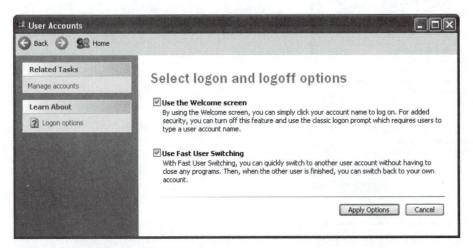

FIGURE 18-6 Fast User Switching

30 MINUTES

Lab Exercise 18.02: Groups and Standard File Sharing

Now that you understand simple file sharing, it's time to increase the complexity by un-simplifying file sharing! In this lab, you'll see the true firepower of NTFS as you use standard file sharing on a standalone system.

Learning Objectives

At the end of this lab, you'll be able to

- Recognize the standard NTFS permissions

- Configure NTFS permissions for a shared folder on a standalone system

- Recognize and configure NTFS permission inheritance

Lab Materials and Setup

The materials you need for this lab are

- The system you used in the previous lab

- Access to the local administrator password

Getting Down to Business

Step 1   Log on as administrator, verify that simple file sharing is disabled, and then use My Computer to open the Local Disk (C:) folder. Right-click this folder and select Properties to display the Local Disk (C:) folder's properties. Click the Security tab, and you should see something similar to Figure 18-7.

Now that you're no longer using simple file sharing, you can control access to any folder on your computer—assuming you have the right to control access! Given that you are logged on as administrator, you have complete control.

Step 2   Note the "two head" icons on the top of the Security dialog box. These are groups. Groups are handy when you want to give a number of users specific NTFS permissions for one or more folders. Close the Security dialog box, navigate to Computer Management, and select Local Users and Groups. Click the Groups folder to see something like Figure 18-8. These are all of the built-in groups for your system.

FIGURE 18-7 The Security tab under Local Disk (C:) properties

The three most important built-in groups are Administrators, Power Users, and Users. Each of these groups has a complex set of things they can and cannot do, but start by looking at what they can do when it comes to file sharing:

- **Administrators**   Have complete control of all NTFS permissions. Any user who is a member of this group has all the same power as the administrator account—use sparingly!

- **Power Users**   Can create users and groups, but they cannot change any NTFS settings unless they have the right to do so.

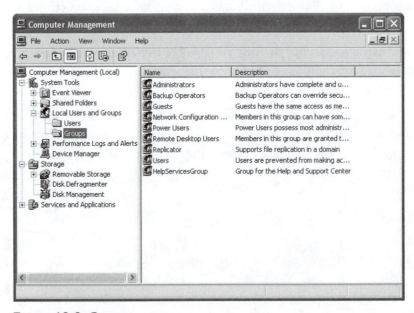

FIGURE 18-8 Groups

- **Users**   Can only change NTFS permissions on a folder if they have been given the right to do so. Anyone with a user account on the system is a member of this group.

You used the User Accounts Control Panel applet to make the FRED and TIMMY accounts. When you created those user accounts, you were given two choices as to the "type" of account you want to make. When you set the type of account, what were you really doing as far as Windows was concerned? Using the Local Users and Groups tool in Computer Management, answer this question: "What group is a 'limited' account type assigned to?"

Step 3   Still using the Local Users and Groups tool in Computer Management, make the FRED and TIMMY user accounts members of the Power Users group. Here's a clue how to do it: Right-click either the Power Users icon or right-click each user—both ways work! How many users were members of the Power Users group before you added Timmy and Fred?

Step 4   Still logged on as administrator, go back to the Local Disk (C:) Security dialog box you saw earlier (refer back to Step 1 to remind you how to get to this). This time, concentrate on the permissions at the bottom of the dialog box.

Step 5   You'll notice some groups in the list that were not in the Local Users and Groups utility. These "specialty" groups are used to help organize NTFS permissions. For example, the System group is used by the operating system itself (yup, even Windows needs permission sometimes!), the CREATOR OWNER is the person who actually created this folder, and the Everyone group is a quick way to set the NTFS permission so that everyone (and I mean everyone, even someone who's not a user—risky on networked computers) may access the folder. How many of these specialty groups do you see? Do you see the three examples just mentioned? Do you see others?

✔ **Hint**

Just for fun, check out who is the creator/owner for the C: drive by clicking the Advanced button and then clicking the Owner tab.

Step 6   If the Everyone group is not yet listed, add it now. Click the Add button, type the word **Everyone** (not case-sensitive), as shown in Figure 18-9, and then click OK.

Adding everyone into the C: drive is *not* something you would do on a normal system, as it gives literally anyone—even remote users—complete access to the entire volume, but simply putting everyone on the list doesn't do anything until you start adding NTFS permissions. For this example, click all of the Allow check boxes, except for Full Control. When you finish, members of the Everyone group will have Modify, Read and Execute, List Folder Contents, Read, and Write permissions; your dialog box should look like Figure 18-10. What happens when you click the Modify button first?

Step 7   Create a folder called C:\LAB. Look at the Security tab under the folder's properties (surely by now I don't have to tell you to right-click to get to properties, do I?) and look at the NTFS permissions. What do you notice about the permissions? This is called inheritance—any NTFS permissions set for a folder are automatically transferred to any folder in that folder.

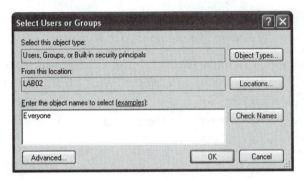

Figure 18-9 Adding the Everyone group

Step 8 Create an empty text file. Open the C:\LAB folder and right-click anywhere inside the folder. Select New | Text Document. Give it the name FIRST. It should look like Figure 18-11. Check out the text file's NTFS permissions. Yup, files get NTFS permissions too! And yes, they also inherit permissions from the folder in which they were created.

Step 9 Sometime we don't like inheritance, so you need to know how to turn it off. Go back into the LAB properties. Go to the General tab and make sure the Read-only attribute is turned off (Figure 18-12).

Go into the Security tab, click the Advanced button, and then check the box that starts with the phrase *Inherit from parent the permission*, as shown in Figure 18-13.

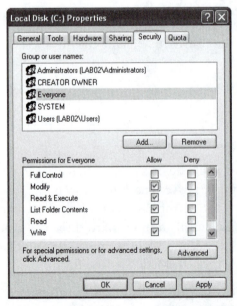

Figure 18-10 Setting permissions for the Everyone group

FIGURE 18-11 FIRST file in C:\LAB folder

When you do this, you get a warning dialog box. Basically, Windows is saying, "Okay, I will turn off inheritance, but what do you want me to do with any folders and files in here right now? Keep the current NTFS permissions (Copy) or just delete everything (Remove)?"

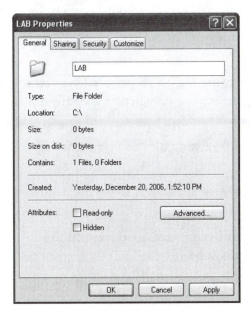

FIGURE 18-12 Making sure Read-only is cleared

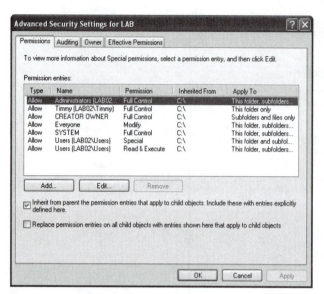

FIGURE 18-13 Turning off inheritance

If you delete all of the NTFS permissions, no one—not even the administrator account—will have access to the folder (administrator accounts have a way to fix this if it happens, called *taking ownership*), so let's just click the Copy button. When you do this, you'll notice all of the formerly disabled check boxes are now enabled.

Step 10 Go into the C:\LABS folder's Security tab, and add the Timmy user. That's right—you can assign both users and groups NTFS permissions. Do this exactly as you did before: Click Add and then type the word **timmy**. What NTFS permissions is the TIMMY account given by default?

Step 11 Go into the C:\LABS folder's Security tab and add the Power Users group. What NTFS permissions is the Power Users group given by default?

Step 12 Time to start setting permissions! Start by reviewing the NTFS permissions that follow. Keep in mind that these permissions behave differently, depending on whether they are applied to a folder or a file:

- **Write** Enables you to change or add to (append) existing files and create new files and folders.

- **Read** Enables you to read any file in the folder. Also allows you to see the names of the subfolders (but not open them).

- **Read & Execute** This permission is the same as Read but also enables you to run executable programs in the folder and to open any subfolders.

- **List Folder Contents** This permission enables you to see the contents of the folder and any subfolders. (This permission seems the same as the Read & Execute permission, but it is only inherited by folders to help the Read & Execute permission work properly.)

- **Modify**   Enables you to do anything except delete files or subfolders.

- **Full Control**   Enables you to do anything you want!

Step 13   The TIMMY account has Read & Execute, List Folder Contents, and Read permissions, so he should not be able to change any files, correct? So log on as Timmy, and see what happens when you try to open the First file. Go ahead and open it, type some text, and then try to save it. What happens?

The issue is that Timmy is also a member of the Everyone group, which still has Modify permissions. When an account has more than one reference in the NTFS permissions, the greater permissions always win. Delete the Everyone group. What happens now? Go through all of the groups to make sure there are no groups of which Timmy is a member that have greater permissions than the TIMMY account by himself. Do not delete the Administrators or the Creator Owner groups from the C:\LAB folder's permissions!

 20 MINUTES

Lab Exercise 18.03: Local Policies

NTFS permissions are powerful tools that can be used to control with great detail what users and groups can do to folders and files. However, NTFS does not cover a number of security issues that are important but that don't directly involve the file system. For example, what if you don't want a particular user group to shut down the computer? What if you want to make sure all accounts use a password of at least eight characters? What if you want to prevent certain users from reformatting the hard drive? These types of security settings are all controlled under the umbrella term of local policies.

✔ **Hint**

There are hundreds of different policies that you may configure for a system. This lab only covers a few of the most basic policies!

Learning Objectives

At the end of this lab, you'll be able to

- Locate and open the Local Security Policy utility

- Create, modify, and delete local policies with Windows XP Professional

Lab Materials and Setup

The materials you need for this lab are

- A Windows XP Professional PC with the C: drive formatted as NTFS. Configure the system as a member of the TEST workgroup with simple file sharing and the Welcome screen logon disabled.

- Access to the local administrator password

Getting Down to Business

As you go through your Local Security Settings, you'll notice a large number of pre-made polices that may not make sense to you. Don't worry about these as even Windows experts don't know exactly what every policy does! Concentrate on the policies used in the lab.

Step 1   Log on using an account with administrator rights. All local security policies are controlled through the Local Security Settings in Administrative Tools. When opened, it should look like Figure 18-14. Open the program.

Click the Account Policies icon to see two icons: Password Policy and Account Lockout Policy. Go into Password Policy, right-click *Password must meet complexity requirements*, and select Properties. Enable this policy as shown in Figure 18-15, and click OK.

Create an account called JANET, and give it a password. Try something simple like "janet," and see what happens. Keep trying to make a password until you get one that is accepted. What do you need to do to make an acceptable password? Hint: Use the help in User Accounts to get some ideas as to what you need to do.

Step 2   Head back to the Password Policy in Local Security Settings, and enable Password History. Go into User Accounts, and try to change a password using the same password you used before. What happens?

Step 3   This time try the Account Lockout Settings. An account lockout is when the operating system no longer allows a certain account the right even to try to log on. Try to change the properties on the *Account lockout duration setting*—it is disabled until you set the *Account lockout threshold* to something other than the default of 0. Try changing it to 3 attempts. Note that Windows now

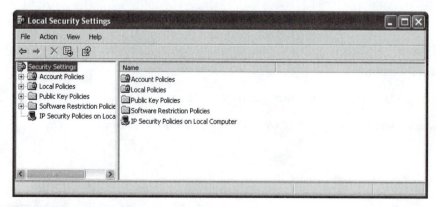

FIGURE 18-14 Local Security Settings

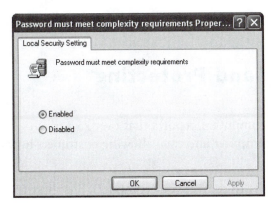

FIGURE 18-15 Enabling password complexity

automatically sets the *Account lockout duration* and the *Reset account lockout counter after* settings to 30 minutes. Use the help in Local Security Settings to determine exactly what these two settings mean.

Log off the computer and, using the JANET account (you do still remember the password, correct?), intentionally attempt to log on using incorrect passwords. What happens after the third try?

Step 4 Log off and log back on as Fred. Try to change the system time (go to the Date and Time Control Panel applet). What happens? Log off as Fred and log back in as administrator. Now try using some of the security policies under *User rights assignment*. Locate *Change the system time* (Figure 18-16), and notice that by default only the Administrators and Power Users groups can change the time. Add the FRED account to those who can change the time.

How can you test to make sure your policy change works? Then go do it!

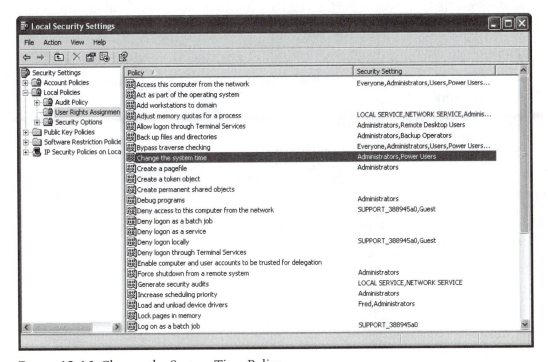

FIGURE 18-16 Change the System Time Policy

 **30** MINUTES

Lab Exercise 18.04: Cleaning and Protecting a Client's Computer

Geek Squad, the popular PC repair arm of Best Buy computers, reports that over 75 percent of their service calls involve cleaning malware off of a computer and then showing customers how to protect their PCs from malware and other attacks.

Windows comes with many programs and features to protect your computer, but these tools are useless if not used properly. In this lab, you will check and clean the computer of malware and then go through the steps to reduce the likelihood of another attack.

Learning Objectives

At the end of this lab, you'll be able to

- Remove malware from a Windows XP Professional system
- Configure a software firewall
- Configure an anti-malware/antivirus utility

Lab Materials and Setup

The materials you need for this lab are

- A Windows XP Professional PC (Service Pack 2 with Windows Firewall not running)
- Access to the local administrator password
- An antivirus suite (this lab uses the popular and free Avast! Antivirus suite with the separate Avast! Antivirus tool, but any antivirus suite—Norton, McAfee, Trend Micro, AVG—will work)
- Spybot Search and Destroy anti-spyware
- Ad-Aware SE Personal Edition anti-spyware

✔ **Hint**

This is a great lab for students who want to bring a PC from home—or one that belongs to a friend—for testing and cleaning.

Getting Down to Business

The tools used in this lab are some of the better known options available and also have the added benefit of being free! However, these are not the only tools available, and as a tech you should always be on the Internet looking for better tools.

Step 1   You are stepping up to a system that has no antivirus tool installed. Whenever you approach a new system, your first act should be to remove any viruses. Every antivirus utility comes with a special scanner tool to be used on possibly infected systems. Do not confuse this scanner tool with a full-blown antivirus suite that's normally installed on systems. Run the tool to find any viruses. Figure 18-17 shows the Avast! Antivirus tool running.

How long does this scanning last? If the utility finds a virus, what does it do? What are your choices?

Step 2   With the viruses cleared, the next step is to clear out any spyware/adware. There is no single utility that does a perfect job, so most techs prefer to use two different products to improve their chances of finding all of the spyware. Run both programs and compare them. Can you identify malware that one utility finds but the other does not? Where are these spyware/adware located? Why are they given a danger/threat level?

Step 3   Install an antivirus suite to protect the system from ongoing threats. More advanced suites provide protection from malware/spyware as well as viruses. What are some of the options you see with your antivirus tool?

Start Windows Firewall by opening the Windows Firewall Control Panel applet, as shown in Figure 18-18.

Simply starting the firewall provides a degree of protection from intrusions into your system, but there are cases when you might need certain services from the Internet to come into your computer—that's the job of exceptions. Click the Exceptions tab to see a list of programs Windows recognizes as programs that may need input from the Internet. In most cases, we use the default settings.

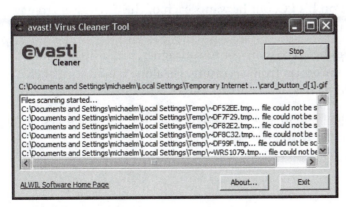

FIGURE 18-17 Avast! Antivirus tool

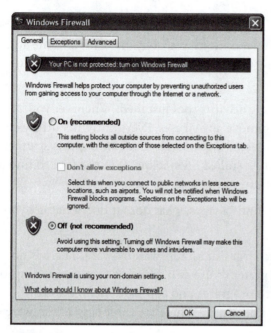

FIGURE 18-18 Windows Firewall

Lab Analysis Test

1. Jen's mother just got a new Windows PC for home use. Her mother used to work on a large network and is rather "security sensitive"; she is concerned that when she starts her system it automatically goes into Windows without asking for a user name and password. What can Jen do to keep this from happening?

2. Frank is trying to install a new program on his computer, but the system tells him he doesn't have the correct privileges to do so. What does he need to change?

3. John shares his computer with two colleagues. John's system currently allows him to share only the Shared Documents folder on his PC, but he wants each of the other users to have access to only one specific folder and not to the other's folder. What should he do?

4. Kyle has a laptop that he sometimes needs to loan out to colleagues, but it holds a lot of information that he wants to prevent others from accessing. He alone has control of the administrator account. What could he do?

5. Kelly has just purchased a brand-new system and wants to protect it from spyware, malware, and Internet attacks. What should she do to protect the system?

Key Terms Quiz

Use the following vocabulary terms to complete the following sentences. Not all terms will be used.

Administrator

exceptions

Full Control

group

inheritance

local security policy

Modify

NTFS permission

Power Users

Read & Execute

Sharing and Security

simple file sharing

spyware

user account

User Accounts applet

virus

Write

1. The _____ group is the second most powerful built-in group in a Windows system.

2. The _____ permission would enable a user to open a file.

3. The _____ permission is second only to Full Control in terms of what a user can do.

4. Windows Firewall allows _____ for programs that need incoming data from the Internet.

5. Allowing a user to change the system time is an example of a(n) _____.

Chapter **19**
The Complete PC Technician

Lab Exercises

At this point you're well on your path to becoming a CompTIA A+– certified technician. You have an excellent understanding of the major technical aspects of computer systems: hardware, software, networking, and the Internet.

When a client launches an application, that person isn't thinking about what happens behind the scenes: "Hey, look at me! I'm using the keyboard and mouse to input data! The processor is calculating all of the information to produce the desired results and present the output on the screen or in hard copy form on a printer. This is only possible because the operating system, applications, and data were successfully stored on the hard drive." You, as the tech, *do* have to think about all of this, but you also need the user's perspective. When you look at the computer system as a whole—that is, as a practical tool that can create and process everything from your résumé to the latest Hollywood thriller—you'll have a better understanding of how your clients envision the computer.

In the real world of PC tech, you also have to work with people: customers, clients, supervisors, coworkers, family members, maybe even spouses. You have to develop the skills for calmly gathering information about the state the computer is in and how it arrived there. Usually, your clients won't use the most technical language to explain the situation, and they may be frustrated or even a little on the defensive, so you need to be understanding and patient. You want them to see you as an ally, and to ensure this, you'll need to treat them with respect and kindness.

Bear in mind that someone who doesn't understand computers can still be quite intelligent and capable in other areas; talking down to a client is a bad idea! The client also trusts in your integrity to solve the problem in the most efficient and cost-effective manner possible and to return their computer and data uncompromised.

Finally, and most importantly, you should cultivate a good troubleshooting methodology. It's difficult to give you a specific checklist, but the following guidelines should help:

- Make sure you have the proper tools for the situation.

- Back up as much as possible before touching anything.

- Analyze, progress from simple to complex, and swap known good for bad.

Don't forget that many times, the client will be there with you, hanging on your every word. Explain the steps you are taking to configure a new system, or to repair damage and recover data from hardware failure or malicious software. When backing up data prior to working on a system, err on the side of caution; make your best effort to determine which data is vital to your client and to their business, even if they are vague about what data needs to be protected. Try to give them realistic expectations of what you likely can or cannot do so that the outcome is a pleasant surprise rather than a bitter disappointment.

✔ **Note**

Due to the tremendous overlap in content on the CompTIA A+ certification exams, the Complete PC Technician Labs for the Essentials exams (220-601) are the same as in the IT Technician (220-602) Lab book.

✔ **Hint**

Ideally, you should have a classmate play the role of the client while you play the role of the PC tech. Work through the scenario in a live person-to-person role-playing of the situation, just as if it were real. If possible, try to work with different classmates through each of the different scenarios, and try to spend time playing the client as well as the tech.

 **30** MINUTES

Lab Exercise 19.01: Scenario #1: Computer Obsolescence and Expense of Replacement

An independent salesperson for a multi-line musical instrument dealer walks into your shop carrying a weathered laptop case. He lays the case on the counter and asks simply, "Is there anything you can do?" You open the case to find a late-1990s model IBM ThinkPad. You open the lid on the ThinkPad and see a semicircle indentation and spider-web cracks all across the screen. The liquid crystal display (LCD) panel has been completely smashed!

As the expert in this situation, you have to make some decisions about what would ultimately be the most timely and cost-effective solution. You then have to explain your recommendations to the client carefully and respectfully, as either solution will most likely be costly and therefore stressful for him.

✔ **Cross-Reference**

Before you work through the role-playing scenarios, go back and re-read Chapter 20, "The Complete PC Tech," in *Mike Meyers' A+ Guide to Managing and Troubleshooting PC's, Vol. 1: Essentials*.

Learning Objectives

This exercise will test your ability to stay cool in the face of a concerned client, even as you may have to deliver news that the client doesn't want to hear.

At the end of this lab, you'll be able to

- Assess the damage and back up the client's data

- Convey the options available to the client

- Provide a recommended solution to the client

Lab Materials and Setup

The materials you need for this lab are

- A partner or classmate to play the role of the client (if you don't have a partner, you can still work through the scenario and complete the Lab Analysis Test at the end of the chapter)

- A notepad or computer-generated "trouble ticket" to simulate the practice followed in many computer support organizations

- A demo computer and/or Internet access to re-create the scenario and research options on vendor Web sites and tech forums (optional)

Getting Down to Business

To begin, have your partner read the Client section that follows. You will then read the PC Tech section and use the specifics to analyze the situation and recommend the best course of action. Sit down and work through the scenario with your partner. If possible, use the Internet or demo computers to make the role-playing scenario more valid.

CLIENT:

You are an independent salesperson for a multi-line musical instrument dealer and spend about 20 days a month on the road. You use the laptop to keep all of your customer data and product information up to date. You were finishing up a particularly busy week when you fell asleep with the laptop on your lap. You placed the laptop next to your bed in the hotel only to step on it in the middle of the evening. Your entire business relies on the information contained in the computer, and having it down, even for a short time, is going to create problems.

Along with the time-critical issues, you are also basically self-employed, since you are an independent salesperson; you pay your own travel and lodging expenses, health benefits, and life insurance. A costly repair or replacement was not in the planned budget until forever. You do know that working with a dial-up connection to the Internet in hotels and using floppies to transfer files between your laptop and your home computer (when you're there) is becoming cumbersome.

PC TECH:

As the technician, you are going to analyze the laptop and quickly recommend that the hard drive be backed up immediately. Using a laptop Integrated Drive Electronics (IDE) harness and duplicating the hard drive to a volume on the shop data server, you can alleviate the customer's concern that all his data will be lost.

You know that the computer is over six years old and that the replacement screen and labor to install it are probably going to cost a fair amount. You use the Internet to research replacement LCD screens and try to estimate the overall cost of the repair. Not only is it expensive, the availability of the screen is backlogged over three weeks. It is also a good bet that other components in the computer will begin to age and fail even if the screen repair is warranted. The laptop does not have wireless access, there is no universal serial bus (USB), and the CD-ROM drive is just that, a CD-ROM drive!

Your job is laid out before you. You need to discuss the options of repairing the current computer, warts and all, or having the client upgrade to a current-day laptop.

 **30** MINUTES

Lab Exercise 19.02: Scenario #2: Hardware Failure, or I Can't See Anything!

One of the marketing analysts in your company calls the help desk and complains that he's unable to get his monitor to work. He arrived this morning and the computer just never booted. There's a mission-critical presentation on this system that is due to be presented today at 2:00 P.M. It's now 1:00 P.M., and nobody has returned his call, even to say that his initial request was received! The analyst storms into the IT department and demands some assistance. You look up from your screen just in time to see your supervisor and the analyst barreling toward your cubicle. Your supervisor asks if you will accompany the analyst to his department and see if you can figure this out.

In cases such as this, the tech's job is not only to troubleshoot the problem and provide a solution, but also to provide customer service and present a good image of the IT department to other employees. As the expert in this situation, you not only have to solve the issue—you must also make your best effort to diffuse the agitation of the anxious analyst.

Learning Objectives

The plan is to have a classmate play the role of the client, and to have you play the role of the PC tech. Work through the scenario in a live person-to-person role-playing of the situation, just as if it were real. Optimally, you will be able to work with different classmates through each of the different scenarios, and you will play the client for some of your classmates while they handle your computer woes.

At the end of this lab, you'll be able to

- Analyze the problem with input from the client

- Diffuse the frustration of the client

- Provide a complete solution

Lab Materials and Setup

The materials you need for this lab are

- A partner or classmate to play the role of the client (optionally, if you do not have a partner, work through the scenario and complete the Lab Analysis Test at the end of the chapter)

- A notepad or computer-generated "trouble ticket" to simulate the practice followed in many computer support organizations

- A demo computer or Internet access to re-create the scenario and research options on vendor Web sites and tech forums (optional)

Getting Down to Business

To begin, have your partner read the Client section that follows. You will then read the PC Tech section and use the specifics to analyze the situation and recommend the best course of action. Now sit down and work through the scenario with your partner. If possible, use the Internet or demo computers to make the role-playing scenario more valid.

Client:

You arrived this morning and started your normal routine: You dropped your briefcase in the corner of your cube, carefully placed your coffee on the file cabinet (away from the computer), and pressed the power button on the computer. You exchanged a few pleasantries with your fellow workers and sat down to get the finishing touches on the presentation you will be delivering at 2:00 P.M. today, only to find a completely blank screen. You attempted to reboot the computer and verified that the power light was lit on the monitor (you do know *that* much about computers). But it was still a no-go!

You placed a call with the help desk and tried not to panic. Some friends invited you to lunch, and you joined them with the hope that the IT department would visit while you were gone so that you could return to a working computer. When you returned, nothing had been done!

You are a little tense, but you know that you are at the mercy of the IT group. You head on down to the IT department and visit directly with the support supervisor. He introduces you to one of the techs, who is now traveling to your desk with you. The only thing you can remember doing differently was authorizing an Automatic Windows Update last night as you were leaving.

PC Tech:

Well, you've certainly been here before—a critical situation with severe time constraints, but now it's 1:20 P.M. and the analyst is very tense. You arrive at the analyst's desk and have him run through the routine that he followed when he arrived this morning. You ask if anything has changed since yesterday when the computer worked. You then run a check of the obvious diagnoses and troubleshooting steps.

✔ **Hint**

It is imperative that you keep detailed records of diagnosing and troubleshooting steps. If you have set items that you check first (remember: simple to complex), then you will perform a quick check of the power lights, power cord connections, monitor connections, and whether the monitor settings menu is accessible to rule out simple items that may have been overlooked in a time of stress.

If none of the simple solutions appears to work, you have two issues on your hands. One is that you need to get the system back up and running, and the other is that your client has a big presentation due in 30 minutes (yes, it took 10 minutes to check the simple items, so it's now 1:30 P.M.). You know that your organization has all of the employees save their documents to My Documents, which is mapped to the server to facilitate backups. You have the analyst log onto a coworker's computer, access his My Documents folder, and fine-tune his presentation with 10 minutes to spare.

You send a calmer analyst to the meeting, complete the analysis of the system, and perform the required repairs. Record the additional steps you would take to complete this trouble ticket. How would you communicate your findings with the analyst? Share the results with your instructor.

 **30** MINUTES

Lab Exercise 19.03: Scenario #3: What Do You Mean, a Virus?

You're just finishing up lunch when one of your neighbors walks into your shop with her computer under her arm. She knows you from the neighborhood, and has heard that you know a fair amount about computer systems (I hope so, since you are working in a computer shop!). She asks if you can take a look at her system.

You ask what seems to be the problem, to which she responds, "It seems to be running really slow. I can't find some of the documents and pictures I used to have, and every time we try to access the Internet, it kicks us off!"

You recommend that she return to whatever she was doing and leave the computer with you; it just so happens that your schedule is open this afternoon, so you should be able to take a quick look at the system. You ask if there are any passwords you'll need, and the client responds, "No, we don't worry about passwords." You fill out a trouble ticket with the contact information and let her know you'll be in touch with her shortly.

Learning Objectives

The plan is to have a classmate play the role of the client, and to have you play the role of the PC tech. Work through the scenario in a live person-to-person role-playing of the situation, just as if it were real. Optimally, you will be able to work with different classmates through each of the different scenarios, and you will play the client for some of your classmates while they handle your computer woes.

At the end of this lab, you'll be able to

- Analyze the computer to determine if it exhibits the symptoms the customer has indicated
- Perform routine maintenance and optimization
- Make recommendations to the client for the upkeep of her computer

Lab Materials and Setup

The materials you need for this lab are

- A partner or classmate to play the role of the client (optionally, if you do not have a partner, work through the scenario and complete the Lab Analysis Test at the end of the chapter)

- A notepad or computer-generated "trouble ticket" to simulate the practice followed in many computer support organizations

- A demo computer or Internet access to re-create the scenario and research options on vendor Web sites and tech forums (optional)

Getting Down to Business

To begin, have your partner read the Client section that follows. You will then read the PC Tech section and use the specifics to analyze the situation and recommend the best course of action. Now sit down and work through the scenario with your partner. If possible, use the Internet or demo computers to make the role-playing scenario more valid.

CLIENT:

The computer you are dropping off to the shop is the family computer and is used by the family members—two teenagers, you, and your spouse. The computer is constantly using a high-speed cable Internet connection, and there are tons of music files, pictures, and stored on the hard drive.

You are not completely computer-savvy, so if asked by the tech, you respond do not know if there is any anti-spyware or antivirus software installed, although it's p ly, you kids have installed something. All you know is that the computer is running te r connect have lost some documents and pictures that you wanted, and the computer w to the Internet.

When you drop it off at the repair shop, the tech attempts to send y n better. way, but you would like to see what he is doing and possibly learn how to make t rything You are fairly insistent, and finally work out that the tech will walk you when you return.

PC TECH:

You set the system up on your test bench and boot into Windows XP. are a large s take an inappropriate amount of time to boot and load all of the programs (. You take a number of items in the system tray, but it is surprisingly devoid of a o it's a good quick note of the version of XP and notice that there are no service bet that Windows Updates have not been running either.

You check Device Manager and Event Viewer to verify that there are no specific hardware issues; everything seems to check out there. You then run Disk Cleanup—which uncovers over 4 gigabytes (GB) of temporary Internet files—and then Disk Defragmenter, which indicates that the disk is fragmented. It is a 20-GB hard drive that is almost filled to capacity, so Disk Defragmenter is probably not going to run. Finally, you double-check to see if there are any antivirus/anti-adware/anti-spyware programs installed, and find nothing.

✔ **Cross-Reference**

Refer to Lab Exercise 18.04, "Cleaning and Protecting a Client's Computer," to review a checklist for cleaning up a machine that appears to have no specific hardware problems using issues, but merely an accumulation of junk files, adware, spyware, and viruses.

---

contact the customer and recommend that she stop back by the shop to discuss your recommendations for the computer. You still do not know if the lost files are recoverable, but you know you'll have to work through the other problems before you get there.

NUTES

Lab Exercise 19.04: Scenario #4: No Documents, No Mail, and I Can't Print!

You work bright and early at 7:00 A.M. to find several voice-mail messages blinking on your phone. One of the desktop support specialists at a large financial institution, and you usually make arriving early to catch up on some of the studying you have been doing to pass your next on exam. However, it looks like you will have to put this on the back burner for today. The messages, and it appears that the entire proposals department is in already, working. stment proposal for a prominent client. The messages are frantic requests to fix the comput. the proposals department. Apparently, none of the computers are able to access the do eam has been working with all week; they could not e-mail their concerns, and the netwo wn!

You what might be happening, but you are going to drop by the proposals depart k some of the individual computers before you make a rash decision. You ch *ing and Troubleshooting Networks* textbook, and walk over to the proposals depart

Learning Objectives

The plan is to have a classmate play the role of the client, and to have you play the role of the PC tech. Work through the scenario in a live person-to-person role-playing of the situation, just as if it were real. Optimally, you will be able to work with different classmates through each of the different scenarios, and you will play the client for some of your classmates while they handle your computer woes.

At the end of this lab, you'll be able to

- Verify that this is not an isolated problem with one or two computers

- Diagnose and troubleshoot from simple to complex, and record your findings

- Follow proper procedures to escalate the trouble ticket

Lab Materials and Setup

The materials you need for this lab are

- A partner or classmate to play the role of the client (optionally, if you do not have a partner, work through the scenario and complete the Lab Analysis Test at the end of the chapter)

- A notepad or computer-generated "trouble ticket" to simulate the practice followed in many computer support organizations

- A demo computer or Internet access to re-create the scenario and research options on vendor Web sites and tech forums (optional)

Getting Down to Business

To begin, have your partner read the Client section that follows. You will then read the PC Tech section and use the specifics to analyze the situation and recommend the best course of action. Now sit down and work through the scenario with your partner. If possible, use the Internet or demo computers to make the role-playing scenario more valid.

CLIENT:

You are the chief financial officer (CFO) for this large financial institution. You have asked your entire team to come in today at 6:00 A.M. to finish up an investment proposal for a high-profile client. Everybody is on point, but as soon as things begin rolling, a number of your staff appear at your door: "The network is down!"

They inform you that they have left numerous messages with the IT department, but you do not expect anybody to be there until 8:30 A.M. or so. Just as you are preparing to call the chief information officer (CIO) at home, one of the desktop support specialists arrives on the scene.

You ask if this person is up to the challenge of determining the cause of the outage, and if so, whether he or she will have the authority to complete the tasks involved to get the network up and running again. This person seems like a sincere individual, so you ask him or her to perform the initial investigation and report to you as soon as he or she has a handle on the situation.

PC TECH:

This issue is going to challenge your professionalism more than it will challenge you as a technologist. You should run through some quick checks of the various computers in the proposals department. Check the physical connections, and log on to a few of the computers to verify that the network connectivity is down.

As soon as you can verify that the entire department is down, make sure you communicate with the CFO to apprise him or her of the situation. This is a case of escalation—you need to get your network administrators online and have them troubleshoot the network. You have checked a few computers in other departments to verify that there is network connectivity in the building, and it is only the proposals department that is down.

You assure the CFO that you're on the issue and will inform him or her when the network admin is onsite. You then make a call to your friend, who just happens to be one of the network administrators; she is only a few minutes from the office, and tells you to hang tight and plan on joining her in the switch room. You're going to have an opportunity to work the issues through to the resolution. Don't forget to update the CFO!

Lab Analysis Test

1. Write a short essay summarizing the problem, discussion, and solution of the smashed laptop screen from Scenario #1.

2. Write a short essay summarizing the problem, discussion, and solution of the nonfunctioning monitor from Scenario #2. Be sure to include detail on handling the analyst's stress level and frustration with the IT department.

3. Write a short essay summarizing the problem, discussion, and solution of the slow computer and connection problems on the Internet from Scenario #3. Be sure to include detail on the steps and updates you would recommend that the client authorize.

4. Write a short essay summarizing the problem, discussion, and solution of the network outage in Scenario #4. Be sure to include detail on the steps you took to escalate the issue to the proper individual, the documentation paper path, and communication with the CFO.

Index